**Books are to be returned on or before
the last date below.**

Developing Leadership Genius

The nature and nurture
of leaders

Developing Leadership Genius
The nature and nurture of leaders

Dr Cyril Levicki

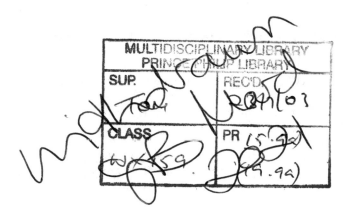

THE McGRAW-HILL COMPANIES

London · Burr Ridge IL · New York · St Louis · San Francisco · Auckland
Bogotá · Caracas · Lisbon · Madrid · Mexico · Milan · Montreal
New Delhi · Panama · Paris · San Juan · São Paulo
Singapore · Sydney · Tokyo · Toronto

Published by
McGraw-Hill Professional
SHOPPENHANGERS ROAD
MAIDENHEAD
BERKSHIRE SL6 2QL
Telephone +44 (0) 1628 502 500
Fax: +44 (0) 1628 770 224
Website: http://www.mcgraw-hill.co.uk

British Library Cataloguing in Publication Data
A catalogue record for this book is available from the British Library

ISBN 0 07 709848 X

Library of Congress Cataloging-in-Publication Data
A catalogue record for this book is available from the Library of Congress

Sponsoring Editor	Elizabeth Robinson
Editorial Assistant	Sarah Wilks
Production Editorial Manager	Penny Grose
Desk Editor	Alastair Lindsay

Produced for McGraw-Hill by Steven Gardiner Ltd
Printed and bound in Great Britain by Bell and Bain Ltd, Glasgow
Cover design by Senate Design Ltd

McGraw-Hill books are available at special quantity discounts. Please
contact the Corporate Sales Executive at the above address

This book is dedicated to
Phyllis and Jeffrey

Contents

Figures, Questionnaires and Tables

Figures

Questionnaires

Tables

Tables (continued)

Foreword

All authors know they owe a debt of thanks to many people. Mine is to the multitude of people whom I have taught in development programmes over the last 17 years, at the London Business School, Cranfield Management School, City University Business School, Queen Mary College, London University, Baruch College, City University of New York, UMIST and The Manchester Business School. UMIST appointed me a Visiting Professorial Fellow in 1997 and Reading University to a full-time faculty position in September, 2001.

In addition to my students, I also want to acknowledge what I learned from the hundreds of clients who have employed me as an adviser on strategy, team development and board composition. I feel my debt is larger because I was learning so much while I was really supposed to be teaching or assisting them! I can only hope that my help to them was as useful as all that they showed me about the dynamics and intricacies of leadership, management and corporate life. Many of them now lead businesses all over the world. I trust that a few of my values adhered to them.

I also want to thank Elizabeth Robinson of McGraw-Hill. She and they have been enthusiastic in their support of me in writing this book.

Finally, I must thank my family. My son, Jeffrey, who at the tender age of nine, understood why his dad needed time alone to write the book. My wife, Phyllis, not only proofreads my words but she tells me when they make no sense; she helps change mumbo-jumbo to English; and she allows me the time and space to pursue the strange pastime of writing books. I can never thank her enough.

As always, much credit is due to others. As ever, all mistakes are my responsibility. In the book, I state 'the perfect leader has not yet been born'. I don't think the 'perfect author' is any more feasible. I hope the reader will forgive my errors and mistakes because they find enough compensating value to have made reading the book worthwhile.

Dr Cyril Levicki, March 2001

Introduction

In some ways, an author is never sure what s/he knows or thinks about a subject until s/he sits down to write the book. When we read a new book we have written it is possible to then decide whether we agree with our thesis. McGraw-Hill has kindly encouraged me in the writing of this book. I have added several chapters to this book which differentiate it strongly from my previous writing on the subject of leadership. First, I have set the subject into a theoretical framework, making it more amenable for different uses for both teaching as well as helping managers and leaders, the practitioners in the field of what I determinedly still call 'artistic science'. Please try to read the opening theory chapter. It is deliberately written in a style and manner to please and communicate with practitioners. I hope it will also enlighten some academics.

I have also carefully separated the different components of what it takes to be a leader. The three major aspects are (1) the genetic qualities we are born with (traits); (2) the developmental influences that happens to a person as a child and growing adolescent (Chapter 4); and, the behaviours we can learn consciously, as an adult (Chapter 3). There is also an entirely new chapter to help readers assess themselves (Chapter 11).

There are not many good leaders around. The larger the organization you examine the less likely you are to find high quality bosses. This book is written to try to remedy that situation by helping those leaders who start with the requisite skills and talents to better develop their potential and become one of the good leaders that are in such desperately short supply. Occasionally I have dealt with leaders who had special gifts that singled them out from others. That is what I refer to in the title of this book as 'Genius'. It harks back to a previous book I wrote on leadership called *The Leadership Gene* (Levicki, 1998), which focused more on the qualities a leader has to be born with. In this book I more carefully delineate the differences between the 'genetic' aspects of a leader (the traits) and the developable aspects of a leader (the behaviours which come from parental development or the skills that can be learned).

The sample from which I am making the generalizations in this book was composed of the thousands of senior managers, and hundreds of leaders, I have worked with, either as a consultant on strategy or top team development, or as the personal adviser to the leader. Amongst my clients have been major international and national telecommunications businesses, such as British Telecom and Cable & Wireless and One-to-One. In the cable telephony and entertainment industries I have worked with the leaders of international and national majors such as TCI, MediaOne International and TeleWest. In manufacturing and engineering, I have worked with the bosses of businesses such as APV, Chloride Batteries, Hawker Siddeley and Reed International. In the world of transport, logistics and distribution I have been adviser and developer to leaders of NFC (National Freight Consortium), Caliber Logistics and Ryder International. In the world of insurance I have worked with Swiss Re, Guardian Insurance and Jardine International. In the pharmaceutical and ethical products industry, I have worked on strategy and team development with SmithKline Beecham, Hoffman la Roche and L'Oréal.

I have also advised, at various times, the leaders of businesses such as Jones Lang Wootten (now Jone Lang LaSalle, one of the world's largest property consulting businesses) and KPMG Consulting (a global auditing and management consultancy business). I have conducted international and global strategy studies and undertaken team assessment assignments throughout the world. I've been lucky enough to have been employed, usually, by the leaders of these organizations. It's been a lot of fun! It has also given me a unique perspective on the composition and mix of the skills, traits and characteristics of the leaders of many of these organizations.

Elliott Jaques, formerly Director of the Brunel Institute of Social Science and an academic authority on discovering who had leadership skills and how and when they would evolve, reckoned that he could always tell exactly what level a leader would rise to and when. I do not go that far. I think it is hard to predict the direction of careers into the future because there are so many accidents that can befall a leader during a career. But, with all other things being equal, I think you can foretell, by and large, that a person has or doesn't have the necessary leadership qualities.

An underlying theme to this book is that leadership and management are in some senses a trade-off, one to another. We might almost say:

> Leaders don't manage and managers don't lead
>
> (see John Kotter's book entitled *What Leaders Really Do*)

This implies that the roles of leadership and management are almost contradictions of each other. Managers need to be team players. They have to get groups of people to work together to achieve their objectives. They are coordinators of other peoples' efforts rather than leaders of teams achieving their own, self-set agendas. On the other hand, leaders have to balance all the stakeholders in their business, those people who have the power to judge them or who have primary rights over the assets they control. But the leadership job is not just a coordination role. Leaders are paid to balance everybody's interests as part of the act of leadership itself. Such leaders must be visionaries and have high quality judgment. They have to know how to set examples and change cultures and atmospheres to help their organization evolve into the form it needs to adopt to achieve their vision of the future. Leaders don't manage people towards a result. They mix and mould the whole set of resources, people, assets, streams of income. The skill they display is similar to a cook mixing ingredients. All great cooks have their personal 'style and touch' which gives them superior results. They all have a touch of originality, which is hard to summarize in ordinary terms. Yet they accept and retain the ultimate responsibility for success.

This welcomed responsibility for successful outcomes is the uttermost differentiator between leaders and managers. All managers, ultimately, have somebody above them to take responsibility for some or most aspects of their role for the organization. It may be their finance director or their technical research manager or their own line manager giving them their instructions on strategy. It might be their marketing or sales manager telling them what to sell and how much for. At the end of the day there is always somebody else to take ultimate responsibility for some aspect or other of the final decision. It is only the leader who bears total responsibility for all facets of the organization's future and its results.

Although the roles of the manager and the leader are differentiated from each other, each contains some elements of the others' cares and responsibilities. A leader has to manage the team around them; a manager has to have some capacity for strategic analysis. However, as we move up the organizational ladder, a manager needs to use more leadership skills and fewer management skills; a leader can drop more and more management behaviours to focus upon leadership in its purest form as illustrated in Figure 1.

This book is intended to help future leaders trace the balance, which they have to retain as they move up the hierarchy towards their personal career goals, either in a senior management role or a leadership role. Somewhere along the road a leader realizes whether they are 'suited to be a leader' as distinct from being 'fit for management'. I sincerely hope that many readers will discover that they have what it takes to become a leader. There are too few good ones about. This book aims to ensure, by the close, that any leader who is reading will be best fitted and mentally equipped to fulfill their destiny and enjoy a leadership career. Naturally, amongst the total readership, there will be some who will have to face up to the discovery that they may well never become a leader. After all, every leader needs the personal

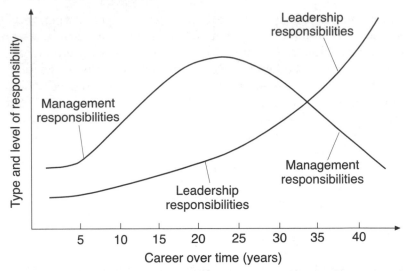

Figure 1 The balance between management and leadership over time. Management responsibilities start early for leaders, in the management phase of their career. It peaks between the 20th and 25th year for those who are climbing towards a top leadership role. Leadership duties and skills should overtake management tasks, on average, some time in the last 20% of their career.

courage it takes to be fully self aware, even of their own weaknesses. The starting point to building either a management or a leadership career, is one of the absolutes of all great leaders' characteristics, the armour of moral fibre!

Remember also, there are many leadership jobs, at different sized organizations, from small business to giant corporations. A manager in a large-scale business may have a much more influential role than the leader of a relatively small company. But the manager will know 'he is not the leader'; and the leader of the much smaller business will know that he or she is truly the ultimate boss in the mini empire they control. The objective of a work life is for people to find a role which suits their talents within or at the top of the organization. It is a constant theme of this book that only happy people work well and do good things for themselves and their business.

1. Theoretical Context of Studies of Leadership

Who is the leader?

The ultimate leader in an organization is the person paid to take the biggest and most important decisions in the organization. Naturally, this book also addresses all those people who aspire to become that type of leader. A great leader spends his or her entire career learning how to be the best possible leader when they finally make it to the top. It is not possible to arrive in the ultimate leadership job and know everything it takes to be great. Besides, a leader is always learning new skills, evolving latent traits and improving his or her mastery of the necessary characteristics of leadership. It is a feature of most successful people that they are always learning and are prepared to take their lessons from wherever they come.

It is important to note here that most of the data and observations in this book relate to the business world of senior corporate leaders. Most of these people are not famous because they don't like to get into newspaper headlines. Wise leaders deliberately don't get themselves into the media, if they can help it. In most organizations we are describing somebody holding titles such as 'President', 'Chairman, 'Chief Executive Officer', 'Chief Operating Officer', 'Executive President', 'Executive Vice-president' or 'Managing Director'. When the strategic leader is *not* the Chairperson or the President, usually that position will be occupied by a 'non-executive'.

The examples and data used in this book originated, in the main, from large size corporations. Usually, their revenue was measured in hundreds of millions or several billions of pounds or dollars. The numbers of employees were often measured in thousands and tens of thousands. Often, the profits were measured in hundreds of millions of pounds or dollars. Normally, they measured their customers in millions, rather than hundreds or thousands.

Paradigmatic thinking

Learning how to think in paradigms is another way of expressing the need to think within frameworks of understanding. We all do this most of the time. But usually it is unconscious and accidental. For example, if somebody is discussing with a colleague an interview of a candidate for a job, they might remark, 'she had some unusual ideas on recruitment'. This brief statement implies a whole framework of understanding:

- What is a normal recruitment method?
- How do we normally do things in our department or business?
- What are the accepted ways of recruiting elsewhere?
- Are the 'unusual ideas' acceptable or too deviant from the norms? etc., etc.

All those ideas are 'paradigms' of accepted thought. Those paradigms are frameworks or working theories that we all have in our heads. Often they will have formed unconsciously, over years of experience. Sometimes they contain important flaws of logic or errors which, because we have never subjected our paradigm to conscious scrutiny, have not been questioned or tested for reliability or accuracy. That is why, to understand this whole area, we have to dig briefly into some complex areas of philosophical thought. It warrants a quick glance at the roots of the subject.

A key philosopher of twentieth century scientific thought was Karl Popper, a Jewish refugee from the German Nazi era who settled down after his refuge years at the London School of Economics. Popper wrote the *Logic of Scientific Discovery* (1959) while still in Vienna. In that book he suggested that all science is based upon a logic of continuing scientific progress. Science moves forward by means of scientists offering hypotheses which should be expressed, according to Popper, as simply as possible. They should also be set up in a form which enables other scientists to test them by exact replication. Popper argues that scientists should try to make themselves 'transparently falsifiable' so that their theories can be tested the more easily by other scientists. Popper also advocates that when there are two apparently equal explanatory theories on the same subject, the one which is expressed more simply (thus having greater falsifiability) should be the one which prevails. Thus, for Popper, science marches forwards, always getting bigger and more comprehensive (although simpler), always edging nearer towards the ultimate truth of all encompassing understanding.

A contrasting viewpoint is represented by the philosophy of Thomas Kuhn, an American philosopher. In Kuhn (1962), entitled *The Structure of Scientific Revolutions*, he represents an opposite view from that of Karl Popper of how science works. He argues that science does not progress forward with theories encompassing more truth. He suggests that science moves in revolutionary stages, neither forward nor backward. Science produces theories that encompass the needs of society at that time. During the period when any one paradigm prevails most scientists do small-scale experiments that move science and society forwards in small practical ways. Once again, society works within the paradigm.

Towards the end of any period of scientific progress under any particular paradigm or framework it gradually becomes obvious to all working within that particular framework that a new paradigm is necessary. Why? Because towards the end of the useful life of the paradigm anomalies begin to arise from experiments that the paradigm fails to illuminate or help to solve. To break out from the crisis of questions that the current paradigm or framework cannot solve science needs a great revolutionary new paradigm.

Kuhn suggests that towards the end of the era of a ruling paradigm, anomalies in the scientific results of experiments or observations of phenomena which contradict the prevailing paradigm or fail to fit within the framework begin to arise. He likens this period to any political pre-Revolutionary phase. When a great scientist comes along with the new paradigm (a Copernicus, a Newton or an Einstein, a Marx or a Keynes or a Friedman), it is akin to a revolution. He suggests that changing paradigm is almost as challenging as changing one's religion. It is equally hard because it requires those 'normal scientists' to adopt the new paradigm like they would embrace a new religion or a new belief system. Most of the normal scientists fail to do it and just work out the rest of their lives within the old paradigm.

What are the implications of the two different theories about science and scientific progress represented above? In fact they are the difference between objectivity and subjectivity. Popper's concept is that science and life moves forwards, onwards and progressively upwards. This contrasts to Kuhn's theory that scientific discovery moves only in relative terms to previous positions. Popper is saying that science moves ever onwards towards greater truth. Kuhn is suggesting that it moves in revolutionary leaps from position to position depending upon society's needs at that time. Kuhn's philosophical implication is that science and knowledge are not necessarily moving forward but merely from one place to another. It might represent progress or it might represent, in perspective, a regression to a less favourable position. That represents a philosophical position of relativism. Everything relates to something else, there is no absolute truth or knowledge.

Popper's position is much more objective and strong. Everything relates to everything else and, at the end, to the greatest knowable eternal truths, when science has eventually made enough progress. There is an absolute truth and that is what all scientists are working towards. The philosophical moral equivalent of Popper's position is that there are eternal ethics and morals and that we should all abide by them. Kuhn's philosophical stance from this point of view could be that morals are relative and may change according to need and circumstance.

These viewpoints form the range that must be considered when we try to understand how a leader needs to think and judge when deciding a vision for his or her organization. It is such philosophies that one is using, without necessarily knowing about the thinkers or mode of thought themselves, when deciding what one's organization must do under particular circumstances or when forming a strategic vision for the future.

The ability to think in paradigms or frameworks is vital to any leader of an organization, state or community. A classical example of what we mean here would be the thinking of, say, John Major compared to Margaret Thatcher. There can be little doubt that John Major possesses great intelligence. However, unfortunately he missed the type of classical education that many of the people around him had received, namely the top civil servants and many of his cabinet subordinates. His pure intelligence could not make up for the easy leaps forward they could make in having so many paradigms at their mental disposal, learned from the hallowed halls of Oxbridge and their various public schools. Compare that to Margaret Thatcher who had the benefit of Oxford doctoral level training. She understood paradigmatic thought easily and knew how to use it to wrap her ideas up in theory-like frameworks which made her ideas seem sufficiently rational to those who were meant to accommodate her wishes. She was thus able to command more respect and obedience from those around her who understand the philosophical game they are all unwittingly playing all the time.

There is an unfortunate consequence of all this. The more complex and clever a leader's capacity to use frameworks becomes, the more it drives out the capacity to use his or her intuition and creativity. That enabled Major to make imaginative breakthroughs in Ireland and prevented Thatcher from seeing how crazy were the results of her frameworks when they led directly to a universally hated 'poll tax'.

Three schools of thought

Leadership theories can be roughly grouped into three categories. They are:

- trait models   leadership in terms of personal attributes
- behavioural models   study what leaders do and theorize therefrom
- contingency theory   examines correlations between situations and leaders' styles

Trait models

The key concept of the traits models is that they try to identify qualities that leaders seem to have as a natural or genetic inheritance rather than characteristics which they acquire by development, training or up-bringing. In essence, this is a 'leaders are born' type premise.

Behavioural models

The underlying assumption of behavioural or models of leadership is that if you study leaders you can learn how to be a leader from their behaviour. In other words, to be a leader you must do as other leaders do. The basis of this theory is that leadership is a learned or acquired skill. The inherent weakness of the concept is that it tends not to differentiate between good and bad leaders. When adopted crudely it can lead to the teaching of poor as well as excellent management practice.

Contingency theory

Contingency theory examines situations in order to discover which style of leadership is successful in each particular type of situation. It is dependent upon agreement about (or even the possibility of finite categorization of) the many different types of situation that can be defined. It is also dependent upon the range of what contingency theorists choose to describe as leadership styles. In consequence of both these variables, contingency theory tends to have as many adherents as newcomers to the field of leadership theory.

When theory does not help

The brief descriptions above help one to infer that the longest running debate about leadership theory is concerned with distinguishing which talents or traits are the natural attributes a leader needs to be born with compared to those which may be learned or acquired. The greatest problem all the theorists have is to agree which particular set of born traits and which group of acquired skills is necessary and similar for all *successful* leaders. They all seem to agree that a strong motivation to lead is vital. Peters and Waterman (1982) *In Search of Excellence* found leaders had an obsession to implement the mission of the organization, clear values and vision and rewarded people narrowly on the key winning tactics for success. What few have described is what made them ambitious in the first place.

A weakness of trait theory (or the 'leaders are born' theory), is that it ignores the possibility that leaders are also formed by their family circumstances and upbringing, their education and the many other external influences during their psychological formation. Furthermore, success as a leader is dependent upon many other factors such as being in the right business at the right time for the particular sets of leadership qualities that any one leader brings to the situation, including having an optimum team of subordinates. Of course, a traitist would say 'But a great leader would have traits that ensured s/he was in the right business at the right time with the right people'.

Pure trait theory also renders itself into a pure hypothesis of accidents. Nobody can control which bed they will be born in. Nobody decides for themselves which types of parents they will get or the type of parental environment they will receive. For example, consider the story Richard Branson (2000) tells in his autobiography, *Losing My Virginity*. He describes how, when he was very young, his mother drove him some distance from their home and said 'now find your own way home'. When ones puts that experience together with love, a wealthy and comfortable background and the installation of a self belief that anything he wanted to do would be approved of and was likely to be successful was great training for the larger than life, large-scale entrepreneur he was to become.

Consider again the plaintive letters that the infant Winston Churchill wrote to his parents begging them to come to Harrow School, where he was boarded, for Speech Day or to acknowledge he was doing well as a cadet in the army. His parents, probably unwittingly, set up such a vast need to please and win approval in Churchill that he was enslaved to achievement for the whole of his life in an effort to win approval from them. Before we judge them too harshly, let's note that their behaviour was normal and conventional for parents from backgrounds such as theirs. Their parental style only appears to be uncaring and selfish in the light of modern parental theory.

Many traits theorists appear to be saying that all the leadership talents need to be latently available from birth. However, usually, a more careful study of their work demonstrates that they are also implying that some of the practical skills of leadership can be acquired during childhood and during the early years of a management career. As was stated in the introduction, every managerial job has some aspect of leadership to it; so does the job of leadership itself. At some stage in an individual's career, when s/he reaches senior levels in the organization, the leadership aspects of the function overtake the managerial ones in terms of the time spent on them and their importance in delivering the content of the role. I described, in *The Leadership Gene*, six 'chromosomes' which compose the 'leadership gene'. They are, youthful energy; courageous circumspection; winning ways; balance; intuition; and, moral fibre.

Other leadership studies

Other theories of leadership suggest the opposite pole of the theoretical span. There are some which are always referred to in the textbook literature on leadership. They are:

- The Iowa Leadership Studies;
- The Ohio State Leadership Studies;
- The Michigan Leadership Studies;
- contingency theory;
- charismatic leadership;
- managerial leadership;
- stakeholder theory.

The Iowa Leadership Studies were conducted by Lewin, Lippitt and White. They mainly studied leadership style and its effect on children's behaviour. The underlying implication was that leadership can be a taught behaviour and does not require genetic starting skills. Unfortunately, these studies were mostly irrelevant to modern business models.

The Ohio State Leadership Studies tried to define the qualities of good leadership in numerous situations and types. They found that 'good leadership' was synonymous with *consideration* and *initiating structure*. A criticism of this work was that it was too focused on *how* leaders lead and not enough on what qualities the successful leaders need to achieve success. These studies thus fell between the two stools of trait and behaviour theory and decided nothing.

The Michigan Leadership Studies led by Rensis Likert found there were four key leadership styles. These were the exploitative; the benevolent autocratic; the participative; and the democratic. Leaders were either task oriented or employee-centred. The studies concluded that leaders who focused upon people were more successful and ran better businesses. This was rather simplistic for practical application. It also lacked verisimilitude. Any single leader may display a multitude of styles and qualities.

A third category of studies about leadership is known as *contingency theory*. A leading researcher in this field was Fred Fiedler who developed his contingency model. The basic model says that leadership effectiveness is dependent upon (1) the leader-member relationship, (2) the degree of task structure and (3) the leader's position power. If all three are high, then the leader seems to be more effective in delivering success. Fiedler (cf. Levicki), developed a concept of *situational favourableness*. This suggests each type of leader can only be effective in a limited number of situations. So, it is necessary for the people selecting leaders or the leaders themselves to be aware of what types of problem and range of strategic problems a candidate is suited to solve and to verify that matches the given situation.

There has been a revival of the theories about the need for *charismatic leadership*. This is an old theory whose modern revival is attributed to Robert House. Charismatic business leaders have superior debating and persuasive skills, which, together with superior technical knowledge, foster attitudinal, behavioural and emotional changes in their followers. I have always disfavoured the use of personal charisma as a leadership methodology. In my experience, charismatic people too easily sway people and it removes the value of subordinates' insights and experience by overcoming them with brute charm.

J. M. Burns pointed out differences between leaders measured by their capacity to either manage transactionally or to be transformational. He theorized that leaders displaying these two key contrasting skills possessed the most relevant qualities of leadership. Hersey and Blanchard have become famous disseminating their situational leadership concepts. They focus upon two dimensions, relationship and task. By using these on a simple grid they create four styles: *telling*, *selling*, *participating* and *delegating*. Their simple questionnaires are in use all over the world. Their practical leadership and management training concepts are widely adopted. The theory itself, although its simplicity is admirable, is rarely tested under suitable experimental conditions and remains unproven.

Another school of theory could be entitled *Managerial*. John Kotter, at the Harvard Business School has conducted many studies of managerial leadership behaviour. He carefully distinguishes management behaviour from that of leaders and points out that there are important differences between the two as well as similarities. The differences are that manager's focus on teamwork, carrying out other leaders' strategies; managers are rather more short term in their outlook than leaders. Leaders tend to be more visionary in their approach; they are consistently strategic and are less involved with people than managers tend to be.

Herbert Simon developed the *Stakeholder Theory* of leadership. He saw leaders primarily as *satisficers* or aggregators of stakeholders' (those holding stakes or having influential power in the organization) relative power. Simon's concept states that, ultimately, leaders always have to make *satisficing* decisions, which are an aggregation of everybody's interests. It enables the leader to satisfy everybody to some extent. Thus, none are so unhappy with the organization's results that they care to intervene or protest. But also no one feels that the others' interests are being unfairly favoured. Thus, the leader is seen as *final arbiter*, the judge in a game of competing internal and external groups of interests.

Finally we have what I call the *Practical School*, which specializes in the 'How to Do It' Approaches to Leadership. These are represented by academics such as Warren Bennis, whose most recent work, *Managing People is Like Herding Cats*. He concludes that 'leaders are the ones with vision, who inspire others and cause them to galvanize their efforts and achieve change. Managers, on the other hand, will follow standard operating procedure to their graves . . .'.

Another practitioner in the 'sharp end' division is John Adair. His core work, *Effective Leadership* (Adair, 1988), describes the qualities that a leader must develop. When dealing with task objectives, the leader must demonstrate initiative and perseverance; in leading a team, a leader must embody integrity and humour; as an individual, the leader needs tact and compassion. As always, it is easy to pick a few buzzwords that Adair misses, such as vision or the ability to deliver shareholder value, but, overall, he offers practical advice on 'how to make a good leader'.

Theoretical aspects of studying leadership

Studying leadership embodies many of the same problems as almost all other business subjects. The prime variable, the leader, is, by definition, unique. In addition, the business or businesses for which s/he works are usually all different in terms of industry sector, size, geography and success. Below I try to isolate those variables which should be held constant if one were trying to develop a better science for the study of leadership and to isolate the fundamental variables which contribute to a greater or lesser success.

The variables of leadership

1. Organizational size

Bolton (1986) defined business sizes as small (businesses having numbers of people between 1 and < 100) or medium (businesses with people numbers of more than 100 and less than 500); all businesses having over 500 employees are defined as 'large businesses'. In this book, it is the leaders of large businesses that I am discussing. I believe that leaders of smaller businesses have different characteristics and interests. The way they communicate and the number of actual variables they have to administer and mix is fundamentally less complex than those of the larger business.

2. Different organizational forms need different leadership skills

Almost by definition different organizational forms need different leadership skills. At the simplest level, political leaders are different from business leaders who are different from social leaders and so on.

The essential difference between business and political leaders is that the former take decisions to achieve profits whereas political leaders manage their behaviour, mainly, to achieve votes at election time. Although sometimes these areas of interest overlap, by and large, the necessary compromises that achieve political success nearly always run against the profit maximizing motivation of most business organizations.

3. Corporate leadership is not the same as entrepreneurship

An entrepreneur has to have the courage and skills to create a business. This includes setting up finance, risk taking and, normally, the power to inspire others to work for him/her. Once the business grows to a 'corporate size' the entrepreneur needs normal corporate business leadership skills. That is often a testing period when the business is highly vulnerable. Most people who become entrepreneurs do so because they like to run their own show, are relatively independent and dislike having people in authority over them. By definition, once the business grows to a corporate size it needs to evolve to a separate form and adopt a hierarchical structure, more or less. If the entrepreneur is unable to adapt (which s/he rarely is) s/he must move aside. If they are unwilling to do so this normally immediately begins to restrict and constrain organizational growth. It will do so as long as they remain in charge. When entrepreneurs are unable to transform into the needed role in their own organization, then they need to bring in someone else to discharge the roles they cannot engage. It is difficult to judge which happens more frequently, the entrepreneur lacking the skills of chairmanship or their inability to accept anybody over them as chairpersons. A classical example is Alan Sugar, former leader of Amstrad. Although he has moved up to the chair role he has remained executive in style and entrepreneurial in mode. Thus, he seems to lose his managing directors on a regular basis.

4. Leadership is not the same as management (Kotter, 1999)

Kotter, at Harvard, has defined many of the differences between management and leadership. He sees them as fundamentally different skill and behaviour sets, although here are many apparent similarities among some of the required skills for both form of work. The key differences are:

- *leadership*   is strategic, influential, visionary, transformational and inspirational;
- *management*   is motivational, organizational, ordered, planned, budgeted and consistent.

[Neither list is exclusive but both are indicative of their sector.]

Summary of key variables of leadership

(1) Stylistic and/or temperamental suitability;
(2) Situational fit;
(3) Organizational size;
(4) The state of evolution of the industry;
(5) Technology (different industries need particular knowledge or talent);
(6) The time horizons of the industry (e.g. fashion garments versus telecoms);
(7) Mission/raison d'être of the organization (e.g. profits, non-profit organization, share value maximization, longevity of individual family wealth, rapid capital gain).

The independent variables indicating leadership roles

The reason it is so difficult to aggregate previous studies or draw conclusions from previous work on leadership is that all too often the variables within the studies have not being controlled in any way that permits comparability. No one has tried to make each study comparable to previous work. To create a real body of social or business science studies of leadership as an independent subject worthy of academic research, investigators, in the future, might try and control their selection of leaders for some of the following the independent variables:

(1) the degree of autonomy of the leader
(2) the degree of importance of the leaders' decisions
(3) who could dismiss the leader from their position?
(4) how frequently does the leader have to make reports?
(5) to whom does the leader have to report (e.g. to the board or to another individual)?

New questions to consider about leadership

There are several different indicators emerging which suggest there is increasing difference nowadays between:

- operational or 'managerial' leaders (e.g. Unilever, BAT); and
- share-value maximizing leaders (e.g. AOL, Liberty Media).

In 'mature' or 'old industry' businesses, the share value maximizing leader is dependent upon the operational leader for results, because the leader talks strategy to the influencers but relies upon the operational leaders to deliver the empirical implications of the strategy to justify their market pitch. In high technology, fast growth or emergent market businesses, the operational leader is dependent upon the skills of the share value maximizing leader, to attract the capital necessary for infrastructure growth and to increase the capital value of the equity to facilitate fast market share growth. That is because s/he knows how to do it but not how to talk it up into share or investment values. In terms of investment values, in *mature businesses*, we want old-fashioned, operational leaders, whereas in *emergent, hi-tech industries*, we would prefer a share value maximizing leader who can be almost ignorant of traditional 'managerial' skills, as long as the leader has the necessary share value maximizing skills.

This is an area ripe for research attention, especially by anybody responsible for selecting new leaders? Is enough attention being paid to the vital differences in nature, style, skill, behaviour and objectives of the two fundamentally different key types of individual outlined in the paragraph above?

New areas of leadership research

Over the past few years many multinational corporations have grown exponentially. For example, ATT spent $120 billion in 1999, buying TCI and MediaOne, to become the world's leading cable business. AOL and Time Warner attempted to merge nearly $200 billion of assets to become the world's leading high-tech media business. Vodafone took over Airtouch and Mannesman in 1999 for almost $200 billion, to become the world's leading mobile telephony company and a key media player.

In the year 2000 the top 10 merger and alliance advisers organized deals worth five thousand billion dollars. Morgan Stanley alone did over a trillion dollars worth of merger business. The top four merger and alliance advisers, Morgan Stanley, Goldman Sachs, CSFB, Salomon Smith Barney did over three trillion dollars of business on their own (*Financial Times*, 29 December 2000). This gives some indication of the quiet but massive far reaching revolution that is taking place all over the global economic empire.

These gigantic, multi billion dollar takeovers and mergers represent a step increase in the rate of large-scale merger. Consider the FTSE 100 in the UK, for example. The top six UK firms represent nearly 40% of its total value (see Table 1.1). That is a vast amount of wealth, power and employment in the hands of just half a dozen individuals who are only directly controlled by the highly inadequate and dubious democracy of a disseminated shareholder power. Such changes, which are matched equally around the world, especially in the USA, represent a

Company	Sector	Market Cap. (£bn)	FTSE 100 Weighting
Vodaphone	Telecoms	145.9	10.1%
BP Amoco	Oil	122.5	8.49%
GlaxoSmithKline	Pharmaceuticals	116.7	8.09%
HSBC	Banking	90.3	6.26%
Astra Zeneca	Pharmaceuticals	60.5	4.19%
Shell	Oil	54.6	3.79%

Table 1.1 The UK's largest companies

According to the *Financial Times* of 28 December 2000, the top three UK companies (Vodafone, BP Amoco and GlaxoSmithKline) accounted for £385 billion of capital and nearly 27% of the total FTSE weighting. In other words, the top three companies were worth over a quarter of the top 100 companies put together. Imagine the power of those three leaders!

fundamental change that is taking place in the relationship between capitalism and democracy. This also presents a need to rethink that relationship (Table 1.1).

These mergers are often arranged through the medium of just one or two key leaders within the respective corporations and a few outside merchant bank 'ideas people', who make their living from the fees earned when business leaders follow up their ideas for industry synergy or increased market control. These innovative strategic business concepts are rationalized by the leaders and their advisers after the event when the idea is 'sold' to the owners (the shareholders).

In essence, vast quantities of economic power are placed within new ownership parameters. They are often controlled offshore in a multinational structure. Frequently they are completely outside the control of any of the nation-state governments which are nominally meant to be regulating and controlling them with regard to social and ethical norms, taxation, employment policies and the well-being of the various industrial states wherein they and their customers are implanted. Who, other than the one or two top leaders, rules or influences these corporations on behalf of their employees, their owners or the legal citizens of the respective nation-state governments of the countries where they conduct their business?

Consider, for example, the behaviour of some leaders. At BMW the leader bought and sold Rover Cars during the 1990s, largely against the will of important internal and external stakeholders. At Barclays Bank, in 2000, the leader closed down hundreds of small branches against the will of the unions and the customers. At Microsoft the leader continues to fight the US government, in spite of the fact that most shareholders believe they would be advantaged if the business was broken into separate and independent divisions.

The supreme example relevant to the theory of democracy comes in the form of Rupert Murdoch, the ultimate controller of News

International. His holding company has interests in newspapers, satellite television, programme and film manufacture and the supply of news and entertainment to many other entertainment distribution organizations, such as the cable industry in the UK. Rupert Murdoch is on public record saying that he can reach 60% of the total world population through the media that he directly controls. It is possible that he controls or strongly influences the actions of politicians in many of the spheres of the globe in which he operates. Yet his Corporation pays comparatively low rates of corporate tax in spite of the fact that his wealth has grown from a few millions in the 1950s to, in the year 2000, over $75 billion. He has Australian and American citizenship (the latter to facilitate his ownership of American broadcasting rights). He recently married a Chinese citizen for his third marriage. It is not difficult to guess where the focus of his business interests will be between now and the moment he hands over his dynastic Corporation to his children.

Each leader or set of leaders described in the examples above appears to be able to manage the wishes of important stakeholders such as the government or thousands of their employees or their customers. They appear to have had little insight or care about the political, social or economic aspects of the decisions they are implementing, other than in ensuring they are never stopped in their ambitions. Yet, these leaders are exercising levels of power equivalent to many Ministers of State as they take decisions affecting the lives of thousands of employees and, potentially, millions of customers.

We have to ask how can any single dimension of corporate governance or political government control such incredibly large-scale business movements? Is it likely that BMW's or Barclays' Bank leaders would be taking different decisions if the social and economic costs of their behaviour were visited upon them through a politically powerful regional organization such as the EC. Vodafone was able to buy a leading US corporation and a top German one because, effectively, there was no global coordinating government to control or oversee what they were doing.

The key point, for the theory(ies) of social democracy and for corporate governance, is that the nature of the role of leader of these vast enterprises is changing. Currently, there is little effective government overseeing the behaviour of MNC leaders. This implies two possible solutions. The first is that external political scale systems must increase to match and control the leaders of these enterprises (e.g. the EC in Europe; federal powers in the USA; the ASEAN in the Far East). The second (and less credible or likely) is that the leaders of large corporations will become more subject to democratic controls through democratic control mechanisms within their organizations. This may have to include the way the leaders are appointed, the criteria for judging their success and the parameters which govern the political, social, economic and ethical 'rules of the business game' which they play out across the global arena.

Unless regional regulatory authorities are able to achieve profound control over modern gigantic global businesses these corporations will become uncontrollable monsters which destroy the very meaning of democracy.

Another solution to the same problem is the hope that modern corporate leaders will become more democratic in their exercise of the power which the role of leader of the Corporation endows them with. However, that solution is profoundly Utopian and has far less possibility of realization than increasing the power of political regulators to control corporate leaders externally.

Summary

This chapter has described the various theories of leadership. The first type is the group of trait theories which believes that leaders are born, not made. The next group, the behaviourists believe that leaders can be trained and given the skills necessary to be a good leader. Finally, the contingency theorists believe that it all depends on the task in hand and the situation the leader has to control. We have pointed out that it is improbable that leaders are born with all the talents it takes to be successful. It is equally unlikely that just anybody can be trained to be a good leader. We have indicated that contingency is so loose in its definition that it cannot be judged as a theoretical set of concepts.

Finally we have indicated new areas which we believe leadership theory must extend itself to cover situations which are arising at the beginning of the twenty-first century. It is unlikely that previous scholars could have a contemplated the gigantic size that corporations are reaching today. Neither could they have foreseen the widely dispersed shareholder ownership of the modern era that leaves power concentrated in the hands of the leaders of gigantic multinational corporations. We believe it is important that new theories are evolved in the arena of both democracy and leadership to match the situations that were never contemplated in previous history.

2. The Traits of Leadership

A working definition of leader and leadership

It is useful to differentiate between quality leaders who have strategic vision from those leaders who have achieved their position merely because of their political skills. I call the former '*strategic leaders*'. These are people who truly understand how to create a mission for an organization and then how to operationalize it to effectively deliver growth and value to all the stakeholders in the business.

I use the phrase '*nominal leaders*' to contrast with 'strategic leaders'. Nominal leaders are those people who get the top jobs but who shouldn't be there. They have little or no strategic vision, their operational skills are usually confined to accounting procedures or using acquisition accounting tricks to cover their inability to truly grow a business organically with judicious, occasional acquisition to cover difficult to penetrate markets. Nor do they know how to create strategic futures without tricks. Nominal leaders know how to look good. They often have an exaggerated opinion about their level of skill. They believe they have a right to be 'at the top'. Consequently they will do whatever it takes to stay there. They often have extremely refined 'political skills'. It was these political skills that they needed to get to the top without leadership talent. Many people around them can see them for all their weaknesses and lack of leadership skills. But nominal leaders cannot see themselves clearly. Or they choose not to.

Effective managerial leadership is often displayed at many levels in an organization. I am writing particularly about those who aspire to and actually do lead successfully at the very top of their organization. These are the people that I have been working with, quietly in the background, for many years. It is my good fortune to have worked with a few, truly great, leaders. Unfortunately, I have also worked with many whom, to keep this account clean, are best described as 'infertile'.

This chapter is talking about those strategic leaders who were probably born with all the necessary traits to become a great leader. In an earlier book I called the aggregation of all these traits *the leadership gene*.

Does a 'leadership gene' exist?

Possibly the oldest, intellectual debate in history is whether the predominant force which influences our behaviour, characteristics, intelligence and achievement levels originates from nature or nurture. John Hunt (1981), in his *Managing People at Work* summarized his research as follows:

> those who make it to positions where all leadership is vital are above average in intelligence (but not too high above average), are healthy, are from middle to upper class backgrounds, have high power needs, and are more often first born or first son.

(Hunt, 1981: p. 126)

There can never be a definitive, scientific final opinion on this tortuous subject. However, after observing, developing and working alongside thousands of leaders, I have become convinced that all good leaders are born with some special talents. In other words there are qualities of intelligence, personality, physical and mental strength, personal determination, energy and intuition which a leader needs to be born with. These trait gets modified as the leader develops as a child and grows into the total leadership qualities package.

The genetic traits it helps to be born with are:

- mental ability;
- physical strength;
- intuition;
- a serene soul;
- a good physique and pleasing physiognomy (being tall helps).

We will examine these 'genetic' or trait skills in this chapter.

The major 'nurture' or skills which can be developed are:

- paradigmatic thinking;
- self-belief;
- communication ability;
- strategic analysis;
- team motivation;
- financial and business analysis;
- people selection;
- balance and judgment.

We will examine these 'acquired' or learned skills in Chapter 3.

Some of the most important influencing factors in people developing the desire and urgent will and wish to be a leader are:

- an unusually dominant mother;
- being the eldest child in the family;

- having a father who achieved high levels of success (and who managed to make his child like him);
- being chosen by a school teacher for special nurturing.

We will look at this group in Chapter 6 on how to inculcate leadership qualities in a child.

The problem with a concept like a 'leadership gene' is that one still cannot easily tell if one has it or not. There are signs of it early in a career. What should one look for?

- an independent spirit with good judgment;
- special signs of leadership such as a person exuding dignity, easy manners, self-respect and respect for others;
- good relationships with bad managers;
- rapid mastery of new tasks and readiness for promotion within a short period after each promotion;
- willingness and keenness to learn new things about anything relating to the job;
- a contented, well-contained, private life;
- attractiveness, everybody wants to be his or her friend (without toadying).

Look at the following list of questions to make a first, quick summary of your suitability or readiness for leadership:

First audit of leadership potential

Ask yourself the following questions:

- Are you always ready to take a free and independent view?
- Do you master new tasks easily?
- Do most people consider your judgment to be objective?
- Do most people perceive you as dignified?
- Are you always well mannered?
- Do people sometimes consider you have too much self-respect?
- Do people find it easy to respect you?
- Do you find it easy to respect people for their particular skills?
- Do you get on easily with bad managers?
- Do you get promoted every year or so?
- Do you enjoy learning new things?
- Do you really think happiness in your private life is as important as your business life?
- Do you make friends easily?

Are leaders born or developed?

This question is close to the eternal debate between nature and nurture. But it has enormous importance here. After all, who decides 'whether you were born to be a leader' or not? Once it is decided you are not 'a born leader', what future is there for you, especially if you are only interested in one of the few jobs at the top of business organizations?

It is the thesis of this book that leaders need to be both born with a set of genetic characteristics and to be nurtured during their childhood and early adulthood to develop what it takes to be a leader. If the potential is not there, it cannot be developed. But if the potential is there and is not developed, it will not come on its own. We concede that it is not always clear that a person is a naturally born leader. It is sometimes difficult to perceive because they may be, accidentally, in the wrong type of job (although I would argue that great leaders don't let too many accidents happen to their career). Unlucky leaders might have an appalling boss who exploits their skills but deliberately doesn't let the rest of the organization learn of the person's talents. But I would argue that a future leader would know how to ensure the rest of the organization finds out. A potential leader may be going through a 'fallow' period, learning some key skills before the next 'spurt of growth in ability'.

One cannot always see clearly who will make a great leader. But, if they are going to be great, it is because they were both born with the traits and have been developed into aptness for a leadership role. It is possible to predict who 'has the leadership gene' and who does not. There is a more general argument for the case that 'leaders are born, and made', provided by the evidence of twentieth century management education and its effects.

We have seen more leadership and management development than ever before, look at the exponential growth of business schools. Is there any evidence that business school training itself has any effect on the rates of growth and decline of large entities? I would argue there is little visible benefit because organizations spend too little time selecting who should go onto leadership development programmes. Far too often they send everybody in an echelon in the company or whoever is on a particular management grade.

Consider the growth rates of businesses in the USA and the UK, where business schools mushroomed during the 30 years between 1960 and 1990, with very little consequent change in the national growth rates. Compare that to Japan and Germany, where there was almost no creation or development of business school education but which had continuous, startlingly successful, growth rates. Interestingly, Japan is now indulging in the Western predilection for the creation of Business Schools and the training and development of some of its business executives therein. One wonders how soon this will have an effect and what it will be? One should also note that Japanese society has an entirely different sociology from the Western world. Facile copying, as advocated by some prominent and self-proclaiming gurus is less than rational.

There are more global and major international corporations than there were before. Although that requires fewer great leaders rather than more, there still remain many small to medium businesses, both in the developed and the developing world. That may be a sign that more people cannot abide the large corporate world; it may be indicative that modern technology facilitates the formation of more small businesses. Yet it can also be taken as evidence that there just are not enough great leaders around, so we get more small and medium businesses, because that is the size their leaders can cope with. Elliott Jaques has argued that organizations will grow to the size of the time horizon of their leader. I certainly agree although I would amend this to read:

> Organizations will grow to the size of
> the leadership potential of their leader

Another observation, before closing the argument. Notice how many leaders seem to get to the top without training or management development. I remember my surprise upon learning that Sir Peter Thompson had risen to the leadership of The National Freight Consortium without any formal management or leadership training. He didn't need it because he knew instinctively how to lead and develop his own strategic vision. He is a typical example of the argument that 'leaders are born, then formed after'.

What about all those individuals, those *nominal leaders* who are in leadership positions but who achieved their position by political sleight of hand rather than objective demonstration of leadership prowess? I would argue that many of them are not leaders at all, just holders of the position of leader. Andrew Kakabadse, a Professor specializing in Human Resource Studies at the Cranfield University School of Management, published data which indicate that over 60% of business organizations are badly managed. Worse, 52% of Chairmen and CEO's 'feel uncomfortable about the effectiveness of the top team leading the organization and the performance of its members' (Kakabadse, 1991). In some ways, this is strong evidence that even those 'nominal leaders' (those in post but lacking real leadership skills) know that they don't have what it takes. After all, Kakabadse's evidence is their own testimony about themselves!

How do these *nominal leaders*' get the top jobs? They probably have political skills and are, almost without exception, highly driven individuals. Yet they lack essential leadership effectiveness. When you examine their career patterns, in spite of their top leadership job, they singularly fail to demonstrate the qualities of successful leadership. Why? Either because they did not start with the necessary genetic qualities or something has gone missing in their personal development which was vital to complete their potential as a leader. Interestingly, it is often the case that others can see the *nominal leaders* are failing, but they can't see it for themselves.

What are the key ingredients of a business leader?

The leadership task range requires multifarious skills. Among the foremost are:

- tenacity;
- stamina;
- long-term wisdom;
- emotional intelligence;
- judgment about what is worth fighting for (and what isn't);
- equanimity;
- character;
- capacity to inspire followership (a form of generalized love for fellow human beings).

Throughout the book we will be elucidating on these qualities and offering explanations of how to improve when one might feel they need strengthening. Use the following checklist (Questionnaire 2.1) to measure yourself at this control point? Are you a future or present leader by the standards of this first list of requirements?

The traits and skills of leaders

Throughout this book we differentiate between the concepts *leadership traits* and *leadership skills*. We regard traits as those inherent talents, or genetic inbuilt qualities, that a leader has to be born with in order to have any possibility of a successful leadership career. We regard *skills* as abilities that can be acquired or learned from experience, education or teaching. The genetic traits we are born with are listed in Chapter 1 but, to remind you, are; mental agility; physical strength; intuition; a serene soul; a pleasant physique and physiognomy (being tall helps); a sense of decency and moral fibre.

If I had listed all the traits above, without this last, key one, of decency and moral fibre, I could have been describing Hitler, Stalin or indeed, any of the failures listed in Chapter 5, such as Robert Maxwell.

Skill	Meaning	Self-applied rating 1 (low)–10 (high)
Tenacity	Capacity for sticking to difficult to achieve tasks	
Stamina	Ability to stick at a job when the occasional career slow down takes place	
Long-term wisdom	The ability to forecast the future of the industry, the development of one's colleagues and the probabilities of success of strategies	
Emotional intelligence	Having a range of insights which explain profoundly the personal motivations of people around you	
Judgment about priorities	Evaluating the business issues that are most likely to torpedo the business, if left unresolved	
Equanimity	The capacity to remain calm in the eye of the storm	
Character	Having values and beliefs that are sound and which guide you at all key decision points	
Capacity to inspire followership	Do people enjoy being led by you?	
Love for fellow human beings	Do you generally like people more frequently and more easily than you dislike them?	
	Add your total score	

Questionnaire 2.1 A measure of leadership skills.

Interpretation:
Scores <50 mean you need to develop more skills fast
Scores between 51 and 69 indicate a good base but needing development
Scores >70 mean you are well grounded to evolve or be a leader

Many leaders, who would be universally condemned as failures still leave massive achievements and differences behind them. But, if they do not have a profound sense of decency and moral fibre, they are capable of being as great a menace to society as a benefit. Maxwell had great operational skills but completely lacked a sense of moral fibre. Thus, he left behind thousands of people, who had given him their loyalty at work, without the pensions they had counted upon to enjoy their deserved retirement.

Again, throughout this book we distinguish between *traits* and *skills*. A *trait* is something which appears to be natural or genetic within the leader. By contrast a *skill* is a behaviour which can be developed or learned. For further example, a useful trait, for a leader, is not to need to dominate either people, situations, rooms, or meetings. That is either a natural genetic quality or something imbued into the child during development when it was outside the control of the leader to influence how his/her mental make-up was being formed. By contrast, it is a leadership skill to know how and when to dominate a room or discussion. It is a trait to have presence without noise, and a tendency to be more of a listener than a talker. It is a skill to ensure that one knows how to be heard, whenever it is necessary, to make an important point.

Wise leaders often have the trait of creating confidence in their subordinate's, thus increasing their ability to achieve objectives while never falsely making them seem too easy or too hard. Yet it is a sine qua non skill to present challenges to subordinates, directly and with honesty. By transmitting their belief in the person's ability to accomplish the objectives they are setting, they, somehow, add to the subordinates self-belief and confidence that they can actually achieve the job they are given. The leader's belief in them becomes a function of their belief in themselves.

The same applies to all those political leaders who lined their own pockets, so many in Africa, who did it at the cost of their impoverished citizens. Or the men who invented and installed apartheid in South Africa, a system so evil and immoral in its unequal treatment of people based solely upon skin colour. These leaders never saw themselves as lacking moral fibre. But their leadership was done within a moral vacuum from which no good could emerge.

It is strange how few of them realized what their problem was. President Suharto, in Indonesia, created an appalling system of nepotism, bribery and corruption. It led, ultimately, to a systemic failure of the otherwise inspirational, economic leadership he had provided, for over three decades, in the fourth largest nation in the world. Ultimately, his lack of moral fibre and the subsequent inability of his family and himself to control their greed and set standards for others, led to so many false indicators in the economic system throughout his country, that nobody was doing business under realistic economic conditions.

The traits of successful leadership

Traits are best understood as natural talents that a person is born with. They are differentiated from skills and behaviours which can be acquired habits that a manager successfully develops as s/he acquires the habits and craft of great leadership. Everything successful leaders do, and every post they pass through, remains effective long after they go away. Their work achievements have much more permanence than the temporary patch up jobs that lesser managers use to achieve their next promotion. Successful leaders are nearly always promoted early, but they still complete their previous task before moving on to the new one. They rarely need to be looking for promotion because it always seems to come to them. They are never arrogant and habitually humble. They usually have 'full lives' giving attention to their family, playing sports, following hobbies and other pursuits. Their rounded lives are rarely narrowly defined only by the leadership job they do. They measure their success in life by their own standards of happiness and well-being, rather than other peoples' perceptions of their 'successful career' (defined by 'reaching the top'). Part of the success of their career is underpinned by the way they value having a full life more than just achieving a successful career.

A modern view of chromosomes

In an earlier book entitled *The Leadership Gene* I likened the talents a leader needs to be born with to the chromosomes which make up any gene. The dictionary definition of 'chromosome' is:

> any of several threadlike bodies, consisting of chromatin, that are found in a cell nucleus, and carry the genes in a linear order; So called because the chromosomes take on color when a cell is stained.

If many of the chromosomes of the leadership gene are, as I argue here, housed within the leader when born, the chromosomes named in that book were and remain:

- chromosome 1: youthful energy;
- chromosome 2: courageous circumspection;
- chromosome 3: winning ways;
- chromosome 4: balance;
- chromosome 5: intuition;
- chromosome 6: moral fibre.

Chromosome 1: youthful energy

Great leader's need youthful energy, all their working lives. It is frequently remarked about successful leaders that they seem to have enough energy for all their team. They exude energy. Is this because leadership jobs are unusually invigorating? If so, youthful energy would be a consequence of leadership rather than a cause. However, if people with an abnormal energy level rise to the top that could be considered genetic.

Later in this book we will discuss emotional intelligence. Recent research suggests that great leaders need to be emotionally mature as well as analytically intelligent. I always advise, both managers and leaders, to evolve their emotional maturity to the maximum as young as possible. Maturity is defined as being able to understand people and events better, earlier and with deeper insight than others, who only seem to grasp what makes people tick later in life. A key to maturing early is to develop and exploit helicoptering skills and a long time horizon.

Your youthful energy can be enhanced if you believe in yourself and start your leadership career while young. Become mature and wise, especially emotionally, by exercising your abilities to rise above any situation you are in at work or in your private life. Observe everything with a wide perspective. Understand each situation from the point of view of both your immediate boss and his or her leader too. Put every ounce of energy into everything you do as if it's the last job your ever and the last day you'll spend on earth. Release your genetic energy. You will find that it gets replaced with even more energy, and then more again. Energy may be a genetic gift, if you are born with it. But if you aren't, make it a personal habit.

Being emotionally mature is sometimes best understood as having 'an old head on young shoulders'. Increasingly, in the twenty-first century, 'being young' has become highly desirable as a quality in its own right. There are valid reasons. The young have highly desirable qualities. They have energy, optimism and passion for life, because they have all their virginal expectations before them. That is both a worthwhile and desirable state. If you can achieve that condition and stay like that throughout your life, then go for it. It is not only good for leaders, it is highly desirable for anybody. However, it is particularly useful for leaders to try to retain their youthfulness, because they need energy and all the other qualities of youth with which to inspire their followers. The young enjoy life. Leaders should enjoy their work. Energy and youth, as well as physical health, make the mind work better. Above all, the young have optimism; leaders need to be optimistic too, to engender belief in the success of their policies.

If youthfulness can be aligned with the wisdom of greater emotional maturity, one has a perfect combination. Recent research (see Goleman,

1996; Cooper and Sawaf, 1997) show that both emotional maturity and empathy can be more important than pure analytical intelligence, as tools of leadership.

You have to believe in yourself, without arrogance. Try to prepare yourself and be ready for the next job you aspire to, while striving for total competence in whatever you're doing now. Whatever job you gain, do it with distinction. It matters not whether it's waiting on tables during your university vacation, or working on the shop floor during an apprenticeship. Bring the same flawless standards to all situations.

It is always appropriate to wear clothes that fit the role, so dress the part and don't be shy about doing so. Never *overdress* for your role, wearing an MD's shirt when you are only the area manager may annoy some MD's. Always do the right deed (guided by your conscience) and never countenance contempt for the managers you are passing as you move up the organization. Your excellent brain and aptitude for leadership are just accidents of birth, with no more merit than if you had been born tall or handsome. Be grateful for your good luck.

Chromosome 2: courageous circumspection

No matter how many leadership qualities and skills you have, your career will still be subject to accidents, luck and circumstances. You will need a sense of circumspection to help you cope with the worst which is coming your way. What will the worst look like?

- idiots getting jobs you could do ten times better;
- malicious conduct by lesser mortals;
- jealousy from those who wish they were as bright as you;
- sabotage from corporate vandals;
- the existence of so many more fools than bright people and far more fools they you ever imagined could exist.

You will need lots of courage too, because most good things won't come easily. There will be setbacks, crises and bad luck. You will have to face terrible dilemmas when there is no one to give you answers and everything is your own responsibility. Imagine, for example, the day when you are facing a major takeover bid with thousands of your peoples' jobs at stake, with all of them dependent on you getting it right. How will you handle the crisis? What priorities will receive your attention first? What will you do to ensure that every aspect of your beliefs and your duty has received the right consideration, your best judgment and the most apt answers? Whatever conclusion you draw and whichever way you go, some people out there won't think that you are the Great Leader you are reputed to be. And you won't feel that you are either.

That is why you will need courageous circumspection. If you diligently and consistently put in the right inputs and take ethically and strategically sound decisions at every step of the path, you will arrive at optimal solutions. But if it doesn't come out right, circumspection will help you to cope, because, being wise, you will judge yourself by your own standards. You will take pleasure from all, including the final job you get. If it is less high than you anticipated, then circumspection will alleviate the pain and ensure that you will have had almost all the fun anyway. It will just be the accolade of the final job that you will have missed. It won't feel so bad or so important.

Courage is vital in a leader because there will always be tough tasks to carry out. Among the toughest will be telling people you have to take their employment away from them, for the greater good of the organization. Some day your duty may lead you to close factories and ruin whole towns. At another time, your board of directors will treat you badly and may ask you to step down. A competitor may buy the company you work for and decide they do not need you. You must hope that you will do it better to others than they will do it to you. Your courage will be fully tested. You will need courage because there is no point to being frightened. No one can predict the weird events that will happen to you during your career. Neither can you foresee the wonderful things that may evolve. Fear should not be part of your psychological make-up. It serves little purpose. A little rational apprehension might usefully keep you on your guard. But don't be fearful, it's a waste of the energy.

Use the helicopter tool (see Chapter 10). That's a mental game to raise yourself above the fray and the daily battlefield. That will help you to keep events in perspective. Whenever you face important or dramatic moments, whether in your personal or your business life, jump into the helicopter and get your perspective back. If you find the helicopter is out of action, turn to a time horizon machine. Ask yourself how awful will this situation feel in 3 months, 3 years, or 30 years time? There will always be some length of time horizon where the pain does not cause so much anguish.

Beware when your temper makes large events look important in your business. Be careful at times when you feel fear, it distorts your vision and belittles your bravery. Fear is always a consequence of not thinking a problem through clearly. When you do, everything will fall into perspective and you will then be able to summon the necessary brain power to deal with it. If it is a business problem, then assemble enough merchant bankers, consultants, colleagues and friends to deal with it. Every problem can be broken up into enough constituent part to get it solved. If it is a personal problem you may need to use different methods. First, share it with a friend, that always helps. Second, sleep on it, the subconscious mind often finds solutions that the conscious mind cannot contrive. Third, if necessary, get objective help from professionals who specialize in your problem, whether it's emotional, physical or just life.

Chromosome 3: winning ways

How can you, in advance, know that you have winning ways and can arrive at the very top of the organization? You must plan a total career on the assumption that you *will* win. You have to ignore the danger that you may end your career thwarted by circumstances and bad luck. Plan it and you will win; wing it and you will be weakened. Most leaders with winning ways map out their life plan as fully as possible. Many who aspire to the top echelons won't make it. By definition, there will always be some disappointed aspirants to leadership. If you're looking for sympathy you will not find it in this book.

One of the keys to giving your winning ways 'chromosome' a chance to weave its magic for you is to plan your total career as young as possible. The most brilliant careers come out best if they are planned that way. After all, there is nothing lost, particularly if you hold your own counsel and don't tell anybody. A total plan will help you to keep events in perspective when your career suffers the accidents that will form the best part of the maturation process that will make you a better leader. All careers take longer to come to fruition than is imagined when they begin.

Chromosome 4: balance

Throughout this book, I have argued from a base of personal philosophy and belief that a leader needs to have a balanced mixture of business interests and private life, humanity and ruthlessness, subjectivity and objectivity. Too much emphasis on one will lessen the success and fulfillment of the other. Nobody can tell any leader what their perfect balance should be. But they will know when they are unbalanced. I argue, later in the final chapter, that you can always do something about it. I describe some of the necessary techniques. You will savour it when you're running a rounded, balanced life, all your triumphs will feel fabulous. When they don't, it's because they are not in the context of a balanced life.

Try not to lose the good habits of your youth, such as finding time for sport, social life and recreation. Build opportunities for leisure into your timetable, in as disciplined a way as possible, as you construct your business diary. When there is fun available at work, enjoy it as a pleasure rather endure it as a chore. Find a partner to share your life, after you have enjoyed the first successes of your career. You may be too busy for the 5 to 10 years, many leaders are. But after that, get on with it. When you are ready to begin the search for that perfect partner, enjoy the best quality 'market research', and select wisely. During your successful career you will put a lot of thought into getting the right jobs, taking the correct strategic decisions and choosing the best members of your business team. Finding a suitable partner to share your life must be worth an equal amount of time and effort.

Chromosome 5: intuition

A few years ago we had a sad event in my family. My father-in-law died. I flew out to the USA to attend the funeral and to be with my wife who had gone out earlier to be with him in his last days. We considered that our son, who was five years old then, was too young to attend. So we asked friends in the UK to look after him while we were away in the USA. We also asked our friends to say nothing about the death of his grandfather as I would fly back immediately afterwards to tell him.

On the day of the funeral in the USA my son was out walking with our friends in Oxford in the UK. Our friend asked Jeffrey why he was looking so sad and young Jeffrey replied to our friend, 'I can hear crying in America'. This is an example of the inexplicable intuition that leaders often have that I am talking about in this section.

Anybody who aspires to greatness must engage their intuition. If you retain the magic and mystery of your intuition you will have a different quality of insight and the use of an ultimate dimension, a genetic gift. Whoever or whatever invented human beings, gave them an astonishing capacity to sense the right way forward. Intuition goes beyond rational reasoning. It is intimately connected to the sources of ultimate survival. The problem is that as we become civilized and sophisticated, rational thinking can sometimes get between you and your instincts. However, if, like my five-year-old son, you can stay in touch it with your intuition, you will enhance your chances of success.

Chromosome 6: moral fibre

Moral fibre is a palpable and vital ingredient of leadership. It refers to a leader needing a complete philosophy of life and morals which act as their template or paradigm to judge the quality, equity and decency of all their important (and minor) decisions. It is not arguing that they all have to follow the same moral code or value system. But they do need a thought-through set of ethics which guide their decisions throughout their career. These will be the controls which prevent abuse of power, unfairness, indecency. On the positive side they will safeguard quality, deliver justice to all stakeholders and guarantee the safety of the organization's future because, thus armed, unethical decisions will never endanger the organization's future.

Up to this point one could add all the chromosome described as composing the leadership gene and assert that they equally describe a monster or a luminary. The only difference between the two is controlled by whether a leader has moral fibre. Without moral fibre a leader may be both ruthless and dangerous. It does not matter that they can make more money for the shareholders if they make it immorally. It is irrelevant if they can amass mountains of money for Mammon if their morality is missing. Moral fibre protects the individual and the organization from the devil within each of us. It protects the organization from the effects of the worst that leaders can be.

Can we say that a leader has to be born with moral fibre? Surely it must be possible for parents to instill moral and ethical values into a child through the way they live and the values they demonstrate? I believe that this is one chromosome of the gene of leadership which can never be properly or fully argued as being part of nature or nurture. However, I am certain that without it no leader can be great or good. I also assert that, if moral fibre is missing from their business then they are dangerous and should never be given power or responsibility.

The gene of leadership

The rest of this book will bring together all the ingredients necessary to make a fine leader. We have described here the traits of leaders. Later we will describe in detail the skills, characteristics and styles of leaders. We will explain the tools of leadership, the time horizons, how to measure the growth of a leader and the means to make them even better. However, when you ponder on the chromosomes of the gene of leadership described above, I trust you will agree that many of these are aspects of character that a leader must be born with. Later we will describe the skills that can be accumulated and developed. However, what is certain is that by the time the leader starts his or her career they will need it to have assembled all the traits, skills and techniques it takes to be a successful leader in an organization. Even so, in spite of successful early accumulation of all it takes, some will fail because bad luck will foul up the best opportunities. Others will stumble because they just don't get the right opportunity for their particular assembly of skills. What is certain is that all those who one day hope to make it to the very top of an organization will need to have assembled a full complement of the chromosomes and skills of leadership.

Summary

This chapter has looked at those aspects of a leader's profile that s/he has to have at birth to have a reasonable prospect of a leadership career. The 'leadership gene' is composed of youthful energy, all through a leader's life; courageous circumspection, which is seeing the best and worst of events with equanimity; winning ways, which could be thought of as making luck for ourselves and our business; balance, which refers to having a balanced life, personally, socially and commercially; intuition, which is about not becoming so sophisticated that one loses touch with one's inner voice and instincts; and, finally, moral fibre, which describes that deep core of a person's sense of ethics, decency and morality which preserves a leader's soul and their business from taking bad decisions.

3. Leadership Behaviours You Can Learn

Introduction

In Chapter 1, I pointed out the many different studies of leadership which exist in the academic field. Some known as *traits* underline an assumption that people are born with the skills of leadership. Other studies, the *behavioural* ones, emphasize more what can be taught or learned as preparation for leadership. This chapter will be focused on the areas that I believe can be developed. We should carefully differentiate between those qualities which seem to come from nurture through parental influence, schools and other childhood events and those changes in behaviour which can come from conscious training of the leader, arranged through employers or themselves. Naturally, a leader can have little (although s/he can have some) influence on personal environmental factors during early formative years. In this chapter we focus on those things that can be learnt within educational institutions, or taught by internal or external development experts within and outside organizations.

The key nurture skills

The major 'nurture' skills which can be developed or improved are:

- paradigmatic thinking;
- self-belief;
- communication ability;
- strategic analysis;
- team motivation;
- financial and business analysis;
- people selection;
- judgment.

Let's look at each one closely and see when, where and how it can be acquired.

Communication ability

The ability to communicate is something that can be entirely acquired through training and development. Many people with speech defects or impediments have managed to overcome them with the right sort of help. If a leader is capable of formulating a valuable idea or devising a strategic vision then s/he can certainly be taught how to put them across to their people in the best possible manner. Personally, I always use the *rule of 3*. The way it works is that everything I wish to express is broken up into three separate parts. If the idea is complex I break each of those parts into a further three ideas each. By and large, I have never yet discovered any set of concepts that was so complex that it could not be covered in these nine points. It will cover any complex programme at university. It will certainly cover the most complex strategic vision any leader can devise.

Of course the leader still needs to exercise his or her judgment about the strategic vision and also how it has to be communicated. Can the organization cope with the ideas in a complex form? Should the whole organization be told about the complete set of ideas as soon as they are ready or should they be broken into smaller parts for different levels of the organization's hierarchy. Should they be disseminated at different times and to a greater or lesser degree of explicitness? For example, Robert Ayling, the former boss of British Airways, chose to tell both his staff and his customers that most of them who went tourist class were unprofitable and he didn't want them any more. Consider the effect of this on his already demotivated workforce and his thoroughly disillusioned customers. What it really told them was that 'we don't really respect over 80% of our customers because we don't make any money out of them'. He was also saying to 80% of the customers 'we don't want you and we don't care about you any more'. This was probably one set of strategic thoughts that the leader should have kept to himself. Anyway, it was just a few months after he made that statement that he lost his job. It took the new leader just a few months to realize that the idea was wrong and had to be reversed.

Strategic analysis

Some years ago I published a book on strategic analysis called *The Strategy Workout* (Levicki, 1996). The objective of the book was to show top leaders how to analyse the strategic situation of the company in as brief and as complex a way as was necessary. In my opinion any corporate leader can scan the strategic situation relatively fast. Strategic analysis was never a problem for any leader. In the book I have devised a series of 1 to 3 page audits which summarize all the important aspects that the strategist has to take into account before s/he sets a strategic vision or mission for the company. Many leaders have been using my methods over many years. What it proves is that the problem of taking account of the inputs to a strategy was never a problem. The problem has always been *the process of implementation.*

How do you make the strategy happen? How do you communicate with the people in your organization so that they understand clearly and simply the optimum way to put your vision into effect? How do you secure their agreement? How do you convince them your ideas are best? How do you convince all the other stakeholders that they should back you? Those are the problems that arise from strategic analysis. The analysis was never a problem. It was always about *implementation.*

Team motivation

A great leader needs to understand how to motivate a team. As I explain elsewhere in this book leaders are not managers. It is not the work of a leader to manage a team. However, there will be a small team around most leaders who have to be motivated to achieve the scenarios that are vital to accomplish the strategic mission.

Over the past twenty-five years there has been a vast concentration by many business development departments upon team motivation and team skills. Much of this was characterized by the use of a business situation substitute exercises, both indoors and out of doors, to help people simulate a problem solving situation. My own executive development company certainly did a great deal of work in this sector and made many profits from it. However, in long-term perspective, when I look back at most of the programmes the business ran, it always looked, at the end of the exercise period, that we had really changed the participants' understanding of how to motivate a team. Often, by mixing insights through psychometric exercises, we also gave them a deeper insight into their own motivation and psychological make-up. I wish I could assert that the understandings into team motivation lasted permanently. It would be even nicer to say that the changes of behaviour we managed to induce for the period of the training lasted for the rest of their career. My observations of almost all of the participants within a few months of their training was that they lost most of the good habits we tried to instill within a week or two.

The same can be said about the insights into their own character from a psychological point of view. We used psychometric exercises to help them understand their own psychological make-up and the workings of the inner subconscious impetus that made them behave, externally, in the way that they did. They often left the training centre determined to overcome the worst effects of their personal childhood environmental development and to be a better manager or leader in the future. I now look back on such training and consider it to have been almost entirely misguided. One can never make profound differences to human beings with a few days training and a little bit of insight.

That is why I decided that 'training' is an inappropriate word to use about human beings. Training is what we do for dogs. We teach dogs to carry out their body functions in places that are convenient to their owners. We train them how to stop at the side of the road rather than run into traffic. We can do that kind of minor training with young children between the ages of 0 and 5 years old. But to change the long-term effects of perhaps 20 years of personal development in a human being requires personal development work over a long-term period.

It is my belief that the only people development that can effectively help them ameliorate and change or moderate their behaviour must be carried out with a programme of at least 6 months and preferably one year of hands-on behavioural intervention. If you want to help a leader change his or her behaviour you have to work with them on a long-term basis. Short-term intervention can only last a few moments. Long-term intervention, with profound work at the deepest psychological level, gives people a chance to change and ameliorate permanently the things they need to examine profoundly in order to become better leaders and happier human beings.

Financial and business analysis

For many years a people development company I led ran 'advanced management development programmes' for some very large international corporations. We described it in our mission statements as 'preparing people to think and behave as managing directors'. We had much success, with most of our clients getting jobs at the level we were educating them to achieve. However, it is hard in retrospect, to say whether the later successes of our trainees depended upon our developmental intervention or whether the companies that sent them on the programmes had already decided that they were going to appoint them to that level of work.

I have always had a sceptical view about accountancy and financial analysis as a means of getting profound insights into how a business works. In my experience, the accountancy and financial analysis tools can be quite as subjective as any apparently softer behavioural analysis. What did surprise me is how entertaining the best accountancy teachers could make the subject. I managed to recruit some of the very best teachers in this area. They nearly always received the highest evaluations of all the teachers.

Looking back in perspective, it is obvious that many executives, managers and leaders truly enjoy working with numbers, especially when shown how to manipulate the financial concepts. Furthermore, I would now conclude that this area is one of the easiest and most attractive to train people in. Not only do they enjoy it but they seem to remember the skills of the financial trade for ever. I believe that this is probably the area where development for leaders is most appropriate and highly effective.

People selection

The selection of people is probably one of the least studied and worst understood of all the separate areas of business science. One of the obvious reasons for this is that people are so complex that it is impossible to make dependable assertions about their future conduct of themselves. Even if their behaviour were predictable, the complexity of the situations in which people find themselves would still render the selection of people as a highly improbable and random aspect of business management.

That is why it is so surprising that one aspect of the 'people selection industry' has become so eminent, that is the 'head hunting of leaders' business, especially at the level of very large multinational corporations. Why is it so hard to select people and predict how they will perform? There are at least three causes of failure:

(1) people are complex;
(2) businesses are unpredictable;
(3) the external economic variables are almost impossible to predict accurately.

These three concepts, clashing to compounded misconception, mean we can never predict how people will behave when they are selected to do a particular job. However, let's focus for a few moments upon the sources of complexity of individuals.

At the practical level all human beings work on several dimensions at the same time. These are normally encompassed under the headings, social, political, economic and personal. Quite often these are mutually contradictory for an individual at any given moment in time. For example, a person's social motivation desires a high level of taxation because few people want others, with lesser life skills than themselves to suffer an impoverished life. At the same time their personal desire is to pay the minimum level of taxes possible. Simultaneously, they may be politically conservative which implies that they desire a minimum level of taxation for anybody and everybody. Yet they may have a seemingly valid economic desire for their corporation to receive a large grant to encourage them to set up factories in areas of low employment (the taxation to pay for these grants, of course, could never come from a conservative political administration which believes in low taxation). So far we haven't moved beyond levels of conscious thought!

Consider then the parameters that control peoples' personal values and learned behaviours that have been instilled within them. Using psychometric exercises one often discovers that people have little idea how the values they have received from their parents were actually transmitted to them. Much of it was far more non-verbal than they realize.

I conducted a set of psychometric exercises with a group of medical general practitioners recently. I discovered that the leader of the practice had a high ability to socialize and appear friendly. However, his true preferred behaviour is to remain alone and never let anybody really know what he was thinking or feeling or even interact with them at all. When I pointed this out to him he was shocked. He thought his feelings were quite opaque. (They were to him, it transpired.) He subsequently explained it with the sad story of his childhood. His father had died while he was still young and he had been sent, with charitable institution money, to a boarding school where the teachers continuously exercised discipline upon him by threatening to send him home if he misbehaved. They would refuse to take the charitable trust money. The damage this would do to his widowed mother and the potential shame, taught him to cover up all his feelings until, in adulthood, he could not bring himself to show them at all.

I met him at the theatre with his wife a few weeks after the psychometric exercise. Although he was able to conduct a friendly enough conversation for a few minutes, he did not introduce me to his wife who was standing next to us. Instead he made his excuses and rushed off to a private corner as soon as possible. I had taken him through the effects of the childhood experience upon his current behaviour and how it looked to others and he had said that he wanted to change. But it was very hard to change the habits and behaviours of a lifetime in just a few weeks.

Had I been a normal patient I should have concluded that socially he didn't wish to mix with a 'customer'. In fact, because I knew him psychologically, I understood it was because he was afraid of social interaction and preferred one-on-one relationships, with his wife or his patients, where he could be in sole control. I was saddened but unsurprised to watch him rush off.

Some months later, in his surgery, he apologized. I told him it was unnecessary to do so as I understood the behaviour from his psychometrics. He then followed the apology with the remark 'You must come over to dinner, some time, if you could stand it'. I was not surprised when this invitation was not followed up with a real date or any further action. He was exercising his inclusion skills, but his childhood had traumatized him into relative insulation as a protection from danger.

This also points to another cause of people's personal lack of predictability. Almost everybody during their childhood and adult years passes through traumatic events which leave psychological scar tissue. We talk more about the subject in Chapter 13 on leadership and life. There we will discuss more fully the nature of the effects of traumatic events upon a part of the brain called the amygdala. For the moment, let us just acknowledge that personal scar tissue from previous trauma can have devastating effects at the subconscious level upon people's behaviour. These effects are nearly always irrational and, for the people being tugged by them, it often seems beyond their personal will to control or change. I grew up in a household where personal emotions were only ever displayed through anger, screaming and occasional violence. Even today, I have to continuously retrain my instinctive reactions to prevent my automatic reincarnation of the learned behaviours of years of childhood in order to try and manage a normal personal adulthood.

Every individual's personal history is different. Consequently one's personal capacity for self-confidence and assertiveness is pitched at a higher or lower level. If we also consider that that same individual has an entirely different set of current circumstances from all the rest of us, the complexity is devine. Is the person single, partnered or married? Do they have children? If not, is it because they cannot have them? Do they have several children who are noisy and expensive? Is one of those children regularly ill or in trouble with the police? Is their domestic partner unstable and difficult? The possibilities are endless.

Another consideration is what the employee thought was required of them when they began the job? Was the job explained fully and adequately? Were the parameters explained fairly to them? One often sees a chief executive being defended by his chairman when he has failed, year after year, to deliver the necessary and desired results. These people nearly always end their careers with a sudden dismissal when the non-executive directors are forced to intervene. Is that chairman really doing his or her job properly when they defend poor leadership?

A further and particular problem of people selection is the impossibility of knowing whether any specific promotion, particularly to an important level of independent leadership, is that promotion too far which takes a person from a level of comfort and competence to the place where they can never work successfully. Most individuals find it hard to measure their own level of incompetence. It must be at least as hard for those whose job it is to select a person to be the leader of a complex and difficult corporation.

Finally, there are the normal other aspects of an individual which can never be fully accounted for. These are the different crises of life and their effect upon the individual. The larger ones are well-known. They are marriage, having children, getting divorced, the death of one's parents, the death of a child, or the death of a partner or spouse. Nobody can tell in advance what the effect will be of any of these events on any individual. That includes the individual himself. Many leaders get to their peak when most people are suffering the worst pangs of 'mid life crisis'. That has been described by a friend of mine, Professor Abe Korman, of Baruch College, in New York (and many others) as 'mid-life crisis; that time in a person's life when their children become parents, their parents become children and you realize that one day, you, too, are going to die!'

Self-control

Gaining control over oneself with regard to discipline over mood is important to becoming a great leader because it is only by the exercise of massive self-control that you can stay calm enough to continuously assess objectively all the data coming at you. It arrives from many different directions, emanating from a vast variety of constituencies, in a suite of sounds, from the shrill to suspiciously quiet. By exercising power over one's impulses a leader can make balanced, rather than emotional, judgments. This, in turn, will maximize and optimize the benefits to the organization from the leader's decisions. Because great leaders want success for themselves and their organization, they will usually do whatever it takes to get it right. If that means learning to exercise vast self control, they will do it. For my son I teach it as Mind Over Mood (MOM).

When leaders tell me how hard they are finding it to learn to exercise total self control I ask them to consider the price they will pay, personally, if they fail. If, eventually, they do not reach the level in the organization that their leadership skills deserve, they will pay the price of *not* having appropriate outlets for the use of their brain and energy. Without the organizational position and the complex problems and tasks that leadership roles confer, the special type of brain and energy that leaders have, can turn from a talent to a tool of torture. It can become searing and soul destroying to have inadequate uses for a fine brain and high energy. Most leaders understand this force within themselves. They are right to worry more about the loss of outlets for their brainpower and energy than the loss of office, status or income.

There is another factor in their thinking. People of quality are often candid and honest with themselves. They know they would not be able to avoid their own assessment of themselves at the end of their career. They would have to face the possibility that, if they had exercised more self-control, they would have had a more enjoyable and useful career.

How do you learn to exercise the necessary self control? First, you have to constantly remember how much you need the work because it fulfills you. It's a great discipline. Use the helicopter tool, alongside the time-horizon machine, to remain dispassionate and to ensure you get your reactions to events into perspective. Never lose your common sense. It's a great litmus test that your key constituencies, customers and workers will accept and welcome your decisions about the business.

Based on the leaders I have observed, it's also a great idea to have an active, social life apart from your business life. Take all the holidays you are allocated by your terms and conditions of employment. Build in lots of short breaks, too. Above all, give yourself enough time to sort any major, personal, problems. They don't go away just because an important leader is neglecting them rather than one of your subordinates, they may have more time to sort their problems, and have a happier life as a result.

Finally, remember that, if you are one of the gifted few who are destined to be a great leader, you need to exercise self control and force yourself to change your personality and behaviour to fit the needs of your opportunities. If you ever feel like giving up (and it is not a characteristic of leaders to do so) remember that your brainpower and energy is not going to go away. You will always have your talent, ability, drive and energy. If you do not succeed in making the necessary changes, consider what you are going to do when you are 50 or 55? Where will you find the outlets to place your drive and energy. How much worse will be your frustration in not having fulfilled your destiny because you didn't control your behaviour, change your attitudes and take total possession of yourself. When you reach 60, how will you forgive yourself for not having made the effort and for allowing your future to get behind you rather than remain in front?

Judgment

Learning to make intelligent judgments requires long years of personal development and scrupulous personal honesty and integrity. A person needs good mentors who care about them and want them to maximize the use of their brain. Quality mentors seek out the best people. But a person has to be in the correct frame of mind to accept advice and mentoring from the best people.

What you really have to do with the help of your mentors and from personal best friends is to learn how to think. That is often one of the hardest things to do, particularly within the context of a busy business. Have you noticed how often people become very disturbed when somebody cancels an appointment in their diary. They immediately go rushing around attempting to replace the empty space with any appointment they can muster. Why? Because the best way to really use the time would be to close the door and think deeply and carefully about where the business is, how the strategy is working out and whether they should be making any profound changes to the course they set at the beginning of the year. But thinking about those serious strategic matters is difficult and most executives prefer not to do it. What do you do when you have an hour or two to think?

If you wish to develop balance and judgment you also have to learn to reflect as well as think. The difference between the two is profound. Thinking can be conscious when you look at the superficial surface data. Reflection examines matters in the round, both the surface data and the underlying patterns and concepts. The former can be done consciously, to get your mind working in the right direction. But reflection means far more than surface interpretation and is much harder to develop as a working tool.

You have to continuously test your personal development to determine it is going in the right direction. That is valuable in terms of your career but also the quality of your life, as your mind develops the ability to cope with larger and more complex subjects. How can you test your progress? By using your mentors, by thinking and reflecting, and by being eternally *dissatisfied* with the quality of where you have progressed so far. In order to use your permanent dissatisfaction with your personal status quo you must learn to accept and appreciate robust and fiercely honest criticism from wherever and whoever you can find it. The fiercer and more robust the criticism, the happier you should be. Among the only people who will give you truly robust and valuable criticism will be old friends who know you well or friendly advisers who have the high quality judgment that you hold in esteem. After all, if they don't have good judgment why are they your (business) friends and how will you learn from them?

Make the effort to keep your old friends. That is not a reason to lose your ability or desire to make new ones. Old friends improve your sanity and quality of life. New ones keep you excited about the future and fresh with different ways of seeing the world.

Elsewhere in this book I describe how you can measure people's levels of frustration and anger. I always advise both managers and leaders to learn to carefully control their temper and the level of their anger. Sometimes people respond, when told their anger levels are too high, 'that they need their anger as (they believe) it is what gives them their energy'. My response is always 'that's nonsense'. There are no circumstances when anger is useful. It prevents you from thinking clearly. It frightens your friends from telling you the truth. It puts people in a state of panic and stops them from performing at their best. Never do it because it will damage your and everybody else's health.

Summary

This chapter has described those aspects of a leader's abilities s/he can learn rather than need as genetic gifts. Firstly, the ability to communicate effectively is described. The skills of strategic analysis and team motivation can also be developed, as can the skill of business and financial analysis. The ability to select the right people can be learned, although more often, it is delegated to experts who can do it better. Leaders are urged to put energy into learning to control their emotional stability for better decision-making. Finally, even judgment is judged to be learnable rather than belief it is necessary as an innate trait.

4. The Development of Leaders

First questions

The environmental development of leaders determines the types of leaders we get. During the 1980s some parts of the business world made heroes of people who had created great personal wealth from issuing junk bonds or by purchasing large businesses in order to break them up for pure financial gain. Let us be clear here. Junk bonds are just slightly higher priced bonds than more gilt edged ones. They serve a useful economic function enabling companies with higher risk profiles to find growth capital which would not otherwise be available to them. Sometimes people who buy large businesses to profit from breaking them up into their constituent parts are also serving an economic purpose. In the UK during much of the 1970s, 1980s and 1990s, among the most admired leaders were people like Lord Hanson, who built up an enormous conglomerate, Hanson Industries. His business consisted mainly of mature businesses like brick making and cigarette manufacture. When these types of business became unfashionable he merely set about breaking up the conglomerate he had so carefully assembled. He made money on the way up and he made money on the way down.

The point of this is that leaders get influenced in their development by the heroes the popular media are setting up while they are developing. In America Ivan Boesky, a stock market investor who manipulated prices and exploited insider information, was a hero for a short while. So was Michael Miliken, the man who invented 'junk bonds' and made himself a billionaire in the process. He provided finance for numerous people which they used to take over and manipulate companies which had underexploited assets. It was during the era of Boesky and Miliken that the creed 'greed is good' developed. It was soon discarded. However, if any developing leader was foolish enough to adopt that creed as the prevailing influential paradigm during their development, the danger to their potential as a leader could have been catastrophic. Moral fibre cannot survive long alongside a value which proclaims that it is good to be greedy.

As we enter the twenty-first century many leaders are aware of the enormous power and influence that large corporations' leaders exercise over all aspects of their employees' (and their customers') lives. They have a major responsibility to develop themselves to be the best possible leader maximizing their personal talents and skills.

This chapter will attempt to offer some guidance.

Personality and character

How does personality differ from character? *Personality* is the more superficial manifestation of habits and surface behaviours. Most of these habits are usually accumulated during childhood by casual learning from parents, and other influencers, such as school teachers and friends. An individual's *personality* is usually what people are reacting to when they form their first impression of somebody. In some cases, personality, because it is the surface or outer skin of a person's total being, can be composed, of fairly superficial elements such as pure physical characteristics, such as height (*top leaders grow tall*) or fashionable good looks (remember Tiny Rowland, the monster from Rio?). To distinguish personality from character, try to think of people you have met who made a deep impression upon you at the first meeting, and then, as you got to know them better, you concluded that 'there is less to them than meets the eye'.

What you saw as you began to know that person was their personality. As you understood them more deeply you began to know what I am calling *their character*. *Character* is much more profound, it refers to the composition of the inner person. It describes the deepest aspects of their underlying psyche. It is the substance, based on their inner values and convictions, which lies within their inner core, below the surface. It is what you find when you scrape away the superficial manners and habitual responses controlled by custom. It is composed of what people deeply believe, their most strongly held life values, because it is based upon the most important influences in their lives. These will be some mixture of their basic, genetically controlled instincts and the few, most concrete, elements of their developmental training. There will always be outstanding events or values imbibed consciously and subconsciously, from their most important mentors and guides. Character is the *meaning* of the inner core of the person.

How can we distinguish between *character* and *personality*? *Personality* can be likened to a person's clothing rather than the body within the clothes. The wallpaper rather than the wall. *Character*, on the other hand, is the inner person, the addition of all their values, attitudes and experiences, the house, not the rooms. A person's *character* represents the values which give meaning to their life and the qualities which govern how they take decisions about important issues. Personality is what people know about you after they have met you for a few minutes. Character is what they know about you after knowing you, or doing business with you, for 10 years.

In the light of this explanation, it is apparent that it is your *character* that you should be trying to improve and render robust, rather than your *personality*. Personality is something that can be put on and taken off, like an overcoat; and, you can buy the best overcoat anytime. But, if you have a shabby body, both an expensive coat and your body will always look disheveled. You can put on a personality for a short show, but if you have a rotten character, everybody will discover the truth only too soon.

I am not advocating that you ignore your personality. There are too many situations in life and business when it is vital to make an immediately favourable impression, using all the resources of personality you can summon. However, true leadership is about character and the long term. It is about leaving permanent differences which do good to the borganization for many years. Your long-term leadership achievements will be more a reflection of your character than your personality. Your long-term work will reflect your innermost values. You can leave your children some money and it will make a shallow, surface difference to their lives. But if you succeed in inserting ethical values and the capacity for wisdom into their minds, and leave them that as an inheritance, it will enrich them forever.

Two questions arise from the observations above. The first is 'can or should your personality be aligned with your deeper character?' The answer is that the more accurately they are aligned, the better because that will ensure that fewer people can make mistakes about who you really are, at first or any other meetings. Of course, this also implies that if you have a rotten character, people will see it fairly soon in their relationship with you. In that case, I suppose, the best advice is to 'learn to imitate a decent character'. However, if personality and character are aligned, it will mean that what you deeply believe in will be what you portray all the time, from first meeting to a twenty year relationship. It may be summarized as 'what you see is what you get (is who you are)'.

The second, and more profound question, is, 'if one finds faults in one's character can anything be done about it?' The answer must be, surely, a resounding, *Yes*. If we cannot believe that we can affect and change our character when adult, we would all be the innocent receivers of genetic probability and childhood environment. Regression would be very mean indeed!

I firmly believe that anyone can improve upon and change their character and the deeper value systems upon which their character is based. To do this they have to examine their roots and inner core carefully. They will need all the help they can get. It always requires ruthless honesty and candor. If you, the reader, attempt it and find important aspects of yourself that require change, be aware that the change process will often hurt and is thoroughly difficult to do. It is the behavioural equivalent of becoming left-handed, if you are naturally right-handed.

What a *good leader* does for an organization is much more a reflection of his character than his personality because it is about the long term rather than the short. That means that a leader needs a quality character based upon sound ethics and values. Their character should be protected by the good instincts of nature and their adopted values about 'the right thing to do in all circumstances'. When organizations interview people for any important job, they should focus far more than they normally do on discovering the inner *character* of the person they seek to employ. It is foolish to respond to an interviewee's personality. That is just the superficial aspect of a candidate. Personality is what they present in the typical, short interviews that are the standard methodology for decisions about employment.

Every leader and leader-to-be has to examine their own character and see how it works for them and for their organization. Everybody should define the type of leader they are at work.

I have discovered seven key leadership styles. No one leader can master all the styles. Most do, however, manage to have more than one. That is important. As we show, later in the chapter, different leaders are more suitable for different business situations and cultures. The seven styles of leader I have encountered are:

- charismatic;
- superior intelligence;
- autocratic;
- shepherd;
- army general;
- princely leader.
- nature's native;

The typology of leaders

1. Charismatic

Usually a strong personality, who is used to getting people to do things their own way. Can be powerful at board level and when dealing with stake holders. Advantages are:

(1) can use charisma to get things done fast;
(2) can use charisma to persuade people that their strategies are optimal;
(3) adds glamour to the workplace and gives everybody who works for them a sense of importance;
(4) can be used to achieve positive PR for the organization.

Disadvantages are:

(1) can leave people feeling manipulated;
(2) can be so strong that all the other charismatic people just below the leader leave the company when they don't get the top job (because s/he has got it) and they then lead the competition. Worse, the company is bereft of good leaders to succeed the charismatic one;
(3) can use charisma to persuade people into the wrong policies.

This style is most successful when a business needs to spend a few years taking important decisions and decisive action. *Charismatic* leaders often have the ability to persuade people to agree rapidly and whole-heartedly with their strategies. They usually are skilled at convincing people to try to perform better than their own preconceptions about themselves. In other words, they *empower* people to perform better than they might with a different leader.

This type of leader can create disadvantages, too. Their charisma tends to outshine those of their subordinates. This can be a disturbing and belittling phenomenon for some executives. They also sometimes cause other charismatic developing leaders to depart the organization. This can thus cause a void where there should be a succession plan. More dangerously, when charismatic-type leaders form wrong judgments about a strategic situation, their charisma may influence people to go along too easily with their flawed plans. They can use their charisma to persuade people into bad plans as easily as good ones. Such leaders must be eternally on their guard to ensure they are allowing the more timid and less outspoken among their executives to have their say and make their contribution. On the other hand charismatic leaders make people feel good and therefore work harder.

Can charisma be developed?

Charisma is as much a manifestation of personality as it may be of character. It can also be quite superficial. This means that one can develop charisma relatively easily by studying the elements which create a 'charismatic ambiance'. For example, what we remember about 'people with charisma' after they leave is often their clothing or their manner of speech or their hairstyle or their car; in sum, *their presence*. Most of these are superficial attributes, which can be purchased or acquired with just a little trouble. However, if you wish to develop a charismatic leadership style, you have to set about systematically acquiring and accumulating these attributes for the difference they make to your effectiveness as a leader.

You have to choose a tone of voice, style of speech and phraseology which ensure that people remember what you say. If you care about clothing and know how to be 'stylish', buy the best quality from the most famous branded tailors that you can afford. It is never too hard to find fashionable hairdressers who will style your hair memorably to reflect who you would like to be. Similarly an automobile is just another personal appurtenance; you can purchase one that makes a statement or gives a message. It could be about economizing the corporation's expenditure or displaying modesty and quietude or whatever. Most sensible leaders usually prefer to display those types of options.

Wise charismatic leaders are careful never to allow their charisma to get in the way of their manners. Be polite! It is astonishing how many people are remembered for their rudeness and their *brattish manners* rather than for their *brilliant profundity*. No matter what personality you bring to your leadership style, if you are rude, it won't be your charisma that people usually refer to when they recall you!

Some readers may consider it somewhat shallow to worry about and take the trouble to develop the characteristics of charisma. There is really not much that is profound about charisma, when one decomposes its elements. It can be as shallow as any other superficial effect. As we say above, it is the profundity of your *character* which you should be developing. That is what has a lasting effect upon people and organizations. Consider for example, Ross Johnston of RJR Nabisco or Peter Guber, who headed Sony's first US Film Studios. These were highly charismatic people who turned out, in retrospect, to have been leaders with a less than totally successful record. But they had loads of charisma. As with everything, selection of leadership style remains with the reader. Some of you will not have the choice because you just won't have what it takes to be a charismatic leader. It is great to be able to, if you can. But if your choice comes down to a selection between character and charisma, go for character every time – it's harder to develop but much more worthwhile.

Some charismatics don't realize they have charisma until later in life. It is useful to be aware early if you do have it because your charisma can have startling effects upon people which, in turn, causes unexpected results. I know one person who emanates intelligence and power, a deadly combination. Because he didn't realize it till later in life, he continuously ran into problems with people reacting to him strangely and excessively strongly. Ultimately, it stopped him doing his best because people didn't give him any chance to explain himself before they reacted, his charisma was too strong and they feared being manipulated or overwhelmed. It's surprising that people around you are often aware of your charisma or power but they are too frightened to tell you. Sometimes charismatic leaders appear to be shallow. If you are one of these, try to balance the appearance with a show of urbane intelligence. If you're not shallow, people will perceive it.

Charismatics are most successful in situations which require leaps of strategic vision where the leadership alone really does know the best strategic way forward. The *charismatic leader* can persuade people to achieve objectives and strategies that they may not themselves believe in without the leader's inspiration. In these circumstances, the leader's charisma may be the only means of convincing them that they should attempt the difficult strategic vision the leader has set out for them.

2. Superior intelligence

The problem with leaders who rise to power on superior intelligence is that their intelligence intimidates people without them (the leader and the led) realizing it. Strangely, they often do not realize their intelligence is different from others until later in life. By this time they will have alienated many. However, leaders with an appropriate emotional intelligence will learn, when young, how to handle their intelligence. The best rule is:

> Don't ever bother trying to show your intelligence.
> Everybody will know it without your needing to show it.

Leaders with the mixed blessing of the superior intelligence style often have to spend extra time explaining things to people because people cannot keep up with their pure brain-processing speed and power. If they fail to realize how fast they have intuited the solution to problems while others have only just grasped the important questions. If they don't take the time to explain, they will fail to communicate their ideas to their team. The team will, in turn, be unable to implement the leader's strategic vision.

Later in this chapter I discuss an example of an extremely angry leader who intimidated his people with his highly superior and quick brain. Consequently they rarely spoke to him or gave him information. His was a classical response, when I told him that he was too angry and was repulsing his people. I informed him that he did not realize how much anger he was displaying because he was expressing it in a covert manner. His response, when told that his subordinates were sensing his anger in spite of it being covered up, was 'That explains the strange phenomenon I get from my subordinates. I always try to run an open door policy. I wondered why I could not get the b__ds to come through the door!' Advantages are:

(1) it creates trust and belief in the leader;
(2) it works well in firms which rely on high levels of education in its employees, like the pharmaceutical or the consultancy industry;
(3) in social situations where deference is acceptable or desirable, it can be efficacious in getting things done.

Disadvantages are:

(1) where the social norms find deference unacceptable, it can be problematic;
(2) it can be intimidating and cause the team supporting the leader to defer to his brainpower too much;
(3) it can also cause people around the leader to become overwhelmed and give less than their best because of the effect of the brightness upon their thinking processes;
(4) *superior intelligence* can sometimes lead the organization to make wrong decisions, too, because, it over emphasizes deductive reasoning and not emotional empathy.

A leader with this classic problem was Bob Horton, ex-leader of British Petroleum and later Railtrack. He, unfortunately, did not live by the dictum above to hide rather than display intelligence. He once boasted to a journalist how he had usually got to the answer on most problems before his subordinates had understood the question. In a company like British Petroleum (BP), which he headed, which was full of highly intelligent, potential substitute leaders, it was a provocative and unnecessary thing to say. He, later, received his comeuppance, when he was ignominiously removed, overnight, in a Boardroom coup which was considered to be partially inspired by the somewhat indiscreet boast recounted above.

Superior intelligence is most successful in businesses where there are large numbers of highly qualified or bright people. They find it easier to accept a *superior intelligence* leader. Having invested so much of their lives in achieving qualifications, they tend to develop an excess respect for brain power as contrasted to the emotional intelligence that is so much more important for leaders than plain IQ.

3. Autocratic

The Autocratic style is usually considered not an appropriate style for the beginning of the twenty-first century. However, appearing to be, or actually being, autocratic tends to be a feature of personality. Given its unsuitability for modern work practices, I advocate adopting the style, only under the most special circumstances, when the organization and its particular situation demand it. Examples of situations when autocracy is the most suitable style for the business are: (1) whenever one is in a rapid turnround to save a business; (2) during a rapid market growth environment when you are trying to grab market share at the start of an industry, during its most competitive phases; (3) when your markets have become mature and your workforce is composed mainly of older workers who respond to values of a bygone era. Advantages are:

(1) it wastes little time;
(2) it is attractive to other autocratic types;
(3) it is often suited to sales-led organizations where the sales force merely require direction;
(4) it can be great in war time or when there's a *burning platform* issue (*burning platform issues* refer to situations such as those on an oil rig when the platform is on fire and every decision has to be taken immediately and may be considered to have dire consequences if the wrong decision is taken).

Disadvantages are:

(1) it annoys intelligent people who don't like taking orders;
(2) it is inadequate when dealing with complex strategic situations;
(3) it fails to exploit the brains of the best people in the organization;
(4) it creates a tendency in the leader to believe in his own infallibility;
(5) it creates an atmosphere with low levels of feedback to anybody;
(6) too many inadequate managers copy the style causing the business itself to take on counterproductive styles and attributes which, in turn, become an inhibition on attracting the right sort of staff.

The *autocratic style* is most successful under circumstances of crisis, when an organization has to change rapidly, whether growing or turning itself from decline to growth. It can also be useful during periods of highly competitive battle for market share, when new products are battling it out in the marketplace. Surprisingly, many staff and workers of a more traditional character find it an attractive leadership style. They know where they are with this style. When staff are rather unquestioning and relatively accepting it can be remarkably comfortable.

4. Shepherd

The shepherd style is most akin, in its behaviour patterns, to the shepherd who tends his flock. This type of leader treats his or her employees, customers and other stake holders with care and solicitude. The shepherd tends to push rather than pull people in the strategic direction the business needs. They allow people time to come alongside the leader's point of view. The shepherd tends to be a gentle but strong soul, who usually understands people profoundly and attracts much love and devotion from the staff and personnel in general. They are usually spoken of in terms such as *strong, gentle* and *dependable*. Advantages are:

(1) builds a resilient business;
(2) safe and sound;

(3) unlikely to be surprised by catastrophic changes in the market;
(4) admired leader, although difficult to copy.

Disadvantages are:

(1) not good in situations requiring very fast reactions;
(2) tends to lose intuitive, fast reactor subordinates who get impatient;
(3) can miss market opportunities because takes too long to react;
(4) poses particular difficulties for market analysts and stockbrokers who tend to work in much shorter time frames than this kind of leader.

This style is most successful when the organization needs steady leadership for a relatively calm period or a period of intense growth when a thoroughly steady hand is called for. This style is most endangered when there is a crisis or a prolonged battle for intellectual supremacy (e.g. the computer software industry) or when the organization contains many, highly qualified people, who like to feel they are in an intellectual hot house. This leader does not lead that type of organization well. Industries which seem to suit this kind of leader are the banking and consultancy industries which do not, in spite of appearances, like to change fast.

5. Army general

This style follows the classical army analogy. The *army general* type leader, like his army counterpart, tries to set great examples but expects his people to follow his commands unquestioningly. Army general style leaders assume obedience and followership. They exude the appearance of having a total grasp of every situation no matter what the context. They exhibit supreme confidence that their answers, solutions and explanations are right, appropriate and brook no questioning. They differ from the autocrat style because their belief in their right to obedience comes from confidence in their decisions and opinions rather than some innate belief in their personal superiority and personal right to lead. Their command style does not come from a need to issue orders to people, nor from inability to listen to others. Rather it stems from their self-confidence and belief in their personal right to lead (which, in turn, stems from their innate ability to do so).

This style is often admired because it allows others to place their own sense of destiny safely under the patronage and skilled leadership of the army general. It is a particularly recommended style for those people who have many high level management skills but who don't quite have what it takes to be to an independent leader in their own right. For them the army general style leader is tailor-made.

In the same way that many lower ranks in the armed forces accept their position unquestioningly (especially after suitable training), so also do the subordinates of this style of leader. Of course, those who can't stand it, disappear fast enough. However, this style of leadership is rarely questioned and easily obeyed. Usually the general is a decent sort, who has a good sense of community and social values of a conservative nature. Advantages are:

(1) people find him easy to follow and want to obey;
(2) tends to specialize in mature industries;
(3) usually a good, precise, and clear communicator, so all stake holders know what they must do to be successful and when;
(4) creates a sense of fairness and gives raison d'être to staff;
(5) usually a great exponent of the art of helicoptering (see Chapter 1);
(6) dependable and reliable-predicted results can be banked.

Disadvantages are:

(1) can be slow to react to catastrophe;
(2) often doesn't understand people who don't share their sense of duty;
(3) may be unattractive to young, brash or extremely bright potential leaders;
(4) doesn't easily admit when he is wrong;
(5) can be pompous and a bad listener;
(6) sometimes bad-tempered.

This type of leadership is most successful defending a dominant or leadership position in the market. The *army general*, like his counterpart in real armies, spends much of his time preparing for battles and wars which, hopefully, won't take place. Similarly, the *army general* leadership style is most successful preventing battles and wars, by ensuring the competition believe they cannot win. They try to ensure their organization is not worth attacking, as a prime source of defence.

6. Princely leader

The *princely leader* is perceived as a natural aristocrat. S/he appears to have been born to lead and emanates a natural style of leadership, with an easy sense of knowing the right thing to do and when. S/he is attractive and seigniorial, exuding a sense of destiny and a natural right to be the leader. S/he can be unapproachable. This serves to facilitate his preference to be carefully selective about whom he talks to, meets or takes data from. This can serve him well, in terms of managing his or her time, but can lead to problems with subordinates or business associates who find the style annoying or who are easily intimidated. They tend to stay away from this type and therefore deprive him of their insights (while simultaneously depriving themselves of the opportunity to be noticed and rewarded for good work). Advantages are:

(1) highly attractive to many followers and easy to work for;
(2) finds time to listen and learn from others (if they seem worth listening to);

(3) makes people proud to be in his camp;
(4) seems such a natural leader that it prevents many from feeling that they could do the job just as easily;
(5) people find it easy to obey (therefore, little time wasted questioning his or her decisions).

Disadvantages are:

(1) natural egalitarians resent this style of leadership and either leave or don't join;
(2) can lead to unquestioning loyalty which doesn't ask enough questions;
(3) sometimes a little unintelligent;
(4) suited to industries with *ostentatious consumption* goods or monopolistic tendencies; this can have unfortunate consequences with regulators (this style seems to be particularly favoured by both Sotheby's and Christies, the two UK based auction businesses which dominate the international auction industry). *Ostentatious consumption* goods are articles which people buy for the opportunity this gives them to demonstrate their wealth to others, such as diamond rings, fur coats or luxurious cars.

The *princely leader* is most successful in long established businesses which have powerful brands and dependable market share. They excel at regal leadership, taking fine decisions to move the gigantic corporate liner a few degrees port or starboard. They are at their most vulnerable when under attack, because they find it hard to respond with alacrity. They are used to having their positions by right and don't know how to cope with upstarts who attack them. Their natural dignity erodes fast and they become bewildered or frozen. A classic of the type was the Earl of Limerick, who chaired De La Rue, the long-lived currency and specialized printing business. When that business ran into competitive turbulence, some years ago, he found it difficult to lead the response. Consequently the business suffered from poor ratings and performance for a more prolonged period than would have, say, a business being led by a *superior intelligence* or *autocratic* leader.

7. Nature's native

The *nature's native* leader is one who always looks comfortable in the leading position. He conducts himself in the leadership role as if it was all he was ever meant to do. A typical leader with this style would be Bob Bauman, previously chief executive of SmithKline Beecham, an international pharmaceutical business, Tony Blair, prime minister of England or President John Kennedy, former President of the United States. They look as if leadership is what they were born to do. People who work for these *nature's native* leaders couldn't imagine having them as a subordinate. They look like they always were leaders. They do it without thinking. They don't panic, they use the helicopter tool with ease, they are rarely strained and then not so as ordinary mortals would notice. They make *nominal leaders* feel as inadequate as they frequently are. They are envied for the naturalness of their gifts and qualities of leadership. But they are rarely resented – they don't excite that type of shallow response in people who work with and for them. Advantages are:

(1) can take leadership role very young and be accepted;
(2) never feels or looks uncomfortable;
(3) always seems to know what to do in any situation (and usually does);
(4) tends to have a multitude of behavioural styles and thinking patterns, depending what is required in any situation or stage in the economic cycle;
(5) usually extremely intelligent and wise and able to take complex decisions with easy facility.

Disadvantages are:

(1) it all looks so easy for them, it almost seems unfair to the less gifted;
(2) can give the false appearance of being more style than substance;
(3) so bright that it takes followers much concentration to understand the complexity and cleverness of their strategic insights;
(4) one is never sure they are pleased with ones' efforts because their own achievements seem so natural, they assume it is equally easy for others, too;
(5) they sometimes forget to say 'thank you'.

Nature's natives are effective under most circumstances. However, they excel in large-scale, multinational or global organizations, because their style transcends local or national attitudes and cultures. They just glide over culturally narrow behaviour. This enables them to fit in with most nationalities and value systems. Leaders of businesses such as Unilever often match this style. A business which would be best led by a leader with this style would be Shell, the global energy business. In fact, in recent years, this has not been the case. This would explain how the leadership of Shell misinterpreted public reaction all around the world to their proposal for disposal of a redundant oil rig in an environmentally unacceptable method of sinking it in the ocean. A truly cosmopolitan leadership, acting as *nature's natives* would never have miscalculated the potential public reaction so wrongly.

Many of the world's leading pharmaceuticals are led by this style of brilliant but natural natures natives leader. Unfortunately, they also incur two of the worst problems and disadvantages of this style of leadership. The first is that the followers are not always sure where the strategy is taking them, which makes it hard for them to follow. I have also noticed that most of the global pharmaceuticals executives I have worked with exhibit the most appalling poor manners, to each other and to all the people who work with and for them.

Summary of leadership styles

It is worth stating that there is no special science about setting out lists of leadership styles. It is unlikely that any list can ever be completely exhaustive. Furthermore, they will change over time as fashions and needs evolve. However, they are useful as a guide to leaders who are developing their own style as they mature and become leaders in their own right. Almost certainly they will recognize more than one personal style which they seem to have developed as different circumstances call for a fresh approach to a particular problem or business situation. Most leaders have some amalgam of a few of the above (Table 4.1).

Leadership styles are, by definition, idiosyncratic. Leaders need to adapt and develop fresh, individual styles of their own. The list of styles laid out above should act as a guide to the extent of the range that tends to be seen in organizations and the effect they can have, for good and bad, upon their followers. All styles have some unfortunate consequences. That is just a function of the fact that the *perfect leader* has not yet been born.

The analysis of leadership styles also leads to the topic of how leaders' analyse themselves. What are the underlying reasons for their adopting a particular set of personal styles with all their various effects and dysfunction's upon their subordinates? Why do certain leaders choose some styles as the vehicle to achieve their leadership goals? How far are they free agents, choosing from the full range of choice? How much is controlled by the nature of their personality and their inherited personal character traits?

In the following sections I discuss the Belbin team skills analytical tool, as well as the more profound psychometric insights of the FIRO-B fundamental interpersonal behaviour and relationships guidelines. In Table 4.2, I name and briefly describe a whole range of other instruments which can be used by individuals and teams to penetrate more deeply the quality, texture and make-up of themselves and their colleagues. Where readers find they are particularly fascinated by any particular one, they can probably obtain details of it through people development businesses local to their own business or from their local business school or from most university faculties of psychology.

The use of psychometric analyses

Psychometric exercises are sets of questionnaires which, when a person's answers are analysed alongside the many others who have

Table 4.1 Summary of leadership styles

Style	Best situation	Worst situation	Comments
Charismatic	Moments of great strategic leaps forward	Steady state, when quality succession planning is preferable	Charismatic leaders drive out other types of quality people.
Superior intelligence	Businesses which employ many bright and well qualified people	Market place fights for low value, highly branded, popular products.	Brains admire other brains, usually. Other leaders with more empathetic qualities, do not value this style.
Autocratic	Great in a crisis because they don't feel the need to ask too many questions.	Inappropriate when work force is well educated and highly qualified	Works well in many situations. Particularly effective in the UK, where people accept class differences easily.
Shepherd	Excellent in a steady state business	Can panic in a crisis or situations needing fast reactions	Great in gilt-edged stocks.
Army general	Great when preparing for war	Not necessarily great in the heat of battle	Usually better at preparation than finishing. Relies on not needing to finish because everybody thinks their preparation is so good they will win the battle.
Princely leader	Long-established businesses with leading brands	Not effective leading businesses with mass demand, such as groceries	A dangerous style for the business because they are hard to remove and do not easily recognize when they are no longer appropriate.
Nature's native	Good in most circumstances, especially well-branded global businesses	Organizations which are heavily sales-led.	Probably the most effective all-round style. They make everybody feel better about going to work, and they keep the owners happy.

previously completed the exercise, enable their responses to be compared with others and their alignment with or difference from the norms to be established. Psychometric analytical tools are most efficacious when trying to analyse one's own or other peoples' personality and/or character.

Some give more profound insights than others. The Belbin Team Skills Test (see Chapter 11 for detailed analysis of this test), for example, is useful but gives little profound long-term insight into character. Rather it informs the user about the current team skills of the recipient which they prefer to contribute to their teams' general needs at any point in time when the test is administered. The great value of psychometric testing is to use it as a back-up to test what your intuition tells you about the people around you and about yourself. They can confirm impressions given during interviews or when working alongside somebody, particularly if there are traits which one cannot explain to oneself but which give cause for doubt or worry.

Psychometric tests are also useful as a means to set up a discussion on important topics about individuals in the work setting. Their use tends to liberate a respondent and their facilitator and 'create' the right atmosphere to talk about sometimes difficult and intimate subjects. Their use can get you into interesting and revealing discussions faster than any other development or teaching technique.

We must always remember that psychometric testing sometimes gives warnings or indications about the sadder and most difficult aspects of people's psychological make-up. It is vital that adequate provision is always made in both time and resources for these major problems to then be followed up with counsellors and other advisers who have the time and skills to help those who have uncovered more than they can deal with alone.

Psychometric tests can be used to facilitate the creation of a balanced executive team or a board of directors. When the results from tests such as these are disseminated in the business and exchanged with key players in the organization, it can give all the key executives a vocabulary with which to express their feelings and their thinking styles. This can be important, later, when working together in emergencies or even more mundane organizational processes. Finally, when used sensitively, psychometric tests can provide major clues on how to handle difficult executives and, especially, how to maximize their individual contribution, as well as that of the whole team.

Uses and warnings about selected psychometric tests

Many of the tests mentioned in Table 4.2 are under copyright control. I have included detailed descriptions of one or two in this book because

Table 4.2 Use of psychometric analyses: the insights from different tests

Insight required	Test recommended
Optimal team behaviours	Belbin teams skills test
Thinking style	Myers–Briggs preferences analysis (see Chapter 11 for detailed analysis of this test)
Emotional intelligence	Cooper–Sawaf Executive EQ test
Thinking skills	Watson–Glaser
Judgment skills	Watson–Glaser
Temperament	Myers–Briggs preferences analysis
Social skills	FIRO-B
Leadership drive	FIRO-B
Capacity for accepting guidance	FIRO-B
Personal emotional maturity/ anger levels	FIRO-B
Need for interaction with others	FIRO-B
Leadership style	FIRO-B
Use of different situational leadership styles	LEAD (Hersey and Blanchard)
Levels and types of conflict style	Thomas Kilman Conflict Mode
Use of political behaviours	Machievelli scale
Motivations for work	Hunt Work Interest Schedule

I believe they are particularly useful to achieve special insights into the deeper nature of the leaders and subordinates. The Belbin Team Skills Test written about in Chapter 2, is one favourite. Another is the FIRO-B Behaviour Questionnaire (see Chapter 11 for detailed analysis of this test).

An extra working tool for leaders: aggregated use of psychometrics

Over the past 20 years I have used the aggregated results of psychometric tests of complete executive teams. This helps clients to gain an insight into the general climate and temperament of the teams of executives in their business. These aggregated tests can sometimes give a profound and accurate insight into the employees' cultural spirit. They often contain a greater degree of accuracy about the tone of a group than one can get from looking at the individuals one at a time. I set out below an example of the aggregates of one set of

Table 4.3 Aggregated FIRO-B results of leaders in a fast growth company

Inclusion expressed*	Inclusion wanted*	Control expressed*	Control wanted*	Affection expressed*	Affection wanted*	Inter-personal score†	Expressi of anger‡
3	2	7	2	3	7	24	28L
6	5	5	1	3	3	23	77H
4	0	5	2	3	5	17	88H
3	1	7	2	0	2	15	91H
4	0	7	1	3	0	15	100H
5	2	8	1	5	4	25	58M
7	7	5	6	8	6	39	33L
6	5	7	5	3	4	30	47L
5	3	2	2	3	3	18	85H
2	0	9	4	2	1	18	96H
5	0	6	3	2	3	19	88H

* The scores in these columns range from 0 to 9.
† The score in this column ranges from 0–54.
‡ The score in this column ranges from 0–100, with H = High = 24%, M = Medium = 30% a
L = Low = 46%.

FIRO-B results that gave an insight into the value and application of such an aggregation. When psychometric results are used in the manner illustrated above (Table 4.3), they become another tool for the analysis of the corporate culture.

I will try to take you through an analysis of the group displayed. They are the senior executives and the managing directors of a quoted company. Firstly examine the *Inclusion expressed* column. The maximum theoretical score for any respondent would be 9. The highest actual score is 7, but most scored 4, 5 or 6. This indicates a relatively well balanced group of people with average to high social skills.

However, when we examine their *Inclusion wanted* scores, we see most of the scores are considerably below those in the expressed column, including several who score zero. This indicates that although people in this group are socially skilled and can express themselves well in terms of inclusion they do not, actually, as a group, really want much social intercourse at all. To paraphrase, they all issue invitations to the Xmas party but none of them wants to go! You can imagine the type of social tension this can place upon the organization and themselves as a group. They can appear to be hypocritical, insincere and, simply, 'never there'!

Now examine the *Control expressed* (control wanted *over others*) column. The maximum score per individual is, again, 9. Notice how many score 5 or more, with many 7s, 8s or 9s. This indicates a fairly high need to exercise control over others, almost to the point of excess.

Compare this to the *Control wanted* column. The contrast is stark. The same people say they want almost no control over themselves from anybody. People who achieve scores such as these are known as *mission impossible* personalities because they are driven to ever greater control and ever higher levels of aspiration, knowing no rational achievement boundaries. They often drive their subordinates to distraction.

When I explained these scores to the Chief Executive (who scored moderately and could both exercise and accept control) he exclaimed, 'Now I understand why I feel I am never in control of them! How will I ever cope?'

Fortunately, there was an answer. This business was trying to build an infrastructure for a new, emerging market. It had to beat the competition to get its infrastructure built first. There was a fair chance that which ever company came second, would become a takeover victim to the winner. In fact, this team of *mission impossible* types was just the right team for the task. They just needed motivating accurately and checking with tight quality control. I recommended that he give them difficult objectives and more tasks than most rational executives would choose to cope with because *mission impossible* types need to achieve excessively, to compensate for a deeply felt self perception of inadequacy. They always take on too much and continuously try to prove themselves against impossible odds.

Finally, examine their *Expression of anger* column. Seven out of 11 have a high anger score. A normal expectation would have been 24% rather than the actual 64%. Only by keeping them extremely busy, could this group be prevented from working themselves and their subordinates to a state of nervous and cowed exhaustion. If they ever achieved their objectives they would all have an angry fight with each other and destroy the business!

Summary

There are no normal groups. But every group about whom I have assembled aggregations, demonstrated tendencies which made their group behaviour more predictable and reflected accurately their company culture. Such aggregations can give leaders a valuable tool with which to decide how to lead their key Executives and their business. Leaders should also take advantage of any insights psychometric scoring may give into the nature of individuals in their teams. Paying heed to their own personality traits and their effects upon others will also be useful.

The key leadership behaviours of leaders

Behaviours and styles are accumulated as one learns to become a leader. They are differentiated from traits because they are acquired from developmental inputs. They are:

- the ability to get into leadership positions;
- better quality judgment than any relevant peer group;
- a capacity for survival (thick skin);
- ability to select effective subordinates;
- ability to inspire 'ordinary' people to perform above par; inspiring followership;
- making a profound enduring difference to the organization;
- a profound sense of decency with moral fibre.

Let's examine each, in detail.

The ability to get into leadership positions

This is best observed in cases of people who gain a reputation for always being 'in the right place at the right time'. I compare it to the days when I ran a wholesale 'cash and carry' business. About four times a year somebody would offer me a deal which, by the end of the year, proved to be worth about 50% of the total year's profits. Furthermore, I only needed 50% of each year to live most comfortably. So why didn't I just relax and do four deals a year? The answer was that if I were not running like a marathon man for the rest of the time, I could never be sure of 'being in the right place at the right time' for just those four deals! The same goes for these leaders who are always just in the right place at the right time. It is not an accident.

Better quality judgment than any relevant peer group

The first manifestations are often at school. They stand out as leaders. They become the captain of the football or netball team. They get appointed as School Captain. Above all, they are noticed early as having a form of maturity and judgment. The same qualities can be observed when they first go out to work. Without excessive deference, they are soon used by their boss to carry out important tasks. They are the first to be promoted because they become known for being a 'safe pair of hands'. It is their good judgment that is observed to be superior.

For those reading this book as a primer on what to do, think carefully about the paragraph above. In terms of most people, it means total and unceasing concentration from the start of their career, on using their best judgment all the time. It means never letting just their feelings rule. It means always reflecting carefully before offering an opinion or carrying out any action at work. Is this what you do? If not, are you prepared to concentrate forever and do this? If you are, there is some consolation. First, eventually it will become a habit and not feel so difficult or tiring. Second, you may just have the necessary genetic strain.

A capacity for survival (thick skin)

We should not imagine that great leaders always avoid controversy or problems. Sometimes it is necessary to confront problems head on.

They survive because they manage to get everybody to realize that they have made the right judgment and that difficult decisions have to be taken. The biggest decisions are usually the ones, which require the thickest skin. Making the larger investment decisions, or deciding to put the corporation up for sale, or moving into or out of major markets, are the types of decisions which cause the greatest angst to leaders and their followers. The mark of a great leader is that they realize it is necessary to get people to understand why they see the final decision taken as being the very best in the circumstances. A great leader does not confront people with the decision but persuades and debates, until people understand. They realize that confrontation is unlikely to bring others around. They explain as long, and as hard, as is necessary.

Ability to select effective subordinates

Having to dismiss a friend who has become ineffective or who is manifesting characteristics that are detrimental to the organization is often the hardest type of decision a leader may have to take. It is one of the worst forms of leadership failure when the leader does not confront these problems. Making the right decisions about people often requires a special combination of intuition and experience. The great leader usually has an intuition about who could fit a particular job and when the person will be ready for it. A feel for people and their development cycle and potential capacity becomes a sixth sense. Wise leaders back up their instincts by sharing responsibility with skilled human resource managers, interviewing both individually and in teams and exploiting psychometric testing. When they can, they appoint people for trial periods to ensure they can be returned to the positions where they were effective previously, if they fail in their fresh position.

I once saw a leader I admired preside over the appointment of a long-term colleague as his successor. That turned out to be a poor choice. Does that mean that the leader (who I admired) was, ultimately, a poor leader? Later, when I asked him why, he replied that he had run out of new ideas and he therefore felt a duty to hand over the reins. It turns out that his appointed successor either shared with him a lack of ideas or didn't know how to enact them. Does that mean in the strict sense of great leadership, this leader failed? Well, it does, in the strictest long-term tests. Failing to organize quality succession, which then destroys what you have built, is not good, long-term leadership.

Ability to inspire 'ordinary' people to perform above par; inspiring followership

By definition, the world consists, mainly, of people of 'ordinary' or average ability. Ultimately, every large organization and the skills of the people in it, regress towards the mean. In those circumstances, how do great leaders make their people perform better than anybody else? They have to, because one cannot always have a consistently, better strategy or superior products, than every competitor. Great leaders do it by the quality of *inspiration*. They are able to make people want to perform better. The exemplar of the contrary is the teacher who tells a child not to expect to do well in their exams. This is guaranteed to ensure the child's failure. The opposite also applies for both teachers and great leaders. They make people want to perform above themselves. They show them how to be better. This skill is closely aligned with the ability of good leaders to attract followers. Getting people to follow, and want to follow, is a prime leadership skill. It results from a combination of charisma, persuasiveness and sheer determination.

Making a profound enduring difference to the organization

This particular trait can often only be recognized post hoc, when the leader has left the organization or department. My favourite example of this quality was a splendid leader I worked with in the transport industry. When I started working with this man, I visited the various divisions and districts he had worked in over the past fifteen years. Astonishingly, people who had not worked with him for ten years or more still spoke of him with awe and affection. All his employees still spoke of the qualities he emphasized. For example, he always emphasized cash collection, often achieving reductions in outstanding debt of over 50%. They still carried out the same procedures in the regions where he had been. In one region I came across an aged secretary who had worked for him more than ten years before. She told me that 'He was the most brilliant leader. It was always obvious'. I asked if she ever saw him (by this time he was responsible for all the overseas businesses and was often on journeys abroad somewhere in the world). She told me that she received a letter from him every Christmas telling her what he had been up to during that year and giving her all his news. I suspect that woman lived for those letters. He told nobody and did not do it to boast about how to behave. He just did it. By the way, they were always handwritten letters. I suspect he wrote them as would many quality leaders, with a whole range of agendas. First, they were a genuinely decent thing to do for an employee who, he knew, probably lived for those annual letters. Second, they forced him to review his own progress, in the eyes of an ordinary employee. Third, they reminded him of the many thousands of employees it takes to make a great and large corporation tick. Finally, it reminded him of his humanity and his roots. To know where he was going to, he needed to remember where he had come from.

Unfavourable indicators for leaders

A lack of intelligence can be a serious problem. Although this sounds facetious, it is meant seriously. I have observed many *nominal leaders* who have reached top leadership jobs through the exercise of will power and determination but with a serious shortfall of the necessary grey matter it takes to do the job. A lack of what we have described elsewhere in this book as *emotional intelligence* is an even more serious problem. This causes a lack of insight into other people and, possibly, a lack of understanding of ourselves. These are hazardous blind spots for any leader. If a leader's emotional balance leaves them with a psychological lack of independence, they can be a menace to themselves and their organization. The symptoms may be displayed through excessive anger or, possibly, excessive emotional turmoil in their life. The manifestations at work are likely to be an excessive need to control everything in sight, matched by an inability to take correct decisions. Sometimes this will be disguised by their requiring subordinates to amass large amounts of data to help them avoid the need to ultimately take what they know will be a wrong decision. Or else they get their subordinates to take responsibility for it, themselves. Immature emotional intelligence may leave them with an excessive need to be admired or loved. This serious problem will induce them to take their decisions for the wrong reasons. It is only equalled by the possible matching defect of having an insufficient need to be liked. A person who needs no love, doesn't need people enough to be in an organization composed of humans.

An excess of charisma can be a problem, too, although, as I explain above, high levels of charisma sometimes disguise a lack of brainpower. On the other hand, too little charisma might make a leader so boring nobody will want to work for them or be able to stay awake when with them. Excessive introspection can be difficult, whether caused by shyness or social awkwardness. But this is only important where it affects their self-perception.

Inordinate fawning fathers foolishness

As leaders move up the corporate ladder, people around and below them become aware of the inevitability of their eventual occupation of a top position. This creates an interesting phenomenon, as they begin to accumulate power. Power exerts a strong attraction to people. They begin to tell the rising leader what they think the leader wants to hear. They start to fawn upon them in subtle ways. The leader becomes accustomed to it. The less aware of the fawning a leader becomes, the less useful a leader they will be.

Why are so many employees so attracted to the power positions of leaders that they give less than honest views, when speaking to them? The answers lie in their desire to influence the leader and to achieve their personal objectives for the business. They may believe their personal aims for the business are also in the organization's best interests. Influence over the leader gives subordinates the power to influence the whole organization. Power is infectious and everybody wants to deliver what they think is best for the business. In addition, leaders are often attractive people and subordinates respond to that attraction. Above all, the many people who have no or few leadership skills, think that influencing the leader is the next best substitute.

All this fawning, lying and general admiration can be highly dysfunctional to the judgment skills of the leader. Eventually they begin to think they are always right. People start to give them the answers they want rather than the data they need. They start to take wrong decisions. After a long enough fawning period, the leader loses the organization's independent-minded, better quality employees and gets surrounded by increasingly mediocre people. Eventually, they lose touch with reality. One key indicator that this has happened is when they begin to believe they are worth a much greater salary and rewards package, just in the year when they deliver terrible results. They may become infected with 'chairmanitis' (a condition wherein they need everybody to call them Chairman rather than by their first name, which was good enough for the first thirty years of their career). Eventually the leader loses the job. It comes as a total surprise to them (but nobody else)!

Lessons for leaders

Is there a key lesson in all the above? First, I cannot emphasize enough how important it is for leaders to know themselves better than anybody around them. If they know their own weaknesses, they can be turned to strengths, because they can surround themselves with people who compensate for their shortcomings and balance their personal strengths. It is useful to use any tools that are available for analysis of both ourselves and our subordinates. This will indicate where the greater efforts have to be made to achieve increasing mastery of self and understanding of others. Aggregation of team results can also give insights into the culture and climate of the organization. A leader should know what their preferred style of leadership is and try to adjust it in the light of the situations the organization passes through. If they realize they do not have and cannot transform into the style that is necessary for a crisis or a change in the fortunes of the organization, it is always wiser to jump before being pushed. Or else, find a transitional leader to achieve what is needed to accomplish the necessary changes. Finally, leaders should always be aware of the power that emanates from the 'leadership' position. Understand that it attracts flatterers and sycophants. Do not be seduced. Learn to use the power wisely. It is easy to be a big personality from the leadership position. Do not become seduced by the nonsense which can so easily attach itself to leaders. Be careful, *today's halo is tomorrow's noose!*

Summary

The chapter begins by explaining that character is important in a leader in a way that personality is not. It then describes the different types of leadership styles that can exist. These include charismatic, superior intelligence, autocratic, shepherd, army general, princely leader and nature's native. I then go on to describe how leaders can use psychometric tests for themselves and their organization to better manage their people. I look at the key leadership behaviours such as the ability to get into leadership positions, the use of high quality judgment, the selection of good subordinates and the ability to inspire people to perform better than they think they can. After warning leaders to be careful about excessive fawning from people around them, the chapter closes by advising readers to get to know themselves well and then select subordinates who can cover their weaknesses for them.

5. *What is a Leadership Career?*

It could be you

Almost everybody who ever worked in an organization, has pondered whether they could do a better job than the leader they faced. Sometimes it's because they don't comprehend the complexity of the problems faced by their leaders. At other times it really is because the leaders don't know what they are doing. Worst, they don't appear to realize how bad they are. Have you wondered how good a leader you would be, if you ran the business? This book is aimed at all those people who are being realistic, when they say to themselves, 'when I run this business . . .'

In my early years as a consultant, I worked mainly with those aspirants and occasionally with their leaders. It often seemed as if the leaders did not really seem to know what they were doing, looking at it from below the parapet. As I worked increasingly, and later almost exclusively, for those top leaders of mainly large corporations, I learned to understand better, the pressures and trials of those at the top. I have now spent many years helping leaders of, usually large businesses, to improve their leadership skills, to survive when under pressure and to assess the team around them, when they suspect there may be incompetence.

Sometimes, of course, I have found that it is the leader who has called me in to help, who is the real problem. More often I find that they need a little help to regain their perspective or equilibrium, following a difficult or disturbing phase in the life of the business or in their own development in their career.

It is useful to immediately differentiate between two types of leader of large business organizations. First there is that group who may be rightfully considered *strategic leaders* who have vision and know how to implement it. The second type are those leaders who may have the title but who are really there only because they have the political skills to get the job but who make little ultimate difference to the results of their organizations. I call them *nominal leaders*. All leaders have an enormous responsibility. They accept, sometimes enjoy, great power for, usually, fine rewards. Unfortunately, a lot of people who occupy the posts should never have achieved those heights; too many people get to the top that should not have succeeded in passing through the filters of elimination.

When should you start your leadership career?

Most great leadership careers begin, unwittingly, during childhood. Psychometric research shows that, frequently, the drive to prove ourselves can often be laid at the doorstep of highly ambitious mothers. When people later fulfill a drive to climb to the top of a large organization they are merely enacting the developmental training that their mothers staged. They brought up their favoured, (often, only) child to want to please their mother at any price. The training is so strongly instilled that the adult child cannot stop trying.

Sometimes, just being an only child is enough to set off the sense of self-sufficiency. Leaders demonstrate a strong *need to achieve* (see McClelland, 1961). It is the classic hallmark of a leader, although, let's never forget, the genetic inheritance is always a prerequisite too.

There is some evidence that a significant number of leaders are taller than average for their generation, without any corresponding proven correlation of size of brain. Can it be that just physical height can explain the large number of *tall* people who appear to have made it to top leadership positions? I am not qualified to make a judgment that physical size may or may not also have a correlation with a larger brain mass leading to high intelligence. However, it seems most unlikely. I suspect that the observations that more leaders are above average height did not distinguish between good and bad leaders. If it did, I would like to believe there are more good leaders of medium height than tall ones.

In most cases, however, leadership potential and style of behaviour, starts very young, although it is not always recognizable as a precursor or predictor of leadership. Some leaders display waywardness during their childhood. They sometimes lack concentration powers in the classroom. Some display a reluctance to settle down to university education because they are so keen to get on with their leadership career. Bill Gates walked out of Harvard. Alan Sugar probably could never have got in. Sometimes future leaders are so different from ordinary mortals that they are seen as 'difficult to manage' children, by those whose opinions count at this stage of their career, like school teachers and scout and guide troop leaders. Usually, however, their parents, and others who adore them, accept and understand that they are destined for greater things.

What are we defining as success?

Success, in the terms of this book, is defined as making a substantial difference to the organization during one's occupation of the leadership post. This may be measured in terms of economic results (profits), creating an increase in gainful and satisfying employment opportunities for workers or making customers happy in the belief that they have achieved the best possible amount of value for their expenditure on products and services. Imagine the contrast of being a leader in one of those businesses where your customer service information tells you that most customers who use your products are unhappy, unhealthy or angry about the product in some way.

What is *effective* leadership?

An effective leader is one who truly makes things happen differently and for the better in his organization. They set the organization along new paths. They make it exciting to go to work because they make sure your working day will have structure and meaning, that all subordinates understand what they are doing, why they are doing it and to what purpose. They make the shareholders and workers rich and make the customers happy with their purchases. They also understand that organizations are more than just economic entities. They realize that, like any politician or social worker or 'life leader', they are running an organization that has many more realities than just economic ones. They are fertile 'imagineers' about the organization's future (see Peters, 1992), while understanding that when they increase working hours for workers they also deprive families of their working parent or spouse.

Effective leaders realize that their decisions have many social, as well as economic, implications. A few years ago I had to help a leader reduce the size of his organization from 6,000 employees to 4,500. It was the only way to save the whole business. He deliberately chose to let the people go early, in October, rather than hold them to their terms of contract and go in December, while paying them the full period, at the cost of several extra millions of £'s cost to the business. The decision was taken in order to ensure they had the maximum chance of finding other employment (the October jobs market is infinitely superior to the December or January situation) and to ensure that their families suffered the least possible during the Christmas holiday.

The effective leader always takes decisions that make the organization succeed economically. What a great leader does in addition is to make the business succeed as a social entity. This leader wants people to feel proud and happy to be working for the organization, as well as prosperous. de Geus (1999) investigated what brings about an organization having a long life. He studied this subject while working for the Shell Oil Company. He discovered that the longest enduring organizations are those which do not attempt to grow at the fastest possible rate but manage their size so that they are able to survive the regular downturns that business life brings. These organizations also see themselves as having a loyalty to their core workers and are careful to try and retain them during economic recessions. In turn, they retain the loyalty of their staff when they could find higher paid employment during periods of economic buoyancy. In general, these organizations have family-type leadership who regard the business as much as a social entity as an economic profit maximizing one.

What are the early indicators of leadership qualities in individuals?

People destined for important leadership roles often get early responsibility in whatever organization they belong to. It could be said that a definition of maturity is being able to see the potential consequences of one's actions faster and more comprehensively than others. It is maturity gives a person high-quality judgment; this is something that people who have leadership potential have from a young age. This quality judgment is the reason that people who are destined for high-level leadership roles are given responsibility early, when they are still young. People know they can rely on these peoples' judgment because it is of a high calibre and they are always dependable.

From a young age high potential leaders tend to lead more than they follow when they participate in teamwork with set objectives. They are the ones who will organize the team's resources. They are the most likely to intervene when the team is going in the wrong direction and should change direction or find more resources. These people are usually deferred to by others in the team who recognize that 'they are likely to go far and they are pleased to have had the chance to work with them'.

People destined to be leaders find the management of people easy. This does not mean that they are more or less sociable or better endowed with the quality of *likeableness* than other people. But their emotional intelligence enables them to understand what motivates the people around them. This, in turn, gives them the ability to understand why the people around them are working and what most people require from their role in the organization. This is what is essentially required in the management of people for successful outcomes at work.

Leaders-to-be tend to have promotion come early and fast with whatever job they get. Usually this is because their talent and skill is outstanding. We often hear it remarked of them, many years later, by people who worked for them as they rose in the hierarchy of the organization 'it was always obvious that they were going right to the top'. I do not believe that this is a post hoc rationalization by those people. It is because these high potential people really do have something that emanates from them in the way they talk, interact with others, exercise judgment and move fast forwards in their leadership career. Additional evidence that this is not 'after the event' rationalization comes from the fact that the same people can also predict who is likely to get to the top without true leadership ability but through social and political skills. These *nominal leaders* career successes are equally predictable, though the consequences of their successful rise in the organization is less palatable and highly damaging to the businesses that employ them.

Leaders never forget why they want to get to the top of their organization. They have the goal of being at the top in their mind. They are driven. However, it is not just their petty ambition to be in charge at any price whether suited or not for that particular organization's needs. Their drive is usually underpinned by the need to use their energy, intelligence and vision for the business where they are employed. It is not usually just a need to control others and to avoid being managed themselves which so frequently underpins the inner drives of the politically ambitious nominal leader who is also uninspired and poor quality.

For many years I was puzzled that so many leaders who were obviously competent and good at the leadership job always told me 'it was not planned and that it all just happened' or 'I didn't really expect to get to the top', or 'it all happened by accident and is a surprise to me'. Were they being honest that their rise to the top was an accident? In retrospect, I have to say that most of them must have been much more casuistic than I thought at the time. Getting to the top of a medium or large-scale organization is rarely an accident. We have to want profoundly to be there. We have to plan a career to assure we get the opportunity to rise further. And we really have to calculate every step to be sure we want to pay the price for the next job. So many of these top leadership roles demand highly concentrated and intense work for very long hours most days of most weeks of the year. Frequently, by ordinary standards, the family has to take second place. We have to think about whether we want the next job enough to choose to carry on.

Above all, these people really want leadership success. They measure themselves in terms of the past historical performance of the business; how well they are doing compared to their peer group of leaders in similar organizations; by polls taken of other leader's ratings; and, by the rewards their remuneration committee give in gratitude for their performance. Above all, like all great champions, they measure their performance against their own judgment about the optimum potential of their business.

Part of the reason they strive to get to the top is because they know they can do the leadership job better than any body else. In good quality people this does not look like arrogance. It is merely the rational assessment of an intelligent person objectively concluding that they, themselves are the someone who is best fitted for the leader's job. Only foolish second-rate people frown on intelligent peoples' objective assessment of their own skills.

Great leaders find it easy to be loyal but difficult to accept poor decisions. For most people this causes a difficult quandary. How can one remain loyal to our manager or leader when they are being blatantly misguided in their strategic behaviour? Wise people always find a way out of the problem. For example, a quality leader was told that the finance director needed extra money to meet that year's budget. He was told to take it out of people development. That broke this leader's rule of continuous development for all his people. Instead, he found the £1 million from the building budget, but he never stopped developing his people. He knew that was the way to the future.

Top quality leaders believe in their company and its products. This stems from various sources. The first is that their personal moral fibre would not allow them to work for any business which made products which are socially unworthy. This creates an immediate problem with both ethical and performance measurement dimensions. For example, I believe that all cigarette products are socially undesirable and physically inimical. I also conclude that anybody in a business making and selling them is concerned in an ethically undesirable business. Does this mean that nobody can, by definition, be a good leader within the tobacco industry? My answer would be that there can be no good leader in such an organization because nobody would want to produce anything which can do real physical harm to their clients. I suspect that this statement is highly offensive to some people within the tobacco industry who may perceive themselves as being good quality leaders. They probably consider they are merely selling legal products that any customer is free to buy or not. The choice, with appropriate information, is for the customer to make.

My position is that leaders have to take a proactive moral stance in their decisions. The performance measurement problem is that success as a leader of a corporation selling ethically undesirable products, such as tobacco, means that leader's success has actually increased the sum total of harm in the world rather than good. How can successful performance in an undesirable organization be defined or be assessed within the realm of 'quality leadership'? Some readers may differ. That is their right.

Great leaders enjoy discovering why things go wrong and they like putting them right. All good leaders have an insatiable curiosity about how things work and how we can make them work better. Similarly, the intelligent manager or leader, when things go wrong, does not get frustrated, angry or bewildered. They want to understand in order to be sure it does not happen again. So they work hard to investigate whether the problem arose from poorly designed machinery or from poor quality human inputs into the machine. Did the system designed by humans go wrong because they stopped using the right machine properly? Good leaders get to the heart of any problem and always put it right or put in place a mechanism to correct it before they turn their attention to the next problem. Even when they cannot turn around a persistent problem immediately they will always plan how to do it better when the opportunity comes around.

People managing a leadership career seem to know where and when the next promotion will come from. When they work in the organization they are always looking ahead. They see themselves in their present position and the organization in the larger perspective. This enables them to see the next rational move in their leadership career. They always know which job would be most suitable and how to avoid being offered jobs that would not improve their wisdom or increase their skills. This should not be mistaken for being excessively political or wily. Rather, it is their capacity for helicoptering above their immediate position and seeing themselves and the organization in an appropriate perspective.

Why would effective leaders need help?

'If these guys are so good, how come they ever need help?' is a fair question often asked. Any leader's adviser has to offer a unique skill of being able to catalyze the development of a potentially great leader. An adviser's task is to maximize the leader's speed of development, thus allowing the potentially great leader to evolve his or her skills earlier than would otherwise be the case. Why should any leader need somebody to help them lead or analyse what they must do? Because sometimes a promotion comes too early or the problems are more complex or profound than the Board explained when offering them the job. Occasionally leaders get themselves surrounded by too many stakeholders who cannot understand what they are doing and the leader cannot find a way to explain it to them adequately. It sometimes helps to have somebody intervene and do it for them.

Other reasons why leaders sometimes need temporary help are related to some of the conditions of the leadership situation, as well as some of the qualities of leaders. The role of leader is lonely; leaders sometimes find it desirable to use a confidant (also discussed later in the book in Chapter 6 on Leadership and Life). Occasionally, some of them have crises of confidence. It helps to check that it's OK with an objective outsider whether what they are doing is within sensible parameters. On one or two occasions, I have been called in to help leaders sort out particularly difficult political situations with their Board of Directors. In these situations, a 'go-between' can be efficacious.

Let's examine a real example of just such a case.

Egos, politics and power

A client had been the Chief Executive Officer in an American telecommunications firm with revenues of about $10 billion per annum and profits close to $2 billion. He himself earned about $3 million per annum and had to be considered, by outsiders' standards, to have had a highly successful career up to that time. Unfortunately, during the last few years he had received a battering at the hands of the media and his achievements had been belittled. The situation had become so fraught that the company president had decided he could no longer continue in the leadership role. It was beginning to affect the share price and the perceived achievements of the Chairman. Furthermore, some of the criticism could be considered justified, because he was considered to be weak when it came to taking tough decisions about people.

Consequently, the Chairman offered him the choice of leaving the Corporation with a generous settlement or continuing his career with them but at a lower level in the business. My client chose to move to a lower level. This was a sign, for me, of a potentially great man. He had his ego so much under control, that he could cope with everybody else thinking he was utterly defeated. To understand how bad his decision 'looked', see Figure 2.

As the figure shows, my client had not only dropped in status from number two in the organization to one of several operating at the third level below the President in the hierarchy, but he now reported to a person who previously reported to him. Furthermore, another of his subordinates had taken over his previous job (and picked up all the long-term fruits of the client's best work). The client called me in, because his boss, previously his subordinate, was trying to both humiliate him and also force him to resign, since the boss believed the media stories that my client was really incompetent at leadership and strategy. My client's instructions to me were to establish exactly what his boss thought. I was then to help him decide what was reasonable to deliver, how much and how little would be appropriate to comply with. Then we would devise a plan to neutralize the situation until he could prove to his boss that he was content with his new job, intended to do it well, was capable of loyalty and of accepting his new position and of doing it brilliantly, if given half a chance.

He then devised a plan which did just that. He had to decrease the size of his management team of 100 executives (not all reporting directly to him) to 50. He had to revise the strategy of his subsidiary and demonstrate within a year that he could make more profit than the parent Division. He had to halve his overheads and to sacrifice

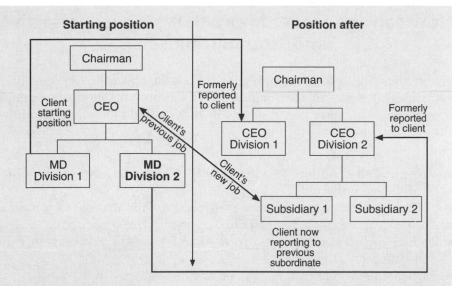

Figure 2 The starting and finishing position of a great leader. The client had risen to be the CEO of the parent Corporation in the USA. He had accepted a position, when I first met him, reporting to the CEO of one of the two divisions his previous empire was subdivided into. To add to the acuteness of the situation, his new boss and the boss of the other Division had both reported to him personally, in his previous role.

his Finance Director who had made an important mistake in the previous year (and delivered a surprise shortfall of cash to the tune of $100 million).

He carried out the necessary action within one week and completed all the recommended changes within three months. He cut his costs from $50 million to $25 million, halved his staff and doubled his cash flow and profits. Within a year, his position was so strong that he could be perceived to be more powerful than his boss. He was once more invited to attend all main board meetings and was seen firmly as a key contender for succession to the Chairman's position as the Chairman began to plan for his own retirement. For me the key learning from him was that great leaders keep their egos firmly under control and their minds fixed on the longer term and the big picture. In addition, if he had not carried out the devised programme, there was a strong possibility that his boss would have eliminated both him and his whole team. That would also have resulted in the loss of the excellent profits he was to bring in for the Parent Corporation.

How can the leader know that s/he is ineffective and stop her/himself?

An obvious first requirement of a leader is a ruthless honesty with her/himself. This is a truly rare quality in most failing leaders (and even in some successful ones). But, if we can do it, we should look for the following signals that we are failing:

- if you really cannot see where the short or long-term profitability will be coming from;
- if you feel overwhelmed *after* the first three months in the job (it is normal to feel overwhelmed *during* the first three months);
- when you start to feel that your subordinate(s) could certainly do the job better than you;
- when you feel continuously tired and depressed;
- when you long for holidays for the first time in your career;
- when you start to think more about past triumphs rather than future achievements;
- when your spouse starts to remind you that you really don't need the money;
- when you know you are sitting in the Board room hoping that nobody will realize that you don't have a clue what to do next (they always do realize!).

Leadership in politics: similarities and differences from business

The question often arises whether the nation would benefit from being run by business leaders rather than politicians. Some people believe that the job of leading an important business is much more complex than the skills to run a government department. Thus, business leaders should be able to do the job of government easily and more effectively. Let's examine some recent 'classical' political leaders and see how they match up to the corporate skills set. If one uses examples that everybody would recognize as leaders, such as Winston Churchill, John Major, Tony Blair, John F. Kennedy and William Hague, we should be able to note the differences better and make one or two predictions as well. Table 5.1 illustrates.

Of course, the table may be questioned in terms of judgment about some of the individuals in some areas. However, by and large, the judgments are reasonably middle of the road on each of the key skill leadership areas. It is obvious that, on most criteria, the majority of people

Table 5.1 Measuring political leaders against corporate skill sets

The key leadership skills	Winston Churchill	John Major	Tony Blair	John F. Kennedy	William Hague
The ability to get into leadership positions	Yes	Yes	Yes	Yes	Yes
Better quality judgment than any relevant peer group	Yes	No	Yes	No	No
A capacity for survival	Yes	No (?)	Yes (?)	Yes	No
Ability to select effective subordinates	Yes	No	?	No (?)	No
Ability to inspire others to perform above par; inspiring followership	Yes	No	Maybe	Yes	No?
Making a profound enduring difference to the organization	Yes	No	Maybe	No	Can't tell yet
A profound sense of decency with moral fibre	No	Yes	Maybe	No	Can't tell yet
Employable as business leader?	YES	NO	MAYBE	NO	UNLIKELY

who succeed in getting to the 'top of the greasy pole of politics', would almost certainly never make it in the corporate world.

Does the contrary apply? The evidence would suggest that corporate leaders find it equally difficult to make the transition into the political world. In part this may be explained by the possibility that both need such long apprenticeships that if one does not start young in either politics or business, there just isn't time to become proficient enough to become successful as a political leader after a corporate career nor as a corporate leader after a successful political career.

So, what are the differences between political and corporate leadership?

Table 5.2 sets out my view of the similarities and differences between the role of leadership in business compared to politics. Representatives from both the political and corporate sides may object to some of my definitions of what makes for successful leadership. But the litmus test is surely how few of either politicians or business leaders manage to achieve successful careers in the other's territory.

Why? It may be because of what each specifically has to offer the other profession after a career in politics or business. For politicians, the main attribute they are able to sell is their range of contacts in Whitehall or their particular experience of legislation they have themselves played a part in enacting. For business leaders, what they seem mainly to be able to sell is an ability to be efficient measured by the dubious quantifiers of 'cost benefit analysis'. The simple conclusion is that the range of leadership skills in the political and corporate worlds are so profoundly different from each other, that practictioners in one are doomed to failure in the other.

A further explanation is provided by examining the measuring tools of success in each profession. In business, success is measured by the relatively objective criterion (in the long run) of profits; in politics, the equally objective measure is *votes at elections*, which, in turn, confer power. These criteria of success are profoundly different in nature and it takes thoroughly different skills and processes to achieve consistent success.

Another key difference between business and political leaders is their time horizons. Corporate leaders must balance the needs of all their stakeholders to arrive at the optimal time horizon for the business, given its markets and the time it takes to develop the necessary infrastructure to supply that market. Political leaders are always constrained by ever decreasing time horizons as their next election approaches. Harold Wilson's famous dictum that 'a week in politics is a long time' is true for all politicians as elections draw near. They are,

Table 5.2 Measuring political leaders' skills against corporate skills

The key corporate leadership skills	*The key political leadership skills*
The ability to get into leadership positions Better quality judgment than any relevant peer group	The ability to get into leadership positions Ability to impress a peer group with personality and brains to create a caucus, thus forcing the leader to offer posts, when the party finally achieves power
A capacity for survival (*thick skin*) Ability to select effective subordinates Ability to inspire ordinary to perform above par; inspiring followership Making a profound enduring difference to the organization, measurable by profits A profound sense of decency with moral fibre	A capacity for survival (*very thick skin*) Ability to make the best of the subordinates we are obliged to use Ability to survive, once in office and wait for the rare opportunity to fight for the final leadership role Only history decides in the long run. No objective criteria (like profits) exist. Short-run criterion is successful re-election Appearance of profound decency with a capacity to suspend it with alacrity for the purposes of survival
Usable as a politician?	**Employable as business leader?**

therefore, forced to take decisions on the basis of the electorate's capacity to accept the consequences, or their ability to 'sell' the policy, rather than because it is what is best for the economy or any particular section of the community in the long run.

Some examples of successful leadership

Sir Winston Churchill, before World War Two had not been considered a great leader. But during World War Two, his oratory, his successful decisions and the eventual victory, provided proof that, for the duration of the War, he was a great leader. This emphasizes that different situations require different skills from the leader or different leaders. Interestingly, the common sense of the British public would not elect him leader, after the War. They voted for a leader, Clement Attlee, who was more likely to give them their rewards for their sacrifices during the War.

Robert Goizueta, led Coca-Cola for over a decade before he died in 1997. His belief in Coca-Cola was an obsession. He led it like a colonizing force, capturing global territory like an ancient territorial general. He increased the value of the firm by thousands of percentage points and it was worth over $60 billion when he died. Leaders who encapsulate and transmit vision and belief, add vast value to their business.

In the year 2000, we could see one weakness which contrasts against Goizueta's astonishing success. That was his failure to prepare a successor of sufficient stature to follow him. His right-hand man, who did succeed him, failed to make the grade and lasted only a short while. During that period the fortunes of the corporation went substantially into reverse. This example demonstrates one of the weaknesses of apparently great leadership (post hoc). That is the tendency for potential excellent successors within their businesses to move on to other opportunities because they recognize they are being led by a great leader. They conclude that their own opportunities to pursue their own leadership career may take too long to come in that situation. They consequently move elsewhere. Thus, great leadership sometimes contains the seeds of diminution of its own success.

Richard Branson, founder and entrepreneurial leader of the Virgin group has demonstrated that *entrepreneurs* can create and lead very large collections of businesses, as long as they make suitable arrangements for *somebody else* to run their *large* businesses in a corporate fashion. Branson achieves this by appointing clever, corporately skilled, managers to develop and grow the businesses, following his founding input. He then concentrates on helping them with the only corporate skill he really has in abundance, which is that of exploiting the media to achieve free publicity.

Sir Iain Vallance successfully led British Telecom, a leading UK tele-communications corporation, without falling out with its regulator, while still exploiting a high level of monopolistic profit potential from the early 1980s to the late 1990s. Unfortunately, by 2001 he had still not succeeded in achieving his stated ambition of making BT into a global player. During the first decade of his leadership his success was un-equalled. He changed the culture of British telecommunications and halved its workforce, bringing it into line with other global telecommu-nications companies. Sir Iain demonstrated steady, profit-led leader-ship, consistently maintaining high standards of integrity, while still ruthlessly pursuing maximum profits and manoeuvring the business into the potential to be a world player.

Unfortunately, during the last decade of his leadership, although his business remained one of the most profitable 'failures' in the history of business leadership (the firm made over £3 billion profit on revenues of between £12 and £13 billion), the strategic direction of the business went out of focus. During his second decade of leadership Sir Iain, who had been voted best leader during the first decade, began to see calls for his resignation and a consensus among the analysts that he had lost the plot. In an industry with time horizons of 10 to 20 years, it will be some time before we can really judge whether his leadership will have been a great success or a minor one. However, by the year 2000 it was becoming obvious that far too many other telecommunications businesses had begun to overtake BT in terms of scope, size and strategic vision. Is it possible that Sir Iain demonstrated brilliant leadership for one decade and lesser quality leadership for the second? He resigned prematurely in 2001, following pressure from key stockowners.

There may be another important lesson here. Elsewhere in the book we emphasize that it is important to find the right type of leader, for any special situation, in the correct size organization, for the particular period you want him or her to lead. During the 1980s British Telecom needed a leader who understood the organization so well that he could lead the vital change in its culture to one more suited to the private sector than the civil service, public sector oriented business that British Telecom was at the beginning of the period. Once Sir Iain had achieved this task perhaps it would have been more appropriate for him to move on to another large job of a similar nature. BT needed to be a more private sector oriented leader to take the firm on to its natural international strategic future.

Sir Peter Thompson, led the first privatization of what was then called the National Freight Consortium (now Exel plc) when Margaret Thatcher was Prime minister. He led it as a *worker* rather than a *man-agement* buyout, thus rendering thousands of ordinary truck and lorry drivers wealthy beyond their dreams, a result that fitted his personal be-liefs. He bought the business from the Government for just over £50 mil-lion. It was floated under his leadership, just a few years later, for considerably more than £1 billion, a twenty-fold increase. The business peaked in value at almost £2 billion. Unfortunately, poor succession to his chairmanship took place, so that much of the wealth he had created throughout the 1980s disappeared during the 1990s. The important lesson here is that great leaders should know their Achilles heel – Sir Peter chose his own successor. Sometimes he was so loyal to his people, he could not see their weaknesses. All great leaders need help in finding their successor. Sometimes they don't realize just how great they have been and what a special person it will take to fit into their clothes.

Examples of failed leadership

Peter Sherlock was brought in to be CEO of NFC by James Watson, who succeeded Sir Peter Thompson, as Chairman of the NFC. Interestingly, NFC contained within it an internal candidate who was acknowledged by everybody in the logistics and transportation industry, to be brilliant. It was considered bizarre by some people that James Watson chose Peter Sherlock. It may have been because people in the City at that time were saying that the National Freight Consortium needed 'fresh blood from outside the business because it was too insular and it too frequently appointed its leaders from within'. Thus, what had been a virtue in earlier days, became a sin. Peter Sherlock came complete with a full range of management jargon, but too small an understanding of the industry or the business. This would not have been a problem had he been the *right* leader. Within weeks of his arrival at the NFC, Sherlock brought in a contingent of consultants from McKinsey, the strategy consultancy specialists. Two years later, and with invoices for consultancy amounting to around £10 million, James Watson was finally persuaded to sack his imported whiz-kid. By this time the original, internal CEO candidate, was a damaged spirit. He left the company and later died in a tragic car accident.

The lessons of failure that should be learned from this example are that no leader should pay too much attention to the City or the brokers' analysts, in preference to sound knowledge and opinion related to their own industry. Another key lesson is that a wrong leader can take a business' value down to undreamed of levels incredibly swiftly even when following a substantial period of great success. During this CEO's 2-year occupancy of the leadership, the share price diminished rapidly. So did morale and the spirit of the personnel of the business. Several years after his departure, NFC's business and share price had still not recovered.

John Major, had a difficult period as prime minister partly because it coincided with a time when the UK had to decide difficult and sensitive issues with regards to Europe. However, he had one superb opportunity for eternal greatness. Having managed to negotiate a ceasefire with the IRA in Northern Ireland, he brought some peace to that troubled isle. Unfortunately he ran into another problem, his backbenchers rebelling against membership of the Common Market. Peace in Ireland would have been a fabulous achievement. Unfortunately Mr Major finally lacked an appropriate political situation to achieve his objective (i.e. an insufficient majority and rebellious backbenchers). He had to find excuses not to sit down and talk with the Sinn Fein representatives of the IRA, because he needed the votes of a few Northern Ireland MP's when his mandated majority was running low.

President Carter, was probably one of the most ethical and sincerely apolitical presidents in the history of the USA. Unfortunately, it would appear that he lacked the emotional insight and the grey matter to understand the complexities of the job. Leaders need big brains!

Robert Allen, was the boss of AT&T for over ten years. He presided over a vast range of strategic initiatives that turned into catastrophes, such as the computer hardware, software and manufacturing subsidiaries, he purchased. However, he had the political skills to survive into retirement, having devastated the company's inherited wealth and strategically strong position. He represents a fine example of failure to understand the basic strategic needs of the business.

Robert Maxwell, was the well-known entrepreneur who 'borrowed' from his business' pension funds to prop up the value of shares in businesses he controlled, while using their value to either expand or borrow more. He did this by exploiting his gargantuan bullying personality and coalescing all power into his capacious hands. Everybody needs checks and balances, for their own sanity. The lessons from the Maxwell story lie mainly in the failure of so many, otherwise respected and intelligent stakeholders, to control this 'larger than life' personality, who bullied and manipulated them so fiercely that they abnegated their duty to the other shareholders.

Symptoms of leadership failure

The first sign that a new leader is failing comes when their words and actions don't match. Their statements about the effects of strategic plans, usually made to City analysts and financial journalists, don't turn out as they predict. Quite soon they begin to blame external causes like the 'strong currency' or 'unfair Common Market regulations'. It is interesting to note that nobody ever says 'we did well this year, but only because the weak currency was in our favour' or 'our farming interests made tons of profit because the Common agricultural policy subsidized us to ludicrous levels last year!'. There are many classic leadership lies and excuses to explain away their failures. My favourites are:

- The government kept the pound too high;
- The market is taking longer to recover than my strategists antici-pated;
- You just can't recruit the right staff nowadays.

(*especially when linked with*):

- The government has failed in its education policies;
- The Board/shareholders/banks/bond holders/customers must take a longer-term view;
- This is a much bigger job than anybody thought when I accepted your offer;
- I've put in all the necessary corrections. The organization is not responding normally.

Another early syndrome indicating failing leadership is given when they do not confront dismissing the people who caused the problems they are being installed to solve. Sometimes they offer the explanation that they want to get everybody pulling together and that unnecessary slaughter would damage the spirit of the organization. However, if the spirit of the organization was so poor that it necessitated a new leader, perhaps a little spilled blood is exactly what is required for the begin-ning of the revival.

Consider the NFC example used earlier. Peter Sherlock was brought in because the City commentators were asserting that the NFC needed to bring in new blood at the top to freshen up its leadership. One reason the CEO who was brought in from outside failed, was that, two years after his arrival, he had not removed any of the previous incum-bents. It is worth noting, for any leaders who ignore this advice to spill a little blood under these circumstances, it was those leaders who had survived, who organized the coup, which forced the Board to dismiss Peter Sherlock.

Any great leader should be able to change the quality of organization results within the first year of his leadership. There are many simple and justifiable ways of doing this, which might be considered short term but which bring long-term beneficial effects. For example, it may be wise to institute a recruitment freeze. This will control costs. Anyway, it is usually advisable because a new leader turning a business around needs time to consider the different type of people the business will need to succeed. In the meanwhile, it is better not to recruit at all. Other ways of making immediate short-term effects upon the bottom line are:

- stop all rebuilding and buildings extension work (until it is decided that these are structures that will be necessary for the future of the business);

- stop discretionary expenditure on PR and product development (until a decision has been taken about what the products of the future should be);
- stop all people recruitment;
- freeze all salary increases and bonuses;
- instruct the accountants to ask for extra weeks of credit and pay suppliers 1 to 2 weeks more slowly;
- stop all new car rental and care hire contracts and extend the period the company uses all the cars it already runs;
- institute controls on all air travel and ask all employees to travel on ordinary seats rather than club class or first class.

These ideas may be considered tactical and short term. However, they achieve several long-term advantages. First, they convince the Board that the new leader knows what he is doing. They win kudos and make it easier to persuade them to accept any difficult, strategic advice that will be given at a later date. Secondly, it convinces the incumbent executive team that the newly installed leader really knows how to make a difference. Thirdly, it signals to all employees that the new person means business; they thus gain their total attention. Finally, it is a strong message to the outside world, especially the financial commentators, that the company really intends to turn the corner and make a fresh strategic start.

What I am suggesting is that there are many formulae available to any competent leader, so that there should be no excuses for not improving the organization's results as soon as one assumes the leadership role. When leaders make excuses, rather than deliver the results, even in their first year, it is a sign that they just do not have what it takes.

Another sure sign of an inadequate leader occurs when many of his or her so-called achievements in past jobs, held prior to the current appointment, come apart at the seams. Such leaders soon become increasingly political in their behaviour and start to blame other people and external events for the failure of their strategy. Failing leaders often then bring in new executives to implement their strategic vision, sometimes with the mealy-mouthed excuse that 'implementation is not my type of expertise'.

Leaders in this same mode often call in McKinsey, the strategy consultants or some other, equally famous group of advisers, to analyse at great cost what's wrong with the company and to develop a theory for change in the business. Surely a leader who has been recruited to create a strategic vision for the business puts himself in question when the first thing he does is to bring people in to carry out that task for him? It should be taken as a very bad initial indicator. Sometimes their excuse is that 'the right type personnel do not exist in a firm'.

This story-line should be treated with the disdain it deserves. People within the organization will never improve their skills in managing and leading the business if they are not taught by the leader to analyse it properly for themselves. Furthermore, if such employees truly do not exist they should be recruited, not borrowed from expensive consultants. At the end of the day the consultants will have climbed up the learning curve that the organization needed to conquer. The consultants will end up more educated but the organization will be as ignorant as it was when the process started. Consequently, the enhanced consultants will then be able to sell their expertise about the industry in general to the next client. Of course, they will assert that Chinese Walls ensure that they will not sell your particular business strategy. However, as they guarantee knowledge continuity by hiring out the same experts to the next business, it is almost impossible that some special knowledge that was accumulated for the original client will not leak into their better understanding for the next. We are not suggesting that the consultant advisers lack ethical responsibility. We are asserting that it is impossible for expertise and knowledge not to leak into the next job.

Finally, you know the game is up with a failed leader and the business he is leading when the newspapers start to regularly put the word 'troubled' in front of all the articles about the organization. Simultaneously, the leader will start to look for his next job (usually by taking on too many non-executive directorships, hoping one will become his next job offer). You know he should be concentrating on his own organization. If you are a stakeholder, try to insist that he focuses only upon the job your business is paying him to do. Look out for the ultimate 'litmus test' of failure when the leader starts to blame anybody other than himself for the failure. He will also certainly refuse to take responsibility for the 'organization's inability' to respond to his leadership.

How and why bad leaders and idiots get to the top

Poor leaders invariably learn the tricks of getting promoted early in their career. Judging by the evidence of Kakabadse (1991), there are a lot of poor managers and leaders with defective judgment around. These people continuously promote fools like themselves, partly because they do not know any better; also because they have poor judgment; and, finally, because brighter people probably frighten and intimidate them. *Nominal Leaders* learn when young how to win political games and claim credit for the work of others. Sometimes, they have been better than average performers for a period of their career (see Elliott Jacques' theory of time spans of discretion, to understand how some people can get to certain levels where their development then stops). When they are at the top, it is very hard to remove them. By the time these 'nominal leaders' get to the top levels of power, they usually know all the political tricks of how to stay there. Once idiots get into senior positions, the inordinate difficulties of removing them from control positions, often conspire to keep them there.

The prime skill of *nominal leaders* is that they learn to look good. They may have even performed well for some part of their career. They will, almost certainly, know the right people in the right places. Sometimes, they are tall, causing them to get noticed more easily. Usually *nominal leaders* are aggressive, immensely ambitious and driven individuals. Occasionally one finds they are intellectual and well qualified with education degrees, and the odd MBA, which gives them a vocabulary and appearance of understanding, without the necessary accompanying insights. Above all, their greatest skill is in managing their career rather than the organizations they damage!

How do you know you have what it takes?

Most individual leaders feel a sense of destiny, they feel driven to lead rather than follow. They can see clearly when those who are meant to be leading are making mistakes, and they work out how to help them lead better rather than make them look foolish. They are often naturally appointed as leader of the school, captain of their school, to represent fellow undergraduates at university.

When they start their first job, other leaders at work adopt them as their mentee. They always have a deep involvement in their tasks at work, whilst retaining control over an important part of themselves, that remains uninvolved. Their early tasks at work may have relatively short completion periods, yet they will conceptualize their role in a context of between 1 and 5 years. They are always ready for the next job because they see how to do it better than the person currently doing it (without wishing him or her to be demoted).

Do they know they have the leadership gene? Most, when they are asked in confidence, answer that they always knew they were destined for a leadership role. They just did not know how and when it would come. Most have had some form of setback during their career. But they have always continued to drive forward because they felt this inner sense they were going to make it to the top, somewhere.

How do others know a person has what it takes?

Leaders who are naturally gifted, seem to command respect without resorting to tricks. They are always able to offer quality judgments and insights in response to an inquiry. They usually remain calm, and tend to focus on objective truths, rather than get sidetracked or involved in self-evidently, subjective opinions. They appear to 'command space' whenever they are in a meeting. They exude 'profound character' and people seem to defer to them naturally, rather than them needing to capture attention with stratagems. Above all, people want to follow them and seem to enjoy being led by them.

Situational leadership

Situational leadership is a concept that was developed originally by Hersey and Blanchard (1977) and is set out in their successful book, *Management of Organizational Behavior: Utilizing Human Resources*. It describes the need for leaders to adapt their leadership style to the situation they find themselves in, as a consequence of the business' needs or the type of people they have working for them. No leader will be competent in every type of situation.

I take the concept a little further observing that particular types of corporate situation are better suited to specific leadership styles. I further suggest that it is almost inconceivable that any single leader will be able to master all the potential styles (my list is both different and wider ranging than that of Hersey and Blanchard) in all the varied situations of start-up, high growth, maturity, post growth and liquidation, that businesses may have to go through, in the course of an industry life cycle which may endure for anywhere between a few months (e.g. a custom-built microchip for a computer) and 200 years long (e.g. the oil industry).

A categorization of types of leader

Leadership styles can be categorized as in Table 5.3. The descriptors are not always flattering, but this is meant to be reflective of reality rather than ideals. These types are those that can be found successfully leading large businesses.

	Leadership style	Description
	Table 5.3 Leadership styles and their descriptions	
	Leadership style	*Description*
1	Egocentric	Self-centred, dominant, runs the empire from the centre
2	Autocratic	Sends the answers down from the top, non-consultative
3	Superior egalitarian (primus interpares)	Participative but always giving impression of knowing the answers, makes people feel superior and worthy
4	Conflictual	Uses conflict, anger and strife to inspire and annoy people towards success
5	Team builder	Mollycoddles and develops teams until they achieve superior results just by wanting to please the leader
6	Strategic	Always communicating the vision and the path forwards, focused and uncomplicated, gains repute for big picture clarity
7	The people person	An *extraordinary* person who appears, on the surface, to be ordinary and makes everybody around feel extraordinary
8	The politician	Always balancing and manipulating the stakeholders to keep the power nexus balanced and controlled at the centre

A categorization of situations requiring different types of leader

There is also a limited number of situations which a leader can normally find him or herself in. Table 5.4 is an indicative rather than a necessarily comprehensive, list.

If we place these two sets of classification of types of leader and situations in which businesses need the leader's skills, we will be able to deduce which styles are the most and which the least effective within the range of situations leaders encounter. It may also be used to reflect the circumstances when good leaders may appear in a poor light even though it is only their unsuitable business situation which is the problem (Table 5.5).

What does the table tell us? First, that the most valuable leadership styles are the strategic autocratic and the people-person. This is an apparent contradiction for the latter two styles are at opposite ends of the spectrum. Yet it is easily explained; there are more situations that require these styles than others.

Consider some examples. Alan Sugar obviously has some leadership skills although not mainly in the usual corporate mode. His two most

Table 5.4 Leader types and their descriptions

Situation	Meaning
Entrepreneurial	Business in start up or strong growth phases under leadership of original founder
Corporate	Large, quoted business, mixture of mature and (possibly) growth products
Turnround	Sick, mature business with either declining and/or a cost structure which renders it unable to compete in its market
Steady state	Mature business, requiring application of mellow management of profitable market
Rapid growth	Immature market requiring clever development of brands in growth markets, possibly with high innovation
Consolidation	Business at close of rapid growth, requiring transition from rapid to steady growth
Slimming following rapid growth	Business at close of rapid growth requiring *rapid* transition to steady state because overheads have built so rapidly, they could break the business
Fattening following excessive slimming	Business which has been excessively down sized requiring rebuilding to avoid dying from lack of resources
Move from product to customer focus	Business evolving to end of competitive phase. Market segments captured through differentiation of product requiring marketing skills to lock customers into brands and service captivity
Move from market share to cost control	Business at close of new market rapid growth development led by product innovation requiring transition to mature market by controlling costs to win mature market fight on price

Table 5.5 Fitting leadership styles and business situations

Business situation	Leadership style							
	Egocentric	Autocratic	Superior	Conflictual	Team builder	Strategic	People person	Politician
Entrepreneurial	fit	fit	rarely	fit	neutral	rarely	fit	rarely
Corporate	fit	fit	fit	rarely	fit	fit	fit	fit
Turnround specialist	fit	fit	fit	fit	rarely	rarely	rarely	fit
Rapid growth	fit	fit	rarely	fit	rarely	tactics	fit	neutral
Consolidation	rarely	rarely	fit	rarely	fit	fit	fit	fit
Slimming following rapid growth	rarely	fit	rarely	fit	rarely	fit	tactics	fit
Fattening following excessive slimming	rarely	rarely	neutral	rarely	fit	fit	fit	neutral
Move from product to customer focus	rarely	rarely	fit	rarely	fit	fit	fit	fit
Move from market share to cost control	fit	fit	fit	fit	neutral	fit	neutral	neutral

evident styles are *egocentric* and *conflictual*. Those styles suit the *entrepreneurial* and *rapid growth* scenarios that are the key times when his businesses have been most successful.

Consider the example of Lord Sterling, the long-term leader of P&O, the transport, shipping, house building and industrial conglomerate. His two most self-evident styles are *autocratic* and *superior*. One of the prevalent situations in his empire is the need for *consolidation* (in those mature, P&O businesses such as house building and transport). The model would predict that his *autocratic* style would fail in the *consolidation* businesses. This may explain why Lord Sterling has been criticized in the Press for his handling of those businesses and calls were made for his resignation. Other businesses he runs are in a condition of *moving from product to market focus* (e.g. the cross Channel ferry business or holiday cruises). Following the opening of the Channel Tunnel, it had to become much more market and customer oriented than formerly. Lord Sterling's *autocratic* and *superior* styles are both *fits* for this type of business situation. Subsequently, he has received strong praise in the media and from other commentators for his handling of these businesses, and has diffused the criticism which was made earlier about his apparent failings.

It is interesting that the least useful style for a leader appears to be that of *team builder*. This conflicts with the pervasive theory of the last decade or two that team building was the key leadership style that could be recommended. If the theory is right for managerial leaders, they should employ a *team building* style. But the point for leaders to note is that although they may need teams to deliver their vision, using the classical *team building style* may be an ineffective way to achieve their objectives.

Mini case study

A leader in the goods distribution industry was the best *team builder* I worked with. He had taken a run down group of distribution businesses and turned them around into a highly profitable, £150 million revenue per annum business, with a national reputation for being customer oriented. It also made high levels of profit. The business was in an industry which was in a state of *consolidation*. He was so good at building teams, it was often commented that he took weaklings and made them strong, through the strength of the teams he built around them. He attracted the most intense loyalty from his team because he never dismissed anybody, even when they had proven to be almost, congenitally stupid.

A few years after this success, he was asked to lead another division which was going through a tough retrenchment, in the office and house removals industry. The industry was suffering from a general economic recession which had caused low levels of house sales (and therefore, low demand for household goods removals). The industry was thus in a state of *moving from market share to cost control*. His skills as a *team builder* went from being a *good fit* to merely *neutral*. His high flying career dragged to a slow march, and he never regained momentum.

Table 5.5 also shows that the *Egocentric* and the *Conflictual* styles are often a good fit in most situations. This is not surprising. The definition of both contradicts most people's ideas about what leadership is meant to be. It is regrettable that they are encountered only too frequently throughout industry. Both are useful for different reasons. The *Egocentric* style runs things from the centre. It is dominant and self obsessed. But it is also economical in the use of the leader's time and effective because it does not tolerate unnecessary discussion or debate. As long as the leader is nearly always right and in situations when there is no time for debate (such as startups, growth or rapid change), it can be highly appropriate.

The same applies to the *Conflictual* style. It best suits all situations of change, which are stressful and require the creation of energy to resolve the problems caused by change. The *Conflictual* style achieves this effectively. Unfortunately, the *Conflictual* style exacts a high price on everybody involved. It increases stress and burn-out and it wastes some excellent potential leaders who refuse to work with other leaders who use that style. It often prematurely wears out the leader as well.

The situation which requires the least skill appears to be that of *fattening the organization following slimming*. Examples abound in the privatized industries in the UK such as British Gas and the electricity utilities and many other monopolies in the USA such as AT&T, IBM and the US government. In essence, this situation consists of taking a company making large profits and spending the profits until the excess organizational slack is expended. Even incompetent leaders should be able to accomplish that relatively easily.

Summary of situational leadership

Some great careers have been built by, having the right leader, in the appropriate place, for exactly the type of situation his or her skills and style and stage in career were getting them ready for. It helps explain precisely the success of Sir Alastair Morton who led the business which built the Channel Tunnel and its associated rail links. He is a fine exponent of the *Conflictual* style and he was exactly the right person to deliver his business' strategic mission. It was an apparently impossible task, with fantastic financing needs and monumental building difficulties in a *rapid growth* situation. The fit between Sir Alastair's style and the strategic situation of the industry and the business, explains why his leadership was a fantastic meeting of the right man for the right job at exactly the right time. It was certainly worth a knighthood!

What types of firm should you work for?

Part of the thesis of this chapter is that great leaders manage their careers carefully. Unfortunately those nominal leaders who really should not get the top jobs at all do the same thing. The advice contained within this chapter, particularly in the following two tables, can be just as equally well used by incompetent as competent leaders. We can merely hope that the quality leaders use it better. More important, we must hope that more organizations will learn better to differentiate good from poor leadership.

Table 5.6 makes suggestions upon which criteria should guide leaders as they manage their career through both biological age and increasing maturity.

As we said above, good leaders mature early. That means they should be able to observe themselves objectively and coldly recognize what they are going to excel in and where they may be lacking the qualities which others have to a greater degree. That is why we recommend that a good leader carefully tries to match the type of work they do with suitable business conditions for their particular range of leadership and styles. It is not hard to understand why it is so hard to make judgments about ourselves. It requires a high level of surety and objectivity to get self-perception right. My personal experience of second rate managers or poor leaders is that their weakest vulnerability is seeing their own worst fallibilities.

Summary

Great leaders manage their careers throughout their working life. This is not because they are political or manipulative. It is because it is very hard to get to the top of any business organization. There are too many other people who, sometimes mistakenly, believe that they can do the job better than you. What we have suggested in this chapter is that you analyse yourself carefully to see what kind of innate traits you were born with and what skills you have developed during your career. Examine carefully all the environmental influences of your childhood and your younger adulthood. Reflect carefully what effect these have had on you. Study objectively all you have done in your career so far. In the long run, what was the effect of your decisions? In what type of situations did you excel and where, if anywhere, have you

Table 5.6 Choice of selection criteria at different stages of a leadership career

Beginning of career	Mid-career	Final stages/peak of leadership skills
Choose firms which have a 'Rolls-Royce' reputation.	You should change only for firms that offer an accelerated route to the top.	Try to choose firms with great brands which are run down rather than great companies which are exhausted.
Choose firms which have the number one, two or three position in terms of market share	You can risk a poor reputation company, but your due diligence should investigate that it is not fatally flawed	The ultimate test question should be 'are you prepared to spend the rest of your career there?'
Get a job which offers management training. It will save you the time it takes to get MBA-type qualification later. Problem is you can't take it with you, as a degree, when you depart.	Only move to businesses whose size can match your business abilities. Not worth being a big fish in a small pond. Get a pond which matches your size.	Don't go to positions where ultimate power resides with the idiot who screwed up the company, before they started looking for you, unless you can see how to remove the problem.
Could you spend ALL your working career there, if necessary?	The level of political danger and attack from lesser mortals will be at its highest point now. Be careful.	Scrutinize the non-executive officers and directors and judge whether you can achieve a working relationship with them. Will they panic before allowing you enough reasonable time for you to achieve the mission?

Questionnaire 5.1 Matching career stage, business condition and leadership style

Stage of career	Condition of the business	Your leadership style	Points allocation	Score
Premanagement jobs	Mature, wealthy People developer Mentoring system in place	Teamwork highly honed Gaining recognition Egalitarian	Three in alignment Two in alignment	6 4
First management role	Relatively mature business in highly competitive industries Profits low but revenue increasing rapidly	Determined Forceful Learning Democratic Partnership approach	Three in alignment Two in alignment	10 8
Middle management	High profits Products moving into more mature phases Many strategic needs	Authoritative Confident Highly visible Sights set on next top job	Three in alignment Two in alignment	14 10
Senior management	Low to medium profits Using brands to maintain position in industry Trying to consolidate past gains	Solid No mistakes Careful Gaining trust Feeling invincible Reliable	Three in alignment Two in alignment	20 14

First directorship	Personal contract of minimum 12 months' notice	Sensitive	Three in alignment	24
	Firm at least solid enough	Knowledgeable	Two in alignment	16
		Strategic		
		Loyal		
		Overtly ethical		
First managing directorship	Business should be in condition to suit your own knowledge of skills and style	Visionary	Three in alignment	28
		Inspirational	Two in alignment	20
		Decent		
		Great user of time		
			TOTAL	

Add the scores you have circled:

<40: your leadership career is in trouble-focus mode

41–80: average potential; time to try harder still

81–100: your leadership career is well launched

failed? What types of businesses and industries have you enjoyed most? Which ones turned you off? Hopefully, this chapter will have helped you select some of the criteria you should use to ask yourself these questions. What no author can do is help you to be objective about your own qualities and skills.

6. Inculcating Leadership in Your Child

Introduction

This chapter is written in partial jest. It is scribed with my tongue partly in cheek because the advice I am giving parents who want to train their children to become leaders is *not* the way I bring up my child. But then, I am not a leader, merely an adviser to leaders. I am *not* advising that you follow the prescriptions laid out in the following pages. They are just the data that I have discovered in my research, working with leaders. It is how those leaders were raised by their parents. Some really wanted their children to be 'winners', as leaders. That's how many of them see the world. For many years I asked the leaders I was working with to describe their childhood and what happened to them before they started their career. This chapter is based upon what they told me. There are definite patterns. Those patterns and repetitions are what I am recounting here.

Many parents who have achieved leadership roles in society want their children to achieve some form of success, along the same lines or, at least, achievements in other, societally recognized professions. Sadly and only too frequently those successful parents turn out abnormal children who have tortured psychologies, a miserable childhood and appalling adult lives. These consequences are often the price that children pay for their parents' success.

I am defining success here along the very narrowest lines. If a person sets out to have a major leadership career within the business world and manages to do so, that can be considered 'success' in the narrow terms defined here. Naturally, if one wished to broaden the concept to 'a successful life', these lives that many materialistic people might regard as successful could be considered an abysmal failure. For most of us success is measured by the level of happiness we achieve for ourselves, our family members and our friends. I concur with those values. However, when dealing with the special subject of leadership we have to define 'success' in the terms of the majority of the people we are discussing rather than by what some might consider to be a more rational, decent and human world.

Success nearly always comes at a high price. Successful people have to work longer hours, attend more meetings than most people, travel widely and allow the organization to occupy most of their focused concentration and time. Throughout this book I urge everybody to retain a balanced life and ensure that they do not inflict the consequences of their success upon their families. To some extent, focusing on a quality life for your family and your children is a very good way of guaranteeing that you will not make the mistakes that so many have made in the past. As Judith Brown says in *I Only Want What's Best for You:*

> As we have seen, children do all kinds of things for parents. They make themselves failures, push themselves to excellence, develop mental and physical symptoms, and relinquish or hang on to their childhood.

> (Brown, 1986: p.69)

Be careful what you ask your children to achieve for the sake of their love for you. They may grow to hate you when with an adult understanding they see what you asked of them.

Context

In an address to the Jean Piaget Society in Philadelphia in 1975, Jean Piaget said:

> There are three classical factors that have always been understood to be pertinent in cognitive development: (1) the influences of the physical environment, the external experience of objects; (2) innateness, the hereditary program; and (3) social transmission, the effects of social influences ... Each one of them implies a fundamental factor of equilibration, upon which I shall place special emphasis.

> (cited in Gruber and Voneche, 1977: p.838)

Chapter 2 laid out the range of controlling variables of leadership. The first referred to natural talents or traits that a child has to be born with to have any chances to become a leader as an adult. These are what we refer to as 'the leadership gene'. We described those in Chapter 2. The genetic traits we are born with are:

- mental ability;
- physical strength;
- intuition;
- a serene soul;
- a pleasant physique and physiognomy (being tall helps).

The major 'nurture' or skills which can be developed were analysed in Chapter 3. They are:

- paradigmatic thinking;
- self-belief;
- communication ability;
- strategic analysis;
- team motivation;
- financial and business analysis;
- people selection;
- balance.

Of this list, the way parents or guardians bring up a child is key to the possibility of a later successful leadership career. How do you bring up and educate your child to maximize its chances of being a leader (if you want to)? If you don't get some of the essential 'developable skills' such as self-belief, communication ability, team motivation skills, and balance and judgment instilled into your child during its period of pre-schooling and during its childhood years, then your child will have a far smaller chance of achieving a leadership career later in life.

Class counts

Cyril Burt found that:

> A child from class 1 (highest) has a 1 in 5 chance of being gifted (IQs of over 130+), whereas a child in Class 2 (lower) has only 1 in 14, and a child from class 4 (lowest) barely 1 in 200.
>
> (cited in Hearnshaw, 1979: p.83)

It is not being asserted here that leaders only come from a highest class of society. It is obvious that there are many who achieve success from different ranks of society. However, my data does not contradict the findings that Burt made. Furthermore, it is not asserted that a high IQ is invariably a feature of all leaders.

IQ itself is not free of the debate about nature and nurture. Some assert that you are born with a high or low IQ and you are limited to what you are born with. Others would assert that IQ is immensely elastic, depending on parental nurture and intensity of education.

A child's (and later adult's) self-belief will come from the careful love that a parent gives to its child. That will reinforce their belief that they can achieve anything. How can one teach them to only achieve excellence? By rewarding excellence and all forms of winning with vast quantities of parental love, affection and approval. Is that reasonable? It certainly is because no matter what happens to a child later in life the knowledge that it had its parents' love, approval and affection will give it a self-belief and ability to cope with any form of catastrophe that life is going to throw at it.

The ability to communicate will come more easily from high-quality schooling where the child is taught in groups with other bright children. Again, I can feel readers' hackles rising as they mutter 'elitism'. Sadly, in so many parts of the developed world public sector provisions of education are poor and averaged down to lowest common denominators (consider urban America or inner cities in the UK). It will not be impossible for your child to learn excellence and high achievement from these ranks. It just makes it much harder.

Judgment

One way to help a child develop judgment can come from teaching the child to achieve approval from all types of teacher whether or not the child likes them; and regardless of whether the teacher likes the child. It also evolves as you debate news and important topics such as religion, politics, philosophy, economics, business, charity, drama, music and all the great subjects that make a whole life. If you always treat your child like the intelligent human being it is, then he or she will respond by accepting the assumption that all it lacks is experience and that its thought-through views and opinions are always valid.

In Chapter 2 we mentioned some of the most important influencing factors in people developing the desire and urgent will and wish to be a leader:

- an unusually dominant mother;
- being the eldest child in the family;
- having a father who achieved high levels of success (and who managed to make his child like him);
- being chosen by a school teacher for special nurturing.

The last of these, 'being chosen by a school teacher for special nurturing', should result from the exercise suggested above when you encourage your child to learn to befriend all their teachers at school, even those who they dislike and who show antipathy to them. Sooner or later one of the teachers will adopt your child as a favourite. It is a great experience for any child to know it had one period of its life as a 'teacher's pet'. This is not to be underestimated. Sadly, the teaching profession is most apt to be subjective, irrational and inequitable when dealing with the potential of the children under their control. There is no limit to the number of children that bad teachers have destroyed by inflicting their poor expectations upon them. All children need protection from teachers such as these. The methodology recommended should help.

The rest of the attributes mentioned above cannot just be obtained on command or by systemic organization of our life. But they are all frequently concurrent patterns for people who become leaders later. The problem that arises is how do you get yourself 'an unusually dominant mother', ensure you are 'the eldest child in the family' and 'have a father who achieves high levels of success (and who manages to make his child like him)'? The answer is, 'you can't'. But you can recognize that these patterns recur time and again in the leaders we have observed, as well as from other biographical data.

There is a self-fulfilling logic to many of the patterns and requirements laid out in this thesis. It explains why the patterns exist anyway. For example, consider the large number of leaders who have an unusually dominant mother who also gives them an inordinately high level of love and approval. Many senior managers and leaders marry high quality spouses. These spouses are usually strong and intelligent, otherwise they would be unlikely to attract the leader or senior manager as a partner. We also know that, increasingly, the work of senior executives and corporate leaders occupy large amounts of their time. This means that their spouses (usually the female partner) spend much time alone at home. Once a child or children arrive it is natural that the spouse pours much of their spare love, affection and intelligent concentration upon that child. It will not be surprising that when this child, later, recalls its childhood, it remembers more about the maternal affection and domination of the person at home rather than the influence of the partner actually achieving leadership success outside the home, who was rarely at home anyway. Perhaps the pattern is not so surprising after all. It also reinforces one of the basic premises of the theory of elite rule that 'ruling elites replicate themselves through their offspring'.

This pattern is being amended slightly as more families emerge with two high flying parents although it has not been around long enough to have many major studies made yet. However, if one is predicting outcomes, it is that such families will have few 'children who become leaders'. These families tend to delegate much of the child rearing process to third-party professionals, whether nannies or schools. I would venture an opinion that they are more likely to have unhappy and maladjusted children than they are to have children who become high flying career leaders following their example of their respective parents.

'Having a father who achieved high levels of success' tends to coincide and reinforce the paragraph above, which explain why people who become leaders later in life often had unusually dominant mothers. When a child is born the parent who stays mainly in the home becomes unusually dominant for that child because that is where she (usually) focuses her energy in the absence of the externally successful partner who is often working away from home. The career-successful partner is then more free to get on with his or her career because the house parent appears to be fully occupied bringing up the child or children at home. Thus the behaviour is mutually reinforcing.

Frequently the contrary proposition is also true i.e. that children from poorer backgrounds, with less successful parents and with lower standards of living are disadvantaged in achieving success as leaders later in life. Burt found that:

> Many backward children come from poor home backgrounds, suffered from inadequate sleep and poor diets; and above all backwardness was closely associated with maternal inefficiency.

> (cited in Hearnshaw, 1979: p.76)

Consider further the proposition that an eldest child is likely to be the best potential leader. A parent cannot guarantee that. It is just the data that stems from the research in the field. Receiving excessive love, care and attention is probably what happens to the first born child in most marriages anyway, and thus results in that child often becoming a leader later too.

Arranging for the birth of a leader

Obviously it is healthy for any child to be born in the context of a loving and stable relationship. Preferably, at this stage in your life, you and your partner will have achieved a high quality home which you are happy to retain as the family home throughout the childhood of your offspring. Evidence shows that pure environmental stability is healthy for children. It is only the children of people serving in such professions as the military who, by obligation, are forced to move themselves frequently. The children of people with these lifestyles tend to overcome the problems of continuous upheaval and can usually manage stable lives in their adulthood.

You and your spouse should have your religious and moral views in full alignment or, at least, in careful agreement where there is discord on what line you are going to take with your children when those dividing lines of demarcation arise. That should guarantee that there are no divisions between you and him/her when you're in front of the child, as it tests you for the standards and parameters you are prepared to accept. It is particularly important in the first years of life that your child find no deviation from the strict system you impose upon yourselves and your child at home and in everything to do with learning the habits of success.

The powerful and strict standards of behaviour which you impose, which derive directly from your religious or ethical values, will enable you to give the child strong standards of behaviour. Liberalism during childhood is the enemy of the creation of strong leaders. The more liberal you wish to be with your child the less chance you give him or her of growing to be a leader.

It is always good for your children to be born while your parents (their grandparents) are still young enough to see them grow up and to give them that special quality of grand-parental love that is likely to be the only 'soft love' that they experience in their lives. If the grand-parents also re-enforce your strong moral values this will be an emphatic additional benefit to the child's leadership development. Sadly, if one of the dearly beloved grandparents also dies while the child is still at an impressionable age, it will add catalytic force to your values and leave the kind of psychological mark upon the child which can inspire it to later ambitious leadership goals. This is just another pattern, not to be arranged!

Tough love lasts longest

In all matters offering strong and clear approval or disapproval in black or white terms for everything the infant does usually seems to stimulate lucidity and clear-sightedness in the resulting adult. It tends to guarantee that the child clearly perceives the differences between right and wrong and learns to compartmentalize clearly about what it should and should not believe. Black and white seem to be the best colours to teach an infant the differences between right and wrong. Again, many readers may consider that the world has more shades of grey than areas of easy to distinguish black and white. I agree. But leaders need to see the world clearly (even in their futuristic vision). Too many shades of grey induce the 'Hamlet syndrome' where a person sees so many angles of why and why not, that he is unable to take revenge for the murder of his father!

In *The Achieving Society*, McClelland (1961) concludes from his studies that 'Ambition describes the goal of the person with a high need to achieve precisely because what he is interested in is something that will give him achievement satisfaction'. Although this argument tends to be circular, it does describe findings that are available from experience. When you offer a child the love it needs as a reward for doing things that are approved, it develops a *need* for that love. Eventually, that need for love becomes a *need to achieve*, which is the major finding that McClelland brought to the field. Likewise, children should receive tough love for failure to use the maximum potential of their talent or ability. This will stretch their use of any innate ability. If you are prepared to do it, expressing disapproval through the withdrawal of love is, sadly, highly efficacious in giving the child a driven desire to obtain approval later in life. Although it is never recommended to actually withdraw love, if you are prepared to go to the wall every time a lack of grit grips the child, you will render your child so immensely ambitious that it will be inspired to never stop achieving as an adult.

Every parent (we assume) makes every effort to discover any natural excellence that the child has and develop it. All children respond when they are extended by receiving all the possible ranges of experience and contact with the external world. When parents can include going to quality musical concerts, attending the theatre and viewing as many different sports as possible, the growth of multiple capacities to use the mind imaginatively and extensively grows exponentially. The infant should also learn to participate in as many sports as possible.

Multiple leadership children?

If there are siblings, the children should not perceive any differences in their treatment. The truth is that you cannot know which one of them will achieve the most. If you did take the risk of concentrating most of your love upon the most likely successful child, you might thus give it an enormous sense of superiority which may boost it later in its leadership career while inflicting appalling sadness upon the siblings during their childhood, which might lie on your conscience forever. Furthermore, anecdotal data shows that the siblings are most likely to recover and have reasonably normal (if slightly sad) lives. The child who received excessive love often turns out to be spoilt and immature, and fail to reach the expected levels of achievement.

Children learn self-discipline by observing it in their parents. I have often thought that children need little said to them by a parent about what that parent believes. Why? Because children take far more notice of what their parents do than what they say. This can, of course, at the extreme, lead to a rather silent home! Seriously, children copy what their parents do. They adopt the values inherent in their parents behaviour. Next time your child does something you do not like, try to imagine which of your behaviours taught the child to behave like that. You will certainly find it within yourself if you are being honest. What you are not enjoying seeing in your child's behaviour is actually something you do not approve of in yourself!

You do you need to display that same discipline in yourself that you expect your child to use later in life as a leader. When you are writing, focus completely. When you are playing, do it wholeheartedly. When you are at the opera or a concert be totally silent and still. When you see a film or a play or ballet, interpret it afterwards until all the nuances have been explored and explained.

Teach your child to read early. Evolve the child on to the most sophisticated materials it can possibly digest as soon as possible. Experience shows that apt children can take in astonishing levels of complex data if they are brought to it slowly but surely and without wasting time waiting for 'next year' or 'when we can fit it in', or 'next year's holiday'. It is also advisable to send children to the highest quality kindergarten you can afford. Quality is often a function of teacher to pupil ratio. This will incorporate an understanding of socialized behaviour, a skill that will be vital as the later leader manages the social part of his or her life. You should arrange for private schooling of the highest quality that you can afford, as soon as the child is born. As you cannot know which particular school the child's personality will fit, choose schools that are adept at creating high achievers but which also have a well-known brand. The schools should have enough self-confidence to ensure its education gets the child to a level which guarantees entry into the best follow-up schools and, eventually, the best possible universities.

Schooling

The choice of schools for your child is probably the second most important decision you can make about their lives in order to make them into a potential leader. (The first is, of course, your choice of partner as joint parent.) In choosing a kindergarten it should be one which knows how to get the child to focus on an introduction to reading, arithmetic, writing and maximizing the development of the child's self-confidence.

The first school, following kindergarten, should be highly skilled at evolving the basic learning skills of reading, writing and arithmetic to an advanced level by the time your child moves on to its next educational phase, probably at the age of about seven, possibly to a new school. Thus the child should be ready to take advantage of the excellent education that the next school is chosen to give. By the time the child enters the new school, aged about eight, you should aim for him or her to have reading and arithmetic scores of an average 11-year-old child. It is only this kind of lead that can form the basis of a really massive total education process that your child should now be undergoing.

From eight onwards the child should receive in-depth teaching (with homework daily) to maintain its reading, writing and arithmetic skills at a minimum of 4 years ahead of the average for its age. Furthermore, the child should receive the maximum possible cultural education, particularly by reading the outstanding authors in the classical texts which will inform much of the literature and science to come in later schools.

Time for another disclaimer. This is what parents of leaders do to their children. It is not meant to be an advisory book for normal child development. This book is not advocating, merely describing the way it is!

Team sports and emotional control

Alongside this elite cultural education should be inculcated a thorough understanding of team sports. The child should be taught to identify its natural talents and strengths and build them into leadership skills in as many teams it joins as possible. All practice of leadership will be useful templates for later life. Furthermore, the child should be imbued with determination *not* to accept the consequences of any lack of natural talent. Where the child finds it does not have natural talent it should be encouraged to substitute energy and determination to compensate for a weakness. The child needs to be taught that a lack of natural ability should not be allowed to get in the way of success at any representative or recognizable level.

Try to choose a school which holds traditional elite values such as trying never to demonstrate true emotions or feelings (*emphatic standard disclaimer from author*). The child will soon learn that such behaviour is considered a weakness. The best leaders use displays of feeling only to achieve results in their people and never to show how they really feel. McClelland (1961) states in *The Achieving Society* that 'There is no such thing as a really permanent friendship. Your friends change with circumstances.' Leaders use any display of emotion as a working tool and not as their means of living their emotional life at work.

Your child should learn to mix and befriend both the brightest and the most stupid children in the school through team sports. It is also advisable to encourage the child to move across all age groups and abilities at school. Later, as a leader, the child will have to work with less bright as well as intelligent people. It should learn to do this at school. The truly vital and valuable skill is that of being friendly with everybody so that nobody knows who the child really likes or does not like.

The child should be encouraged to develop its determination to win. 'Winning ways' is a habit, a need and a drive. It is learned young and grows over time. One way of encouraging the development of this vital skill is to encourage your child to win the approval of every single teacher in the school. It may not be possible but it is certainly worth a try. This is particularly applicable to those teachers that do *not* like the child. It will teach the child how to change people's opinions about him or her, one of the most complex and difficult skills on earth. Adults hate to change their minds! It just requires ruthless self-control and a determination to discover whatever it is that pleases each individual. To be able to turn somebody's set mind to think differently is a key leadership skill best learned at school.

If it has reasonable chances of being a winner, encourage your child to enjoy receiving any form of trophy or prize. Encourage it to try to win school prizes for academic achievement, certificates for music and cups for sport; anything which reinforces its self belief and enjoyment of achievement. The child needs to learn to enjoy (or need) recognition from as many aspects of the world that might be willing to give it. It is a noted characteristic of leaders that recognition is a powerful incentive for them. It is not just about earning more money or holding high position as the leader of an important organization that counts for leaders. For them all recognition is good. That's what leaders need. Most leaders I have met have that extreme neediness for recognition.

Emotional intelligence and maturity

Great *leadership* requires emotional intelligence. Emotional maturity helps you to have a quality life. Elsewhere I develop my thesis of the difference between *strategic leaders* and *nominal leaders*, Another clear difference between these two species of leader is that *nominal leaders* have *a need to lead*; *strategic leaders* have *a need to achieve* (see McClelland, 1961). The *need to lead* of nominal leaders often arises more from a 'lack of emotional balance' caused by behaviours such as parental manipulation of the child's desire to please ('Why was your friend made captain of football? Why wasn't it you?'). The *need to achieve* of *strategic leaders* is more anchored in a childhood upbringing based upon emotional balance, thus enabling the child to acquire a full range of emotions. This, in turn, enables them to match their talent and their expectations of themselves and others.

Leaders need to realize, at a fairly young age, that they have prospects of having a full life. They may not interpret this to mean that they are likely to finish their career close to, or at the top of an organization. More likely, they will realize that with reasonable luck and self-control they will have a materially secure and emotionally contented life. They will choose the paths in their career and personal life accordingly. Quite early in their career, if their parents get their development right, they would have realized that they are above average in potential and skills. If their range of skills and qualities is lacking they will know whether it can be remedied. If they need further training they will know where they have to go to get it. If their emotional intelligence and maturity is not as well developed as their pure strategic thinking power, it will have to be strengthened to make them truly fit for leadership. Above all they know they will need a thorough balance to make really correct strategic judgments.

What is emotional intelligence?

The root of most people's emotional make-up is formed during their childhood. The largest influence, by far, comes from parents. That is followed by teachers at school, particularly primary school. Other influencers are then family and friends of the parents and the personal friends that children make around their home, sometimes at Sunday school, Scout and Guide troops and in football, cricket, baseball and other sports clubs. At school, children often befriend other children from neighbourhood associations. Children also group with children with similar interests and intelligence levels.

In his book, *Emotional Intelligence*, Daniel Goleman (1996) describes some of the ways people acquire their functional and dysfunctional emotional profiles. He describes the Emotional Intelligence Quotient (EIQ) when fully formed and employed by people at work as consisting of four components:

(1) organizing groups   (the skill of initiating and coordinating the efforts of others);

(2) negotiating solutions (the talent of preventing conflicts or resolving those that flare up);

(3) personal connection (the talent of empathizing and connecting);

(4) social analysis   (the ability to detect and have insights about people's feelings, motives and concerns).

He goes on to explain:

> Taken together, these skills are the stuff of interpersonal polish, the necessary ingredients for charm, social success, and even charisma ... They (people with these skills) are the natural leaders, the people who can express the unspoken collective sentiment and articulate it so as to guide a group towards its goals ... (they) evoke the comment, 'What a pleasure to be around someone like that'.
>
> (Goleman, 1996)

What parents need to know

The roots of emotional intelligence come from a capacity to empathize with others and to feel their experience. It also comes from controlling our moods and ensuring that passing shallow feelings do not control our behaviour. People with emotional intelligence take their decisions about themselves and others based on balanced views about what they really think and feel, not on temporary, passing moods. How do mature people know it is a genuine insight rather than a mood based upon a 'passing feeling'? Goleman explains that moods are caused by automated, non-controlled and, sometimes, irrational reactions to previous events in your life. These may have been occasions of deep sadness, cruelty or nastiness by some people around you or just an accident which left a traumatic scar upon your psyche.

These psychological scars from the past can cause a person to react and behave in an automated manner to a particular current event which sets off those switches in their mind based on the traumatic event from the past. Even though they may realize that this is happening to them, until they learn to control themselves fully, they will remain unable to do anything about it, other than go with the force of the passing mood. They will know that they are reacting in a way the current event does not merit, whether too weakly or strongly. But they will continue to feel powerless to fight such emotional 'drives' until they have learned how to control the mood, rather than have it control them.

Furthermore, such events may cause profound stress or other deep feelings which cause a person to react inappropriately to other happenings or circumstances. For example, having a bad day at school. They go home and shout at their mother. The latter has nothing to do with the causes of the bad feeling. A mother's role is not meant to serve as catharsis for a bad day at school. The behaviour is thus entirely inappropriate. It may also make them feel even worse because they probably know that the behaviour will be counterproductive. Now they will have a bad evening at home, as well as a bad day at school!

Getting control of ourselves, and behaving sensibly under all circumstances, can be defined as emotional intelligence and maturity. This does not mean not knowing how to have fun. It means a person has their fun under safe circumstances and when the delight is pure and can have no adverse consequences for themselves or others. We are not advocating cold-blooded excess control. We are merely saying that quality people, who are destined to be or become great leaders know how to manage a balanced life. This will include ALL the pleasures life offers, whether they are based on physical or mental pleasure; or the profoundly conceptual or utterly superficial. Once again, we are really talking about a balanced life.

Most adults dismiss the possibility that they could control themselves better. They feel it is too difficult, when, and if, they acknowledge there is any problem at all. They tell themselves that, even though they are intelligent and can recognize that their behaviour is unreasonable, or stupid, they cannot control their moods in the disciplined way being advocated. It is very hard to control everything. Those who wish to make themselves fit to be great and effective leaders, steel themselves to do it and succeed, in the main. These people realise that those irrational reactions to the wrong stimuli are almost always based upon behaviours and reactions learned, subconsciously, during childhood. The lessons were wrongly learned and can be unlearned. Strategic leaders do something about it. They retrain themselves to be fit for their purposes, i.e. leadership. As a parent, our job is to ensure that our child has no trauma that cause latter irrational reactions. It is also a duty to provide the emotional insight for the child to grow up understanding how to cope with the dramas that will inevitably come along, without becoming permanently imbalanced.

Mini case study

Alastair is a client whose job is to lead the entertainment division of a large privately owned business with interests in different industrial sectors. I had been introduced to him by a previous client who now worked for him. The ostensible objective was to help him revise the strategic vision of his business, a division of a group on whose Board he sat. However, when analysing the psychometrics of Alastair and his team, his personal results caused me deep concern. They indicated a man who had high levels of anger and who also appeared to be profoundly unhappy. I asked him if he had suffered from any physical sickness which could be associated with stress. He had been treated for high blood pressure the previous year and depression. These symptoms confirmed the psychometric results were accurate.

Upon investigation I discovered the underlying cause of his stress was his feeling (at the subconscious level) that he had to spend his life repaying his mother for sacrificing her life to give him an education. She was widowed at a young age and had to earn a living scrubbing floors. She died just as he finished his university studies, having maintained him throughout. Alastair summarized these his feelings in the phrase, 'she died giving me an education'. He felt obliged to exploit that education and never stop moving ahead in life. He had to repay her martyrdom by achieving ever more to justify her sacrifice.

The consequence was that he never relaxed at work. He allowed himself no sense of humour. He could not understand any subordinates who did not do their duty constantly. He even dismissed one of his directors (whose wife had just had twins), because the director was taking time off to be with his wife who was having trouble coping in the first few weeks. Although he had married a charming and relaxed lady, for 27 years he had shouted and ranted and raved at her, usually as a consequence of things not going well for him at the office.

When he was told the analysis of his psychometric results, he broke down and admitted that he was a deeply unhappy man. He confided that his wife had just told him she could not take any more. Because she still loved him, in spite of all the unhappiness he had caused her, she would not leave him. Instead she was threatening to commit suicide (her problems are not part of this case).

I encouraged Alastair to recount to his wife, for the first time, his interpretation of his mother's life and how he believed she had made a sacrifice of her life for him. He had never told her this in the 30 years they had known each other. In telling her the story, he realized that he had wrongly interpreted his mother's actions. His mother had truly loved him and would never have perceived her actions as a sacrifice. She did it because she wanted to. His mother had never reproached him. It was purely Alastair's interpretation of his mother's life that was erroneous. All his subsequent behaviour in life had been conditioned by that subconscious belief in his mother's sacrifice of her life for him.

Alastair had now begun to learn to relax and have more fun in his private life. He now apologises to his wife when he shouts at her and shouts a lot less than he used to. He is practising the idea of relaxation and taking life a little less seriously.

Choosing a university

'Paradigmatic thinking' is a vital ingredient of the leader's capacity to understand the world. It means the ability to form frameworks of understanding in order to assess the economic and social phenomena in the world. It is against backgrounds such as these paradigms that leaders form the strategic vision which is the nub of their drive of the organization into the future. That is what must be considered when you assess the likely effects of particular universities upon your child. How can that episode best be managed by parents, given that the choices are being made at a period when they usually have the least influence upon their children's choices?

It is recommended that you set your child's objectives on high levels of educational achievement at an early and impressionable age. For example, encourage the infant to admire the best places, with interesting visits to places such as Oxford, Boston, California and Paris. Make it an assumption that no form of university other than the very best in the world would be suitable or as much fun. We refer here to universities such as Harvard, in the USA, the Hautes Polytechniques in France, or Cambridge in England. Later, the child will understand how important the best brands are. The branded degrees they get at their first and second degree colleges will see them through the rest of their life.

The best universities your grown up child attends will teach them to think at the highest possible level in the most complex ways prevailing. They will learn the great theories, especially if they take popular subjects such as economics, business, philosophy, politics, the sciences or mathematics. These subjects are always framed in theoretical paradigms which are often set within their own beautiful logic. They will learn also that all subjects are framed within a context of relationship with all the other aspects of their particular world. There is great joy available in learning and understanding these matters. If you have done your job of bringing up your child properly, then he or she will now be ready to independently savour and enjoy the fun of gaining knowledge and understanding for its own sake.

Post-university experience

Strategic analysis is the final key in the list of subjects that can be learned through development rather than being natural traits. This subject, however, is one which is best obtained after university. That is why it is so important, when deciding upon a first job, to ensure the future employer offers high quality postgraduate training or education. By this time, of course, the child is forming independent opinions of his own and a parent's capacity to influence is probably quite small.

Strategic analysis is best learnt at work. That is why it is important to choose an organization for one's first employer which offers high quality management development training. Almost certainly this will include the basics of strategic analysis as well as the best development in our career. The same applies to financial and business analysis.

A final stage in a typical modern leadership career development should come a few years later. Once your child has gained a few years experience at work, it should consider taking an MBA, once again, at as high a brand university as it can gain entry. If everything else has been done properly, it will certainly manage to gain a place at Wharton, Harvard, MIT or the London Business School, all of which are well-known world leading brand schools which also offer the best in education, social life and networking opportunities.

What does it all amount to?

Throughout its childhood your child will have gained the sense that it is separate and special. That separation is based upon the sense of security founded in the knowledge that the child is loved. S/he will also take pride in the distinctions gained from achievements throughout its childhood. The child will know that it is special and that s/he thinks differently from others. Will your child be happy? Who can say? Is it likely to feel lonely sometimes during its life? Almost certainly, but who isn't? Is it likely to become a leader? Probably. Isn't that what you wanted?

In his book *The Organization Man*, Whyte summarized the problems that the development of the twentieth-century corporate leadership styles have brought. He writes:

> If America ever destroyed its genius it would be by intensifying the social virtues at the expense of others, by making the individual come to regard himself as a hostage to prevailing opinion, by creating, in sum, a tyranny of the majority ... [T]his is what the organization man is doing. He is doing it for what he feels are good reasons, but this only makes the tyranny more powerful, not less ... Ultimately any real change will be up to the individual

himself and this is why his education is so central to the problem. For he must look to his discontents with different eyes. It has been said that dominance of the group is the wave of the future and that ... he might as well accept it ... It is wretched, dispiriting advice to hold before him the dream that ideally there need be no conflict between him and society. There always is; there always must be. Ideology cannot wish it away.

(Whyte, 1956)

It is sad to end a chapter on such a cynical note. If you take my advice you may create a leader for our times. Isn't it a terrible sadness that the methods described above could be efficacious and necessary? We have to ask whether we might be helping to make them worse by creating more leadership models to join the game!

Summary

This chapter has outlined what parents have to do to provide an appropriate background for their child's development into a leader. The chapter outlined the need for paradigmatic thinking, clear belief systems and a sound education. The child needs a special love, founded on achievement and stretching for distinction constantly. The parents should be class conscious and firmly place the child psychologically in the middle classes. The mother should be allowed to dominate the child's upbringing and influence the child to constantly achieve to please her. Schooling should be traditional and at the highest standards that money can buy or otherwise obtain. It helps if the child could be given some emotional intelligence and insight into how to behave empathetically towards others. But it is not likely to stick, given the other parts of the upbringing the child is getting. Finally, the child should be encouraged from an early age to aim for the best branded universities. It is the brand that counts far more than the education. Post university, the child should be encouraged to go for an MBA – once again, only at one of the finest business schools. The author asserts again, this is not how he brings up his own child. But it is how leaders have usually been brought up!

7. A Leader Is Always Preparing the Finale

Prepare for the ultimate goals

It is important to get a sense of destiny early in a career. That helps a leader to behave in a manner which is always appropriate whatever positions they gain later. Good leaders usually seem to be 'mature for their age', at each point in their career. What is that maturity composed of? Maturity can be defined as 'a person seeing the larger-scale and longer-term consequences of their actions earlier and more clearly than their peer group'. Throughout their career great leaders always need to have a part of themselves that is helicoptered (see Chapter 10) above the action, observing it dispassionately from above. They reflect carefully and try never to behave in a way that could leave damage in their wake or act as a hostage to fortune later in their careers.

Does this mean that they are timid people, or excessively calculating? No. It means that all their key decisions are taken in the greater perspective of how they see their whole life evolving. They coordinate their overall need to use their brains, expend their energy, and give reign to their personalities. They see everything in the round. These people's capacity for leading balanced lives requires focus and deliberation and more care and reflection than most people manage to give to either their career or their personal life. Although high achievers are lucky to be endowed with more natural and developed potential than the average, it doesn't always feel like that to them. Sometimes it is perceived more as a curse. Why?

- Because they can never switch off their intelligence and understanding.
- Because their insight into others can be destructive of relationships.
- Because their leadership destiny sometimes forbids them developing certain friendships.
- Because, above all, their insight and intelligence can never be switched off.

Their gifts can be a lifelong pleasure and a curse!

There is one area I would single out as being of crucial importance. A leader's choice of partner is extremely sensitive. The wrong partner can not only damage a career but make the rewards of a successful career not worth having, because there is nobody to share the pleasures of material success with. I would assert that wise leaders are extremely prudent in choosing the right partner/spouse to share their success in life. How do they do this? I don't think they get involved with people they don't love. Rather, they are careful about who they allow themselves to fall in love with (see Chapter 13 for more on this).

By contrast, it is remarkable how many failed leaders we meet who seem to be allied with the wrong partner. When people with high quality life skills, intelligence and energy want to use their potential to the maximum, choosing a wrong partner can be a terrible curb upon their career as well as constraint upon their personal happiness. For any readers who know they have made a wrong choice, we have to assume that they are so good at leadership and life that their personal misery is not holding them back. They will have learned how to overcome the problem of managing their life while living with somebody who is causing them grief. Their long-term question ought to be 'How long will they have the spare energy that goes into coping with the emotional drain of an appalling personal life? Do they need to consider how long they are prepared to live with the price of their love?'

Mini case study

I worked with a client for some years who had a wife with a massive addiction to alcohol. He was incredibly tolerant of her behaviour. He never failed to bring her to corporate events whenever it was normal to do so. She never failed to get drunk at every event. Once drunk, she would sexually molest any male in sight. That went from insignificant subordinates up to the chairman of the company. In fact, this man's tolerance of his wife's problem endeared him to many of us. We considered that he was being both brave and kind to never react or disgrace her publicly. Eventually, however, we realized that his personal misery in their private life and the realization that she was a major deterrent in his career were becoming obvious to him. When he was made marketing director in Europe for a global company he met an interesting French heiress. That was his signal to end a very unhappy marriage which he had managed well in kindness to the spouse and without damaging his own career too badly.

Stay balanced!

Usually, good leaders run an emotionally balanced life with time for family and hobbies. They keep their body as well as their mind fit and don't become entrapped by an excessive love of luxury. This ensures they are rarely obliged to take career decisions for money rather than for intellectual excitement or the fun of the challenge. They have hobbies, not only because they enjoy them, but also because they need distraction from the grind of corporate and business life, which can only too frequently be arid and dull. The corporate world contains some of the world's greatest minds but also its worst philistines and bores. Leaders need to have interests outside of their businesses. It keeps alive the spirit of curiosity, the need for intellectual fuel and the balm of aesthetic beauty.

Leaders can too easily become single-minded in their pursuit of a career. They too easily forget that they need their career because it probably gives them a suitable outlet for their unique drive. Other workers often have less energy and range than a 'classical' leader. They may need to devote more time to their career or to their private life to make it work well.

Occasionally, we form the impression that somebody appears to have tremendous leadership potential, because they display a great capacity for intellectual and cultural pleasures and pursuits. However, they may choose not to pursue their potential in terms of leadership skills. They may place less emphasis on their career. They may be disinclined to become over-focused on it. However, such people probably have less genuine leadership ability than the average in spite of their possibly healthier and more rounded view of priorities in their personal lives. An analogy is all those people who assert 'I did my studies for a PhD and gathered all the data. I just didn't get around to writing it up. I could have got one'. My response is 'that is nonsense'. Only those with all the perseverance and guts to finish the job and present the written up thesis to the examining committee to win the award of the title PhD *know* they have what it takes. All the others are living in dreamland.

Successful leaders have happy and balanced private lives. They don't fool themselves that their business colleagues are their personal friends, nor that their business life is contiguous with their private life. They don't make the mistake of using the corporate hospitality tent as their preferred tool for private socializing. They know their private life is meant to be *private*. They respect their personal friends and their time with them and tend to keep their social and their business lives separate. It is frequently a disappointment for a leader when business associates cross the boundary to personal friendship. Why? Because the leader can never tell if they are acting as a friend and are really sincere. The incentive to 'act sincere' is much stronger in business relationships – it's based on money! A 'seemingly sincere business friend' may well turn out to be a shallow personal friend. There is less to motivate them to behave befittingly. Without the business interest in common, we often find there is nothing else to cement the friendship.

We always grieve the loss of personal friendships. However, one which I probably reflected on more than most is one business relationship which I allowed to blossom into a profound family friendship between the friend, his family and mine. It continued for 10 years and gave my family and myself considerable joy. Not long after this friend was made redundant from the corporation where I consulted (I could do nothing to protect him) he and his wife cut themselves off completely. I telephoned and called to ask what was wrong but never received a coherent explanation of what had changed in our personal relationship. I eventually heard nothing further from him or his wife and children. I felt terribly abused. I have always since wondered whether his friendship was based upon using me as a conduit to the top of his organization rather than truly shared interests and mutual enjoyment of each other's company?

We usually find that competent leaders have enough social skills to find as many private friends as they need to maintain their social life. The life of most successful leaders could be most easily summarized as 'a life in equilibrium'. This is not intended to paint a false picture that great leaders lead idyllic lives with no clouds on the horizon and have no family troubles; neither do they all have perfect marriages and have all their children grow up in harmony. Leaders, being human, are subject to the normal travails and problems of life. No one can avoid the travails that all humans are vulnerable to. What matters is how people handle their troubles. That's what makes the difference. Leaders get divorced because their marriages break up, like anybody else. Leaders have children who get into trouble with drugs and other adolescent problems, as so many others do. Some leaders' sexual preferences are not in harmony with common practice. They learn to cope, as does everybody with similar dispositions. They manage their lives. They deal with the problems. Hopefully, they survive and triumph, as do most other people, when confronted with the real world of normal struggles.

Leaders manage all the processes of their career

Most leaders that I have worked with, at first made statements like 'I did not expect to become a top leader. Promotions just kept coming.' When we examine their career patterns they often look as if it was obvious they were going right to the top. Various authors and academics have pondered this quandary. What is it that drives so many leaders so hard, even though they cannot even see it themselves?

I refer elsewhere to McClelland's (1961) work on the *need to achieve* which drives so many people at work. Elliott Jaques (1976, 1982a, 1982b) is another eminent academic who has developed theories and tools of analysis about human beings' capacity for leadership at work. These theories help to explain some of the phenomena being observed.

Jaques developed a theory of *time spans of discretion* which describes how different employees cope with their job responsibilities, for varying lengths of time, before needing supervision from a supervisor or manager. Jaques developed these concepts into a theory of individuals personal development in terms of the maturation of their capacity to see forwards in the future when taking decisions (Jaques, 1976: pp.165–6). In my own research, I rename Jaques' 'individuals' personal developmental stages in maturation of capacity' as *time horizons*.

Jaques developed tools of measurement whereby (he asserted) he could predict the length of time horizon a person would evolve to (i.e. how far forward they would be able to see when taking decisions). He could also predict how rapidly their time horizon capacity would develop over the course of their career. His theory implies that leaders have different time horizons spanning different periods of time. The longer the time horizon of the leader, the larger the organization they could successfully lead. An individual's capacity for decision making is called their time-horizon stratum. Jaques '[came] to the conclusion that the array of time-span progression curves expresses a fundamental regularity in the patterns of growth of compctcncc in adults, as measured by the time frame – the maximum time-span of intention which the individual can muster in working activities, that is to say, goal-directed activities' (Jaques 1982a: p. 151).

These strata can be defined in terms of the following periods of time (over which the person was capable of taking decisions on behalf of the organization) (Table 7.1):

Table 7.1 Time horizon strata stages and lengths	
Stratum	*Months/Years*
1	0–3 months
2	3–12 months
3	> 1 year and < 2 years
4	> 2 years and < 5 years
5	> 5 years and < 10 years
6	> 10 years and < 20 years
7	> 20 years and < 50 years

A person can reach his or her stratum peak, or maximum work and skill capacity, at any age. Plainly, most reach it in their more mature years. One obvious danger with Jaques' theory is the general belief that it is better to have a long stratum, because people think it makes them appear more clever. Thus people are tempted to exaggerate any evidence which helps place them in a longer stratum. It is also worth noting the well-nigh impossibility of testing the accuracy of the longer term time horizon predictions because most social and business 'scientists' just don't live long enough to run the experiments!

Elliott Jaques (with whom I worked while researching data for my PhD) always advised me to sort out false claims by asking people what concrete steps they have taken to implement the objectives of their longest time horizon. I used this test on the leader of the shipping subsidiary of a major oil corporation (Figure 3). He had tried to impress me with the length of his time horizon by describing the unknown and unnamed minerals, which his shipping business was going to explore for. It would extract these hitherto undiscovered minerals at previously unfathomed depths of sea, for use in, as yet, undeveloped industries. When I asked him what he or the business had actually done to further this incredible vision, the answer was 'nothing so far'. Ultimately, his time horizon was closer to a *stratum 3* (1–2 years) than the *stratum 6* (10–20) years he was claiming.

People destined to have leadership careers probably understand intuitively many of the theories being described here. Such people manage themselves and their career carefully. They know when they should be advancing towards their ultimate destination and when they should be biding their time, learning fresh skills and waiting for the next spurt in their leadership development.

Time horizons' importance in decision making

Few academics have addressed the subject of time, surprisingly, given its importance in everything people and businesses do. However, there are a few besides Elliott Jaques, described above. Paul Lawrence and Jay Lorsch (1967) wrote their book, *Managing Integration and Differentiation*, explaining the phenomenon when people in organizations take mutually contradictory decisions, even though both parties to the decisions are taking them in the best interests of the business, as they see it.

For example, when a marketing manager wants to maximize revenue, s/he will recommend the largest possible range of products, colours and sizes to offer to appeal to the maximum number of customers. The production manager in the same business wants to make the smallest possible range of products in the fewest conceivable number of sizes and colours, in order to minimize production costs. Both consider their

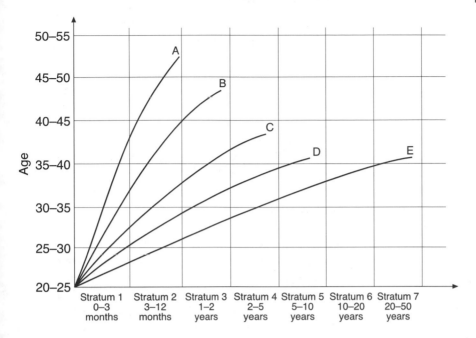

Figure 3 Elliott Jaques' theory of time horizons and personal development over time. The theory would predict that each of these leaders would demonstrate competence throughout their career, at the level predicted by their time horizon potential development line. Obviously A will take longer to achieve a lower level of competence, at a later stage in their career. Person E would be, by any standards, an astonishingly bright, high flier, who would demonstrate outstanding leadership skills, from a young age, throughout a glittering and youthful leadership career.

A represents a person who will reach a maximum time horizon leadership skill of stratum 2 between the age of 50 to 55.

B represents a person who will reach a maximum time horizon leadership skill of stratum 3 between the age of 54 to 50.

C represents a person who will reach a maximum time horizon leadership skill of stratum 4 between the age of 45 to 50.

D represents a person who will reach a maximum time horizon leadership skill of stratum 5 between the age of 40 to 45.

E represents a person who will reach a maximum time horizon leadership skill of stratum 7 between the age of 40 to 45.

preference to be in the best interests of the organization. Both believe their advice concurs with the guidelines for their role in the business. However, as a consequence of each of these people doing their job correctly, as they see it, the organization's leader is receiving *differentiated* advice which puts him or her in an invidious position. Differentiation refers to the process whereby the two managers of different functions in an organization respectively arrive at a differentiated (or contradictory) decision. *Integration* is the process whereby the leader then has to *integrate the differentiated* advice to arrive at an *integrated* decision in the best, overall interests of the firm.

Lawrence and Lorsch made the interesting discovery about time horizons that managers in different functions tend to think in different time horizons. This partially explains what causes these managers to arrive at differentiated decisions on behalf of the business. For example, consider a research scientist and a sales manager. The former thinks in terms of time horizons of many years before hoping to see the fruits of their research. In comparison, the sales manager probably thinks forward over a time horizon of a few months when considering his or her decision options for the organization.

Research I undertook at the London Business School, built upon the foundation work described above, of both Elliott Jaques and Lawrence and Lorsch. I wanted to explore the relationship between the decisions taken by leaders and the lengths of forward time horizon over which those decisions were meant to affect their businesses. I found that the best leaders listen to the long and short time horizon advice of their functional managers and then take decisions that integrate the contradictions into a coherent policy which maximizes opportunities to achieve organizational objectives. I also researched how long were the time horizons of managers at different and lower levels of the hierarchy of the business. Did they see their part in the decision in shorter time horizons, the lower down the ladder they were? I found that they were better aligned in the best performing organizations and poorly aligned in under performing organizations.

I found that where the time horizons of the hierarchy of managers and leaders of a business were in alignment, the profitability of the business was maximized. In other words, if the time horizons are aligned, with the longest at the top and the shortest at the bottom, that organization was likely to be more profitable than one where the time horizons were not so well aligned.

To summarize, my key findings were:

- Time-horizon-aligned organizations are more profitable than non-time horizon-aligned businesses.
- There is a strong correlation between the level in the hierarchy a person occupies and the length of their time horizon. Leaders nearly always have longer time horizons than the mass of people lower down the hierarchy.
- When functional managers are asked to think in integrated organizational terms, rather than in terms of their functional roles, they usually overcome the differentiation problem. The differences in their time horizons are levelled out. Therefore, organizational policy should be to ensure that people learn to think in organization-wide terms rather than merely departmental, functional terms.

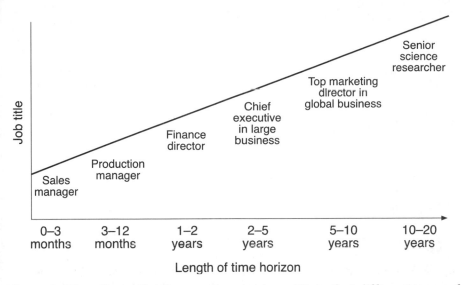

Figure 4 The effects of role upon time horizons. Note that different types of job have a particular time horizon associated with the role. This is caused by the nature of the work or function and how far forward in time they have to think to carry out their function properly.

All the above research findings have profound implications for every developing leader:

- Leaders should try to remain continuously aware of their personal current and evolving time horizon.
- As leaders develop in their managerial roles, they should always stretch their imagination to replicate the time horizon of their boss and see their decisions in terms of their boss' time-horizon context, rather than their own.
- On occasions, when an executive realizes they are seeing further forwards in their thinking than their leader, they should understand this will make them appear to be threatening in the eyes of their boss. They will need to exercise extreme caution. It should also indicate to them that they are probably ready to do their leader's job.
- When they realize they are seeing further on behalf of the organization than anybody else within it, they should be its leader (see Figures 4–6).

Reflect on your personal time horizon. How far does that indicate your potential growth? How far forward, in time, do you go, in your own mind, when thinking about the future of your business? Do you have a vision of what the business or industry will look like in 5 years' time? Or are you more comfortable thinking about the 1–2 year period? How fast is the length of your time horizon growing? What was it 2 years

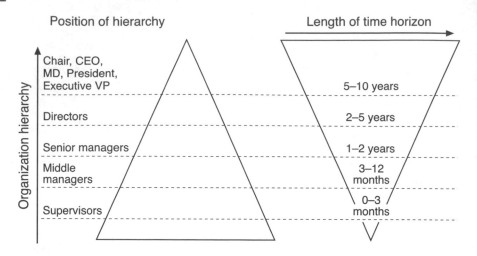

Figure 5 Time horizons and their associated job titles. Note: The higher up the organization, the longer the time horizon. Different jobs have their own time horizon associated with the job. The most effective businesses have leaders with the longest time horizons and their subordinates having ever decreasing time horizons at each succeeding lower level in the hierarchy.

ago? How does that compare to now? How far forward do you think you will be able to cast your mind when you reach the height of your leadership powers? To get a more accurate assessment of your personal current and potential time horizon, complete Questionnaire 7.1.

With the results from this questionnaire you now have an indication of your current time horizon. It cannot be entirely accurate because some of the variables in the questions are partially an accident of current events in your business and industry. However, if you have the right leadership potential, you will always find yourself working towards where you are most comfortable in the types and degrees of importance of the decisions you have to take. As you reflect on your result, consider also how old you are and how rapidly you have been developing over the past 5 years of your career. What is the frequency of promotion in calendar months or years? How many more years are you likely to work? This will indicate to you whether you are likely to move up further strata and what level in the organization you are likely to achieve.

Of course, different industries do not use the same job titles. Further, some of the titles in the table may not be relevant to the reader's industry. One should take into account that the leader in a business with revenue of £300 million and 1,000 employees almost certainly requires a much shorter time horizon than someone leading an organization with a revenue of £10 billion and 100,000 staff. Yet both may carry the same title 'managing director'. Management science has not yet developed classification definitions which equate different businesses and

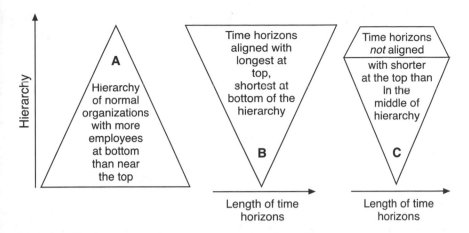

Figure 6 Time horizon aligned organizations are more profitable than non-time horizon aligned businesses. **A** represents a classical hierarchy with most employees at the bottom of the organization, narrowing to far less management employees at the middle of the business and, then, just a few leaders at the top. **B** represents a classical time horizon alignment of a well-aligned business. This would, typically, assume that most of the workers, at the production end of the organization, need a very short time horizon to do their job. For example, a production worker needs only to plan his or her work over a day or two. Their supervisor will be planning a production shedule over the oncoming month or two. The supervisor's manager will be planning a complete production cycle over a year or two. The Director of Production, in charge of the production manager, may be planning a complete cycle of long-run production, renewing machinery and plant, looking for new countries to produce more economically, and researching new technologies to achieve competitive edge. Finally, the CEO will be thinking in terms of the longest time horizon of, say, 5–10 years, about the survival and success of the business in the long run. **C** represents a business where the leadership team (probably the Executive Board of Directors) is thinking in shorter terms than their senior executives. This will lead to frustration in the lower levels, loss of good personnel, fear and excessive politics by the leaders who will only know the level just below them, which understands the business better than them, and, eventually, lower profits and a less efficient organization.

industries with any precision. People pay attention to job titles because they and many others care unduly about such matters. I have known people leave their organization, when offered promotion, because the larger and more interesting task on offer did not carry the title 'Director', they felt they would be losing an important variable in their career development.

Managing a leadership career over a long period is complex and difficult. There will be mishaps and periods of faster and slower growth. The right choice of the type of industry or business you work in will make a considerable difference to your chances of success.

Questionnaire 7.1 The time horizon questionnaire

Think about each question carefully. Try to answer honestly and accurately. Having considered each statement, tick the box which accurately describes the time period in each case.

	Up to 3 months	Up to 12 months	Up to 24 months	Up to 60 months	Up to 120 months
I can accurately and confidently predict the future of the *industry* I work in over the next					
I can accurately and confidently predict the future of the *business* I work in over the next					
I can accurately and confidently predict the future of the *division of the business* I work in over the next					
The most important decision I have taken in the past year will have an effect upon the organization over a period of					
My best subordinate will effect their part in my decision over the following time period					
My boss understands my decision will affect the organization over the following time period					
I like my boss to review my work every					
I feel comfortable when I review the work of my best subordinate every					
My best subordinate's most important decisions affect the organization over a period of					

My boss' most important decisions affect the organization over a period of					
Add the ticks in each column					
Multiply each tick by the number and divide by 10	*3*	*12*	*24*	*60*	*120*
Find the time horizon stratum which is closest to your average	TH1	TH2	TH3	TH4	TH5

It is not just a choice of type of industry which is important. Businesses have different needs at different stages in their growth. This too must be taken into account as the leader tries to fit his or her career to his or her ability as well as to an organization's needs to create a pattern of leadership career success.

Business growth patterns and leadership styles

Every stage described above needs a special form of leadership. It is up to the leaders to decide what form is best suited to their skill range and aptitudes (Figure 7).

What types of company should you work for?

It is to be hoped that most industries contain some good leaders. They tend to distribute themselves randomly. The criteria of choice at the beginning of a career should always be what interests you. It is vital to choose industries which attract you and arouse your curiosity. During the early part of your career you should be deeply involved in the nitty-gritty detail of the business. When you are that close to the rock face truly enjoying the subject matter of the business for its own sake will keep your energy and innate interest going.

If your preference is to retain latitude, try to choose an industry which is at a relatively early point in its development cycle, or about to undergo a long-term renewal of impetus in its development. If you have choices, select businesses which are considered to be either the best performers in their industry, or organizations with a leading

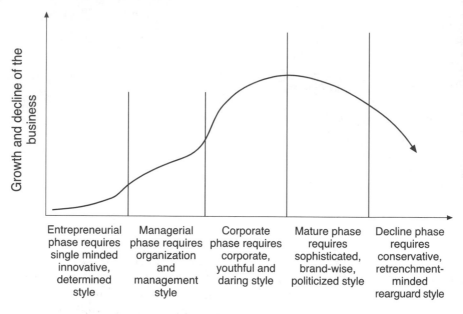

Figure 7 Business growth patterns and leadership styles.

market share, or some technological innovation which ensures their competitive edge. If appropriate, try to belong to international firms, they have the most potential in the twenty-first century. Also, most modern leadership careers will involve some spell of duty abroad. A litmus test should be to ask yourself whether you are excited about the products of your business and industry and about working for it (but without losing your dispassion).

The type of business, and its stage of evolution, will become less important as your career advances. The challenges later in your career will be about achieving strategic vision and ensuring that you make a success of leading whatever workforce you have at your disposal. You will learn to choose your leadership style according to the culture of the business and the state of the organization and its industry. Your choices will be made from a wide and varied repertoire because great leaders are not constrained by the smaller range of choices that lesser managers, without the same level of power and self-control, have to choose from.

Type of industry

As each generation of future leaders and managers starts its career, (a continuous process, by definition), people have to ask themselves 'what industry or business will enable me to maximize the enjoyment of my working life and optimize the return on my talents'. In earlier days it was probably easier, because technology and industrial cycles evolved more slowly. Someone entering the nineteenth century rail industry could be reasonably confident that they would have a lifetime's career within the industry and probably the same organization. That may have applied to the airline travel industry in the twentieth century. But who can predict how long some of the industrial sectors of the twenty-first century will endure? Patterns of employment have changed. Employees are less willing to spend many years at low levels of salary before the organization promotes and pays them what they are really worth. Similarly, organizations are no longer willing to keep employees at work when demand for the goods they are making decreases or dies. Degrees of loyalty from both employee and employer have diminished substantially. It is unlikely that they will return.

That has important implications. The first is that people starting careers at the beginning of the new millennium should be prepared to change their career path, industry sector and functional skills several times during their career. Second, those who desire stability should be looking to the great staple industries like retail grocery (people always have to eat) or the emerging industries which will dominate the twenty-first century, if they wish to maximize the stability of their career. The great industries of the twenty-first century will almost certainly be among the telecommunication, cable and fibre, satellite, broadcasting and data transmission worlds. The staple industries will be all those relating to food manufacture, distribution and retailing, transportation of goods and people and basic tourism and leisure.

The reasons for trying to find a stable path for a career are still valid. If you choose an industry which really interests you and you can sustain it, it is more fun than being forced to turn to your second or third choice. Later in your career you may be forced to change jobs. A stable career in one industry leads to continuously increasing industrial knowledge and thus enhances even further your personal value. Consequently, this will give you a greater return on the economic 'rent' of your body of knowledge. As more people learn about your existence and the level of erudition you have, they will be prepared to pay premiums for your accumulation of experience. Finally, it is advisable to stay with new industries because, by and large, they will be where the higher profits will be made over the longest period.

Condition of business

Try to choose relatively healthy businesses in the early stages of your career. It is a thoroughly miserable experience being made redundant during the early part of your development. It can also cause a major loss of self-confidence. Healthy businesses are unlikely to be living off past glories. Choose businesses which have excellent development programmes for young employees, especially management trainees (if that is your preferred entry point). The business should be one of the top three market controllers in its industry, because they are usually the only earners of reasonable levels of profit in any industry. The business should have a reputation for being sensibly staffed and free of any notoriety for being ruthless about discarding people. This should indicate a decent humanitarian approach to people. Many leaders do not shine in their first few years at work and can ill afford an unwarranted dismissal early in their career which will show as a black mark on their résumé. You need an organization with a reputation for dealing fairly with people.

Potential great leaders are treated better and with more understanding in better quality businesses than in second-rate, 'hire and fire' organizations where the management may not be capable of recognizing potential. In mediocre organizations leaders get dismissed for being wayward, a common enough fault in younger high potential individuals. There will also be more opportunities in larger, more successful companies to be discovered and mentored by a senior manager who will recognize your potential. In more benign organizations you are less likely to attract jealousy from lesser managers who might try to forestall your career in the early stages when we meet many excessively 'political' people who may just do damage for damage's sake! Quality organizations get rid of such individuals, if they get in at all. Finally, almost all the Peter Principle people (those who have been promoted to a job at their level of incompetence) will be clustered in the lower levels of management.

If it is your preference to move around in your career, from one business to another, there are different considerations to take into account at each stage. The type of organization you join should depend on the particular stage of your career you have reached. At each change point of your career you should be asking yourself four key questions. They are:

(1) What particular skills you are developing?
(2) Are you undergoing trauma without being aware?
(3) What is your instinctive feel for your colleagues'/subordinates' work skills?
(4) What kind of people and skills are not represented in your team, thus leading you to ask what types you need to recruit around you?

How do leaders avoid career accidents?

Leaders need all the circumspection they can engender. At any time in their career, whatever they do, they owe a duty to themselves and others to try to foresee how others will perceive and react to their actions. Poor leaders are constantly being surprised at their staff's reactions to and interpretations of their behaviours or actions. For example, I remember one leader who gained a reputation for sexual abuse of the secretaries at his head office. He was tackled on this subject, at the request of the non-executive directors of the company, who were worried about (1) his possible lack of concentration on the company's performance and (2) the possibility of the company attracting adverse publicity if his behaviour got into the media. When asked about it he explained that, in fact, he had been separated from his wife for over 2 years. He had been living with one of the company's senior managers, who was employed separately in one of the corporation's regional offices. It was a permanent relationship and he had not indulged in any improper conduct.

It was explained to him that, as a senior leader at MD level, it wasn't just his actual conduct which counted, but how it was seen by his employees. Since some employees always indulge in speculation and are always ready to circulate rumours, it is vital that leaders behave with circumspection and never fuel the rumour mill. It is too easily forgotten that a leader is always the centre of attention in an organization. Whatever they do will be carefully scrutinized. This is just the 'goldfish bowl' in which leaders live their lives. It can be heavily onerous. However, compared to the fun and rewards of leadership, a little circumspection gets it all into perspective. It is just part of the job description of being a leader.

Dealing with setbacks

Everybody suffers setbacks in their career, sometimes as a consequence of the actions of other people; at other times from our own lack of ability. Occasionally, it's just the nature of events going against you for a while. Always be ready to return to the drawing board. You may need fresh strategic insight or to test anew the latest economic and social circumstances of your decision making. One of the cleverest men I ever knew became a leading professor at Oxford. He always retained the habit of attending undergraduate student lectures whenever a new topic or research area emerged that he felt he ought to understand. Sitting at the back of the lecture hall, with the rest of the students, did him a lot of good, as he ingested fresh knowledge. It also had an amazing effect upon his staff and other lecturers. If the great man himself could return to the drawing board to learn new things, they were all put on call to have their knowledge base honed to the leading edge. They were also motivated to keep their humility carefully wrapped around their tendency to self-importance.

Stephen Covey (1976), in *The 7 Habits of Highly Effective People*, suggests that everybody should 'begin with the end in mind [because it] means to start with a clear understanding of your destination' (p. 98). This would help any leader in the vital need to avoid accidents. Never take on the bigger jobs in your career until you are ready. Early exposure to jobs and responsibilities you are not prepared for, and cannot yet master, always carry the danger of breaking a leader's spirit and moral fibre. With that gone, you will be utterly lost.

You must understand that leadership skills are generalizable and can be applied to many industries. The older and wiser you get, the more generally applicable they become. This means that if you intend to construct a career by hopping about among multiple jobs in various businesses, you will need the courage and application to learn the key to several different industries. It should be great fun. It may prove (to you, no less than others) that your leadership skills are a multi-purpose set of tools that can be applied to many situations and industrial sectors. It may also offer a more stimulating career.

Some personal likes

There are several guidelines which I have learned from business leaders. They are personal preferences which I was particularly looking for and seeking. This is thus a standard customer warning to discard any views of mine stated in the next two paragraphs that you disagree with. Most of the wise people I know who work in leadership roles, rarely, if ever, overindulge in alcohol. They never take drugs. They also never lose their temper although if they need to *appear* angry, they know how to do so under carefully controlled circumstances. When they appear to lose their temper (it is usually only on rare occasions) it is done to influence the behaviour they want from their people, or to emphasize the importance of some action by them or their subordinates. Genuine temper is never a useful tool, because it is hard to predict any individual's personal response to anger. Any learning a person may take away from any temper you display is totally unpredictable.

Another dictum I have learned is that wise leaders don't join companies where the installed leader looks like a nominal leader (as defined above). Those kind of leaders only wish to exploit your skills for their own glorification. They will give you neither credit nor job satisfaction. Similarly, do not work for insecure bosses – they are the most dangerous beings on earth. The better a leader you are, the more they will fear you. Their fear will make them behave irrationally, jealously and nastily. Only really bright people cope well with their rivals' and subordinates' easy and natural brilliance. If you cannot see some sure-fire way of removing a nominal (and inferior) leader, when s/he offers you a job, don't take it!

Summary

This chapter has set out the steps that a leader must take to create a leadership career. It recommends that a leader have a balanced life, counterbalancing business and private social activities, as well as calculating what s/he should be aiming for as a career peak. Every leader has an optimum time horizon to which s/he will develop as their leadership career opportunities evolve. The chapter recommends that leaders measure their potential by the accurate assessment of their time horizon or their ability to see forward in the future. It also advises potential leaders to be careful in the early part of their career when choosing what kind of business to work in as well as which industry to enter. Choose the best business in the larger growth industries. This chapter has tried to demonstrate that leadership is a genuine career choice, available to those who have 'the nature and nurture' for leadership. I advise prospective leaders to manage their careers from the beginning, by carefully nurturing their skills, developing a high quality personal life and living always by carefully considered ethically based values.

8. *A Leader Is Not a Manager*

Why differentiate?

It is surprising to see how many management's books still refer to the three separate skill sets of leadership, general management and entrepreneurship as if they were one and the same thing. Many text books move between each of these concepts as if they were all interchangeable. For example, Jones *et al.* (1998) in *Contemporary Management* state that 'A manager's *personal leadership style* (their italics) ... shapes the way in which a manager approaches planning, organizing, and controlling (the other principals tasks of managing)' (p. 404). For them power is the key component of effective leadership.

It has become my practice to retain a clear demarcation between the three concepts, leadership, management and entrepreneurship. Books which refer to leaders as just general managers with more power and a bigger position at the top are misguided. Other texts on management which elide between self-evident entrepreneurs and corporate general managers are failing to use a key differentiating tool of organizational analysis. Entrepreneurs are people who start their own business and maintain the leading position in it. We should not assume that such people have the same qualities as others who have risen up the corporate ladder. Table 8.1 lays out the key features of the three business operations control areas which differentiate between the three different types in terms of attributes, qualities and skills.

As Kotter (1999) puts it in his latest, popular work on *What Leaders Really Do*, 'Once companies understand the fundamental difference between leadership and management, they can begin to groom their top people to provide both' (p. 52). He goes on to say 'Good management brings a degree of order and consistency to key dimensions like the quality and profitability of products. Leadership, by contrast, is about coping with change' (p. 53).

Table 8.1 Differences between leaders, entrepreneurs and managers		
Leaders	_Entrepreneurs_	_Managers_
Visionary	Self starter	Plebeian
Strategic	Obsessive	Tactical
Inspirational	Drag people along	Motivator
Good communicator	Poor communicator	Messenger
Good with people	Interpersonally inept	Enabler
Corporate	Ideas manic	Sensitive
Organizational	Anarchic	Political

Entrepreneurs

Entrepreneurs are, almost by definition, self-starters. However, the literature on entrepreneurs has often alluded to the possibility that entrepreneurs are really people who lack the social skills which permit self-preservation within larger corporate entities. In other words, people are often forced to become entrepreneurs in their own businesses because they cannot survive in anybody else's.

Successful entrepreneurs require a degree of obsessive energy. Contrary to popular belief, the entrepreneur needs just one or a few ideas that obsess him or her to an extent which does not allow them to rest. They have to strive every minute, day, week and year until they can extensively and obsessively achieve the reification of their idea.

It is an illusion to believe that most entrepreneurs have ideas flowing out of them all the time. In fact the kind of person who has that type of creative and restless style of mind is usually unsuited to be an entrepreneur running their own business. The essence of entrepreneurship is having a few ideas which they obsessively pursue until they fulfil their dream. If they are diverted too frequently along the road by other ideas which interest them equally they would never actually make any one business successful.

Entrepreneurs need the skills and personality to be able to drag people along with them. They have to be able to persuade people to join them in the dream and work as obsessively as they do until it is fulfilled. Surprisingly, one finds that they are often poor communicators. This is partially a function of their lack of social skills but also a consequence of their lack of balance and equilibrium that makes them obsess about their ideas to start with. It may well be for this reason that they find it so difficult to persuade bankers to grant them the money to capitalize their businesses.

Their lack of communication skills, along with their often poor level of interpersonal ability makes them difficult to get along with. As we say above, they are frequently not over imbued with ideas. This means that they often lack the imagination which would give them the personal skills to cope more successfully in a normal business.

However, although they don't have many ideas, they are manic about those they do have. This means that when they do enact their one or two ideas for a successful business, it is a psychologically 'manic' quality they bring to their business. This is most useful to them when they have to work long hours for many years, often for very poor returns on the investment of their labour. Eventually, the crazy drive that makes them work so hard for so long pays off and, sometimes, they become economically wealthy. People who do not have the same drives might feel that they have sacrificed too much. Obviously, a classical entrepreneur would not agree.

Finally entrepreneurs often have an anarchic quality about them which means that they can build relatively large businesses without needing the typical structures that more corporate organizations naturally use, such as divisions into functions, products, geography or a conventional hierarchy. These classical forms are naturally understood and formulated by normal organizational members. That is why, when the time comes to float an entrepreneur's business on the Stock Exchange or to bring in more conventional management, the new corporate managers are often shocked and dismayed at the state of apparent chaos that they encounter. For the entrepreneur this anarchy has never been a problem because their obsession with their ideas cuts through the barriers and chaos of the business that they manage. Their energy enables them to overcome the substantial barriers that the anarchic framework imposes. For the classical manager it can be a nightmare.

Managers

David Holt (1987), in his text on *Management, Principles and Practices*, defines management as 'getting things done through others ... It includes the processes of *planning, organizing, leading* and *controlling*' (his italics, p. 10). As one can see from my list above, I largely agree with his definition. My experience of senior and middle management is that they are often plebeian in their approach to the problem of implementing the strategic vision of their leaders.

Their basic approach is tactical. They deal with the minutiae of carrying out the larger ideas of their strategic leaders. Tactics mean that they have to break down a large-scale strategic concept into small enough pieces for their subordinates to understand and achieve within a given time, cost and profit constraint. In time horizon terms, senior managers take the longest time horizon strategy of their leader and break that down into shorter time frames for their managers to understand and enact.

Possibly the most important skill that managers bring to their job is the ability to motivate their subordinates. We can never underestimate how difficult and creative the art of motivation is. Not only must a manager understand him or herself profoundly enough to be able to master moods and eliminate their own psychological obstacles, but they must also profoundly understand the people who work for them in order to know what will inspire them to want to achieve the objectives they set and know which methods would best motivate them and which frighten their subordinates the least.

In essence, the manager is a messenger. He carries the message of the strategic story from the leader of the organization, down the hierarchy into the operations which must enact the facts which will make the strategic vision into a reality. But it is not a simple messenger job. They are really translators of the vision and deconstructionists of the message. If they fail to understand the strategic vision (which requires a conceptual capacity in the manager), they will pass the wrong message into the organization. If they enhance or change it for personal egotistical reasons, they could destroy or damage the strategic vision and cause their leaders failure. If they do their work too simply they will fail to be noticed and their skills will be taken for granted. It is not an easy thing to be a good, straightforward and clear messenger for a great leader.

A manager is an enabler. He knows how to make things happen. Whether he or she is led by a corporate leader or an entrepreneur, it is the manager's ability to translate and understand how to operationalize a strategy that enables the strategy to be implemented and enacted. We often find that leaders lose this skill once they have been in the leadership role for any length of time. Leaders become totally dependent upon their managers to make things happen.

A manager has to be sensitive. This sensitivity must incorporate the ability to sense the temperature and mood of the organization that s/he is operating. He or she must feel when people are unhappy. They must sense when factories cannot bear the pressure that is being put upon them. They must sense when a particular national system cannot respond to a special set of demands for a period of time. They have to sense how the organization needs to receive messages from the top and what form they will be willing to receive them in. The senses of the manager must be exquisitely and carefully honed on behalf of the organization, his or her bosses and his or her subordinates. It is a special sensitivity.

Finally, a manager must have political skills. They must know how to pour oil on troubled waters. They must know how to tell the leader when their ideas are impossible to operationalize or that the organization lacks the core competencies to carry out the strategic concept. A manager also needs political skills to balance the rivalry, aggression and competitiveness of their subordinates. They must know how to mediate with new lines, products and different functional groups. In a typical modern multinational corporation they must also know how to manage in different countries, with different cultures, in multiple languages, with different codes of law and different business practices.

I hope, therefore, that readers understand when I use the word *plebeian* about managers. It is by no means intended to be diminutive. The plebeian qualities of a high-level senior manager are profound and valuable. The plebeian quality that they have is the capacity to transform the complex and difficult into the simple and doable.

What about the leaders?

What is it that differentiates the leaders' skills and qualities from those that we have described above of entrepreneurs and managers? As John Kotter put it, management is about order and consistency whereas leadership is change. The prime differentiatior is the *vision* of the leader. Leaders have to be visionary whether in a large, medium or small business. This is not the 'vision' of dreamers or religious fanatics. The vision of a leader is practical and worldly and carefully tuned to the capacity of the organization s/he is leading. It is also honed to fit the potential offered by the external world within which they are steering the ship of their organization.

The vision of the leader of a large organization is the simple message of what the organization can be if it operates and succeeds for a long enough period to achieve the maximum that its latent capacity commands. It is a vision that stretches people to work their hardest and to feel pride and achievement when they finally enact the dream of their leader.

A leader must be continuously strategic in contrast to the tactical qualities and skills of his or her manager. What is the difference? To be strategic is to always see the big picture of the industry and the wider world in which the organization operates. It is to understand profoundly how the strengths and weaknesses of the organization can be stretched and manipulated to achieve greater economic opportunities. It is the ability to change an organization so that the worst part of its culture and the restraints on its potential are broken down faster and more efficaciously than any competitor. To be strategic is to always see the big picture of what the organization can be at its very best.

If the leader can achieve a strategic vision of the best that the organization can be s/he must also have a special capacity to inspire senior managers with the dream and desire, the belief and bravado, the challenge and courage to want to operationalize the strategic vision. The ability to inspire the people is the equivalent of the motivational power of the manager. But it is different. Motivating your people as a manager is giving them the skills, mentally, to know how to carry out their tasks practically. The inspirational skills of the leader do not have to be practical. They are not meant to be motivational. Senior managers should not need motivating. If they are at the top of the organization it is because they are ambitious enough to carry out whatever is reasonably required of them. But they still need to be inspired with belief in the strategic vision. They have to believe in it like a religion or a personal ego need. That requires the leader to inspire them.

Being inspirational is not enough for a leader. S/he must also know how to communicate simply and without undue complexity both the long-term objectives that need to be achieved and also the simpler day-to-day, week-to-week reminders of the journey they are embarked upon, the road they will use and the rainbow which ends it.

Leaders must be good with people. This does not mean that they have to be cheerleaders, full of personality or charisma. They may be shy or reticent. They don't have to be hail, hearty and jolly. It is a misconceived idea that they are all extroverts and great wits. What they simply have to be is *good with people*. That means understanding how people hear when they are spoken to; it means knowing how the individual starts to believe in the strategic story; it means trying to make people like being with the leader even if the leader lacks one or two interpersonal skills; it means that people look forward to having time with them and never wish to avoid them; it means that they enjoy people and look forward to being with them; and that they are comfortable when they are with them.

Leaders need to understand how to be corporate. That means knowing how the organization works. They need to understand the mechanics of how one part meshes into another and how messages are disseminated throughout the organization, through both its formal and its informal networks. They need to understand the history and culture of the organization. They must know the mechanics of corporate life. What is the power of the shareholders? What are the rules of the institutions and the Stock Exchange? What can and can't the banks actually do to them if trends turn down? What do the non-executive directors believe is happening and what will they tolerate? How do the various committee systems of the Corporation work and what is the power of each? What are the special rules of this particular Corporation? Where do we have to be careful and about what exactly? Do we have to ask permission from the shareholders in order to move into any new sectors? These are all aspects of why a leader has to be *corporate*.

Finally, a corporate leader has to be organizational. S/he must know *how* to achieve within an organization. They have to enjoy being part of a business system and understand how the systems' mechanics work. They should enjoy being an organizational mechanic and not get easily frustrated when the mechanics of the system slow down the implementation of their exciting strategic ideas. They must have the patience to accept and the wisdom to steer through the depths of the organization, accepting its pace, its mood, its culture and its style. If they are sufficiently skilled in organizational behaviour they will know how to achieve their ambitions through the organization.

The transition from manager to leader

John Harvey-Jones (1988) said in *Making it Happen* 'For the first time in your business life, there are no limitations of any sort on how you can spend your time, or to what you should address your attention'. Until that moment, in every leader's career, there is always somebody who is responsible for some part of their overall responsibility. It may be that the finance director is covering the accounting side or the operations director is checking that your marketing decisions can be manufactured. When you are boss you decide all the priorities, how you will spend every hour of each day.

Some leaders take a considerable time to make the transition from manager to leader. I have described above the different qualities of each role for both manager and leader. The ones which most leaders find hardest to transition from are from messenger to communicator; from motivator to inspirer; and from tactician to being a strategist. But the hardest of all is to go from being an implementer of other people's strategic ideas into being a visionary on behalf of the whole organization, all its resources and the whole of its future.

John Heider (1993: p. 29), in *The Tao of Leadership*, says 'The leaders teachers ... could clarify events for others, because they had done it for themselves. They could speak to the depths of another person, because they had known their own deeper conflicts and blocks'. This is when a leader has to leave his 'teachers' and mentors behind. He can no longer allow them to show him the way because, by definition, he will now have surpassed them in the organization. This is particularly true when the mentors came from within the business where s/he has just been promoted to leader. There are rare exceptions when he has won a leadership appointment to another organization. If that is the case, they can in some circumstances, continue to rely on their old friends for comfort and guidance. For most that will not be the case. To continue to rely on people who used to be superior in position, and then equal and who are now subordinate, would probably be an unacceptable show of weakness and lack of proper readiness to be the leader they all expect you to be.

This is not a case of inappropriate hubris. It is that leadership bestows a special responsibility, a type of 'fatherhood to the business' which requires the leader to accept mentoring roles to other people within the corporation and to throw off those s/he had previously enjoyed themselves. In some special situations where we have a relationship with a mentor who is perhaps a non-executive director or a long-term senior figure within the organization, it might be possible to allow the mentoring role to remain for a short while, as we manage the transition from manager to leader. However, in my mind, it is best to accept we are now on our own.

If a leader has been following the type of advice given in the chapter on the development of leaders or the management of a leadership career, they will be ready to slide easily into the role of strategic visionary leader. If the company is one where they have served for many years they will have been waiting for this moment for some time. They will know the capabilities of the company and its people. They will have already analysed the opportunities that the new world is offering. The job of strategic visionary now becomes one of convincing the key stake holders, deciding the best communication methods and convincing everybody that they should go in the strategic direction the leader has laid out.

If the leader is taking a leadership role in a company which is unfamiliar to them, becoming the visionary strategic leader for the first time, it can be much harder, particularly if they have also entered an industry with which they are not familiar. It is vital to search out the brightest and best executives within the company (and elsewhere) that they can find. They have a very short time in which to discover and understand the key variables of both the business and the industry which they have entered. Many people will be suspicious that they are a poor appointment, particularly the internal candidates who lost their opportunity of appointment to the leadership position against this new leader. In this situation it is most vitally important that they work hard, long and fast to master the intricacies of the industry, the specific capability of the business they are leading and an assessment of the best executives within the organization to execute any strategic mission that they are able to conjure up. It is at times such as these that leadership careers are made or destroyed.

If the leader is lucky there will already be a working mission and set of strategic objectives for the organization. It is unlikely that they are the best or most appropriate otherwise the organization was unlikely to have needed to look outside for a new leader. As I say later in Chapter 9 and in my own work on strategy (Levicki, 1996: p. 134), 'there are not many choices about how to increase the size of the business'. There is rarely a multitude of choices for the strategic mission. It won't be hard to decide where you want to take the organization. Much the hardest part of your job will be to decide who are your best executives to take the organization on the voyage on your behalf, how much you have to grow organically and how much through acquisition? The only complexity will be 'should you do it in 3, 5 or 7 years?

Once you have decided the strategic mission of the company 'the job of chairman, or chief executive, is to "manage" the company through the board'. (Harvey-Jones, 1988: p. 235). If you have got it right, the job of leader should now become fairly mundane and boring. All you have to do is to communicate, communicate, and then communicate some more because your real job is now to tell everybody the objectives and how you think they should make them happen. Your job is merely to focus on your employees' understanding of what you want on behalf of the organization and what they must each do for their part of the work. Too many leaders think that they have to continuously take decisions and let everybody know that they are being busy. In fact, when they are being busy they are probably making a nuisance of themselves by interfering with other people who are getting on with the implementation of the big idea. Once you have told them what you want them to do and how you want them to do it, good leaders are careful not to take too many other decisions.

How big leaders think

Good career management for successful leaders involves the leader always looking and seeing at least two steps ahead of the position which they currently occupy. That is to say, if you want to understand and anticipate your current boss' situation, decisions and problems, then you should think of the strategic situation from their point of view. Remember, the advice is to see and think, and not to *do* as your boss should do if you had his or her position.

As you approached the senior or top leadership job you have been aiming at throughout your career you will have trained your mind to begin to *think as a leader*. Similarly, you will have begun the transition from general management to top leader by reviewing your value system. It is your value system that dictates your behaviour and style as a leader. As leader you will want to become objective rather than subjective in your approach to everything you do. You can no longer allow yourself the charity of your head being ruled by your heart when the business' survival depends on you. You must take objective decisions about your executives, the economic, social and political scenarios which face the company and about its assets and constraints. The latter is the hardest aspect of objectivity you will find, particularly when you have been made leader of a company where have you have worked for many years. It is hard to look objectively at the work of colleagues and friends who, up to now, have been among your peer group. You used to take at face value that they were competent and were achieving what they said in the psychodramas of the boardroom. Now you have to evaluate them objectively and decide whether they can be part of the future of the business.

You will need to retain a capacity for *dispassion*. You will want to remove emotion and colourful thinking from your mind. The dispassion you need is that of the objective judge who is using a highest possible level of logical judgement to evaluate a situation, which, in this case, is the business you have been appointed to lead. When we observe quality leaders it is their ability to be dispassionate which is most striking and frightening. We know that, with this quality, if the leader had to do so, they would have you removed or destroyed instantly and as un-emotionally as a New York criminal boss would order the murder of a turncoat. This dispassion keeps many people at a distance from the leader. It is something they have to be careful about, although it is vital that they manage to achieve it.

A leader must be both *emotionally mature* and *naive*. This paradox enables them to examine objectively the vast range of assumptions that exist in every business. The longer we have been in a business the worst are the assumptions that get caught in our mind. It is frequently the most naive questions about the largest assumptions that will eventually reveal the biggest ideas for the most optimistic strategic mission that the company could hope to achieve.

For example, is IBM in the computer hardware business or the IT consultancy industry; is HSBC bank in the business of looking after people's money or helping people manage their lifetime earnings and savings for retirement plans?; is the insurance industry in the business of managing risk or helping people avoid accidents?; is the pharmaceutical industry in the business of the alleviation of sickness or the creation of health? With regard to my latter example, the first suitable company that becomes a pioneer in the health care industry would almost certainly become the most eminent and successful pharmaceutical business in the world.

As a leader you have to learn to be *wise rather than clever*. Clever people know lots of facts and a vast quantity of data. Wise people have good quality judgment and know how few facts they really need to take a quality decision. Clever people have high IQ's. Wise people have high Emotional Intelligence Quotient (EIQ). At the top of the industry it is wisdom and not cleverness that is needed. One often feels it is a pity that the medical profession does not adopt a similar value system along these lines.

A person should be more an *individual* than a *team player*. This may be the hardest challenge for any leader to make as he moves from management to leadership. Up to this point in their career, they have been disciplined to always act with team spirit within the Corporation. Businesses only survive and thrive when all their people play as a team. But the top job requires a change in the habits of a career.

This is not to say that what seemed to work is now wrong and that cooperative behaviour is inappropriate. Rather what we are saying is that leaders need to be individuals. They should have an individual style, with entirely individual solutions for the organization to adopt. Only an individual can raise him or herself above the general melee and compete successfully at this level.

Finally we want to see *more character than personality* in a leader. This follows from the discussion in Chapter 4. Briefly, a personality is the surface of the individual. They can be interesting, charismatic, shy or dull. In a leader character is more important. And above that one must ask the question, 'Do they have moral fibre?' Do they have a value system that reflects the values of the organization? They have to make people proud to work for them? If they are unexciting we still need to know whether they have a profound character or merely a superficial personality? The answer, for customers or staff should always be 'grab the character and forget personality' on every occasion.

A few extra considerations

Some aspects of the leaders learning curve are particularly important during the period of transition from senior executive general management to the top leadership role. They are: emotional stability; maturity; patience; creativity; tolerance of ambiguity and overcoming frustration. Although it only takes a short sentence to write them it takes a lifetime to prepare and have them at a peak of readiness at this important time in a career.

Every time a leader begins a new job it is a destabilizing process. You often feel frightened and worried that for the first time you have accepted a promotion to a job where you cannot deliver results. The odds are that you can and will. However, you will need the maximum of emotional stability and maturity to remember that it nearly always works out. You will need much patience because the most important people around you, on your board and your senior executives will be frightened when you are appointed even though some of them were probably instrumental in getting you the job. They are frightened because they fear for their own jobs and because your success or failure will confirm or deny the quality of their judgment about you. When people are frightened they usually become cagey, reticent, critical and supersensitive. They will not easily offer you the information and opinions you want from them fast. Without patience you will soon alienate them. They represent the important team you need to deliver your ambitions for the company.

But the fear which is intimidating the people around you will also have its effect upon you. You also will be frightened in your new position. You will be asking yourself difficult or impossible questions. Are you suitable for the job? Is this industry one which you cannot understand? Is the organization so lacking in resources that nobody could succeed in the job you have been asked to do? These questions and many more will cause you much fear and anxiety. Those feelings could destroy the very creativity which is the most valuable asset you need as you set about the task of creating a new strategic mission for the organization. That is why you must focus on remaining calm and creative.

Your tolerance of ambiguity will be sorely tested during the period of maximum insecurity. A leader's unanswered questions are important when s/he takes over a large corporation. People will be judging you against the success of the previous incumbent. They will be asking themselves whether you have come in on a false reputation created by the people who introduced you or whether you are genuinely the strategic visionary that the head hunters promised that you are. Consider the example of P. Y. Gerbeau, who took over the leadership role at the Dome in London after the media had panned the previous leader. First it was claimed that the board had appointed the wrong leader. Then it was asserted that he had only had responsibility for operational aspects of his previous business and had no experience in marketing or general leadership. Yet, within a year of accepting the job he had made such an impression upon everybody within government, his employees and the public at large, that he had been voted a hero by BBC Radio 4 listeners in their end of year poll. Only a good people motivator who also knew how to control all the 'first leadership role nerves' (and how to manage the media) could have achieved so much.

As a leader you will have to overcome much frustration as you settle into your first important leadership job. For many years you will have dreamt of how much autonomy and independence the final leadership role will give you. What you discover is how much more responsibility without power you really have at the top of an organization. You will find people who are not very good at their jobs but who you cannot get rid of because they have too many powerful friends. You will find bankers who will not give you any more money to grow without proof of potential but who refuse to allow you to use your potential to prove your ideas are worth accepting. Your people will mislead you about the budgets that they can achieve this year. You will find dead inventory because your accountants have refused to write it off for years. You will find that previous leaders did not keep up building repairs because they wanted to include that money as profits when they should have kept the organization's physical structure in a good state of repair. Finally, you'll find that your own brain does not work as well as it used to when it had slightly less responsibility. All the above will cause you profound frustration. You must overcome it or your leadership career will end as quickly as it took ages to start.

Table 8.2 Differences between businesses and corporations	
Businesses	*Corporations*
Limited products	Complex strategies
Smaller	Larger
Business leader	Corporate leader
Focused	Disparate
Easier to lead	Hard to lead
Often national	Often international

Simple and complex leadership

If you get the opportunity try to choose your first leadership role as head of a business rather than a corporation. Watson (1990), examined the significance of the 7-S organizational framework, beloved of so many consultants throughout the 1990s. The seven 'S's stand for *Strategy, Structure, Systems, Style, Staff, Skills*, and *Superordinate Goals*. He concluded that 'If one believes there is a difference between leadership and management, then there is some question as to whether managers can achieve 7-S performance at all' (Watson, 1990: p. 26).

Examination of Table 8.2, above will clearly show that almost everything about running a business is simpler than running a corporation. Almost by definition the corporation is more complex, larger and more disparate. It is more likely to be international and need a complex strategy which goes across both industrial and national boundaries. The advice must be, for your leadership career, if it is in the least possible, start at the level of business rather than the corporation. Occasionally I have seen a leader who is really only ready to run a business rather than a corporation get landed with a complex corporation instead. In those circumstances, they have tended to break the Corporation up into business size chunks (and therefore smaller time horizons) which they could understand and run effectively. In some cases, however, this slowed the Corporation's growth against the potential speed it could have been. When a leader accidentally has too big a job as his first leadership role, it takes them much longer to evolve into complex corporate thinking than if he had a chance to practise leadership at the business level first.

Summary

The chapter starts by carefully differentiating the different leadership aspects between corporate leaders, entrepreneurs and managers. It carefully delineates the differences, particularly pointing out that leaders are visionary whereas entrepreneurs are obsessive and managers plebeian. The chapter continues to explain the processes of translating our career from management to leadership. It looks at how big leaders at the top of large organizations think. It points out the need for dispassion, wisdom, individuality and character. Finally I point out the particular importance of emotional maturity and tolerance of uncertainty, particularly if we become the leader of the complex corporation rather than a relatively simple business.

9. *Strategic Decision-Making for Leaders*

Leadership, decisions and business success

Throughout this book I have emphasized the differences between leadership, entrepreneurialism and management. I trust that by now readers are convinced that leadership at the top of large corporations is an intrinsically different concept from decision making by entrepreneurs or managers. In this chapter I wish to examine the basic methodology of decision-making and discover whether leaders should adopt any particular methods.

We certainly know that leaders should always focus upon the strategic decisions rather than functional, tactical or operational decisions. That immediately differentiates it from managerial decision-making. On the occasions when I have attended board meetings with leaders to help them improve their decision-making techniques, I have nearly always been dismayed by the type of foolish detail that some leaders get involved in. I nearly always advise, after these meetings, that the leader focus more upon policy and general rules rather than descend into the detail of operational situations. If a policy cannot be applied to an operational situation, then the policy is wrong. Every single operation, even if particularly difficult or complex, should be controllable by general policy guidelines in a large corporation. If your managers have to evolve or guess the general policy upon the basis of particular past operational decisions, a leader can never be sure that their preferred policies will be followed at all.

People managing a total leadership career should always take their decisions with the whole perspective in mind. By this we mean that at any decision point, the leader should be thinking about the organization's total strategic mission, the social and economic well-being of its employees, his or her personal career situation and whether, in 5 years' time, the decision will be defensible in absolute terms no matter what the environmental, economic and prevailing social mores are at that time.

For example, a retailer in the mobile telephony industry recently issued a pamphlet entitled 'Mobile phones and health'. The language of the leaflet is, to put it mildly, opportunistic. It does not seem to be intended to really inform the public or remove the genuine doubts that customers of mobile phones should have of the dangers that mobile phones pose of causing brain tumours if excessively used. It says, for example, in reference to memory, 'the results (of experiments upon rats) showed that RF (radio frequency) could modify signals in the cells in a part of the mind that is responsible for learning and short term memory. This study has not yet been replicated by other scientists and its relevance to humans has yet to be established'. If it is proven, eventually, that the use of mobile phones can cause brain tumours and 'kill the customer', will this kind of obfuscation be considered any more unwholesome than the behaviour of the leaders of cigarette companies who perjured themselves in Congress in the USA when they swore on oath that cigarettes do not cause cancer and there was no evidence of any possible proof (that nicotine was addictive and that smoking causes cancer), even though that evidence was sitting in their corporate safes? (see Kluger, 1997).

It is also worth issuing an early warning. One of the things that senior managers or executives often think is that when eventually they become leader, they will be able to be busy all the time and take lots of decisions. Many of these people get an adrenalin kick from being occupied and seizing the initiative all the time. That might be an appropriate behaviour for a middle or senior manager. It is rarely the way senior executives should conduct themselves. At the very top a leader should be moderate in the number of decisions s/he takes. The general rule is 'the less the better'.

Mini case study

You can never take too few decisions

Great leaders take few decisions because they realize that any decisions they take as leader can cause great disruption to the organization. They therefore try to take few but excellent decisions. A former Group Managing Director of British Road Services (a large transport supply business in the UK), was said to have taken only two key decisions in 5 years as leader. The first was to reduce the number of regional divisions from 7 to 5. This enabled him to remove two, slightly less than adequate leaders, without singling them out for punishment. It also sent a warning signal to the five surviving managing directors. They subsequently worked ferociously hard during that leader's remaining years, in case he again decided to reduce the number of regions. Apocryphally, it was said that the only other decision he took was *not* to take any more decisions. In retrospect, those were, relatively, the best years ever in the history of BRS.

Strategic decisions

Strategic decisions, for leaders, are defined as those which may affect the long-term health and prosperity of the organization. The mini case above illustrates that, by and large, it is probably a wise counsel for leaders to stick to the big and important strategic decisions, whenever they can. These will usually involve the following topics:

- long-term product and market development;
- the development of human resources for the organization;
- movement from mature industrial sectors into developing industries;
- expansion into new growth sectors;
- closure of mature, undesirable market interests;
- changes of corporate culture to adapt and prepare for the future;
- major additions to the *core competencies* of the organization. *Core competencies* are the most important aspects of 'know how' within the business. They represent the skills, knowledge and techniques that form the organization's individual competitive edge and ability to make profits (see Hamel and Prahalad, 1994).

The reasons for advocating fewer, but better decisions, is that when leaders get down into the minutiae of detail of their organizations, they can do considerable harm. This is not to say that leaders should not know about the detail of their businesses. Nor that they should not take detail into account when taking decisions. Rather, it is suggested that they should not take decisions about small, relatively unimportant matters. It removes focus from their (super)vision of the major and important factors. It also diminishes and damages the skills of their subordinates. Why? Because every time leaders take decisions that are really the province of a subordinate in the organization, they deprive that person of a learning opportunity. There is also a greater chance of the boss making the wrong decision than the subordinate. The leader probably knows less about the detail of the problem and brings less expertise and knowledge to the decision than the subordinate.

Finally, a leader's greatest service and kindness to a subordinate may sometimes be to allow him or her to take the *wrong* decision. Most leaders learn their trade by getting things wrong as well as right. Most of us learn more from mistakes than from accidentally getting things right. Allowing a subordinate to learn that way, at the expense of the organization (in the short term) is the kindest gift a leader may give a subordinate.

Short-term decisions with long-term consequences

Many apparently short-term decisions can have much longer-term potential consequences. The leader's expertise should be to know which they are and focus on those with the most profound strategic long-term effects. For example, all culture change decisions are likely to have long-term effects. They can cause profound corporate scar tissue. Although decisions to change the culture ('the way we do things around here') might be taken lightly and look like they can be accomplished in a 1 or 2 year process, it is rare that a corporate culture can be changed, in medium or large organizations, in less than 5 to 10 years. Sometimes there may not be enough time to change the culture before the organization dies.

Occasionally, an organization gets into a rapidly accelerating spiral of decay. There may be many different strategic causes of this. Examples could be among the following:

- the permanent loss of market share;
- the growth of rival firms which are competing more successfully;
- the growth of bad practices within the business;
- the discovery of accumulated mistakes in the accounting process;
- technological disadvantage as a result of rivals' R&D break-throughs;
- the unexpected death of the business' leader (before a competent successor is nominated);
- a one-off catastrophe such as product failure which is badly managed.

Comment

One-off catastrophes which break large corporations have become an important feature of corporate life in the last two decades of the twentieth century. This is mainly attributable to litigation and the willingness of, particularly American, courts to award punitive damages against corporations which fail to exercise corporate responsibility and ethical conduct towards stakeholders, such as their workforce, their customers or people living within the environment which they affect. They can affect the organization's well-being for many years or decades.

For example, when contamination was found in some bottles of Perrier water, the slow reaction of their leadership had a catastrophic effect on the long-term confidence of consumers in the product. This can be compared with the exemplary, extreme reaction of the leadership of the pharmaceutical company producing the pain killer, Tylenol, when somebody deliberately poisoned a few packs in a blackmail threat. They withdrew and destroyed all stocks of Tylenol from shop shelves. When they put their product back on the shelves, with an innovative safety control device, their product was welcomed back to triumphant acclaim. The visible sign how much they cared was symbolized in the tamper-proof packaging. Perrier came back onto the supermarket shelves with no symbolism showing any difference to the packaging or evidence that the accident could never happen again. It never recovered its market share. In the USA Goodyear's catastrophic mishandling of the problem with its tyres, which were proven to cause dangerous blow-outs on the Ford four-wheel drive cars they were fitted to, will probably cost the company its independence. In the UK, Equitable Life, a major insurance company, lost a legal battle which it brought to try to avoid paying up on guaranteed bonus promises it had made to investors. This led to the whole organization having to put itself up for sale at a knock-down price.

It could be argued that several of the situations listed above would never have become catastrophic if the organization concerned had a good leader who would have perceived and reacted to the problem long before the crisis. But that would imply an organization in a state of continuous perfection. One way a leader may be judged is how s/he deals with unforeseeable crises and problems. Few organizations manage to live without any. It is only under the kinds of extreme circumstances listed above, that drastic *cultural* action is recommended. It should usually be considered foolhardy to risk 'killing the patient completely, by removing limbs, to save the 'body of the business'. Incidentally, many of the radical *downsizing* operations of the workforce, that multitudes of businesses undertook throughout the 1980s and 1990s, were akin to 'removing several limbs from the body of the organization'. Many died!

Decisions about product and service quality are usually strategically important. At L'Oréal, one of the world's leading beauty products manufacturers, a decision to change just a line of the hairstyle on the picture of the model on their ElleNett Hair lacquer (a world leading brand), goes to the main board, in Paris, for approval. L'Oréal has become one of the leading suppliers of hair and body preparations in the world. They maintain their position by being obsessively focused about the detail of their key products and brands.

Drastic changes in human resource policies can reverberate for decades. Many years ago, when John Harvey-Jones was in the Chair at ICI, he decided to change the ICI human resource policy of 'jobs for life'. He was to declare the first £1 billion profit year in the history of the business. He achieved that goal, in part, by making thousands of people redundant. This was the first time, ever, in the history of ICI that that level of profit had been reached. We cannot judge, however, even now, whether it was right to change the astonishing guarantee that ICI offered, of 'a job for life'. But there should be no doubt that the amazing loyalty and dedication to ICI that all workers felt before he took that action, was probably changed for ever.

Decisions to change the structural design of an organization are always complex and difficult. For a start, the structure of the business is the main guide to everybody within the organization to how the business works. It organizes people into appropriate work units. It describes the promotion system and where the next job prospects within the organization might lay. It also states levels of authority and who is in charge of whom. It delineates where the power lies and who may use it upon whom. Thus, structure is a sensitive matter. When leaders decide to change the structural design of a business, they should first prepare their planned changes privately along with their human resources adviser, and then, *implement the changes quickly*. Structural change always induces massive insecurity before, during, and after the event. People behave more politically and dress up their results to ensure their 'place in the new structure'. They take their eyes off any budgetary or other motivational objectives they may have had before the announcements about the structure change. I always recommend to leaders that they should take all structure change decisions themselves, with the assistance, perhaps, of a human resources expert. That should, at least, ensure minimum disruption (see Levicki, 1996).

If the new structure involves losing people as well, it is wise not to drag out the process. Do it humanely and with the minimum damage to people (it always looks bad afterwards). Morale can be ruined if people remain in their posts for long periods of warning notice. It is as important for the business to look after the survivors as those who leave. There is evidence that shows that those who depart tend to, psychologically, get on with the rest of their lives. But those who stay remain fearful, uncertain and untrusting. For ages afterwards they believe that the sword might still fall upon them and they are often more demotivated than those who have been made redundant.

Long-term decisions with strategic import

These involve anything to do with new markets, international expansion, developing new skills and core competencies or investing large percentages of the organization's capital resources (therefore locking up the firm's wealth flow for many years). In fact, anything the analysts, Wall Street, the London Stock Exchange, stockbrokers, investors and analysts regard as changing the nature of the company, should be considered a long-term decision with strategic import. These are the really substantive decisions of which the average leader will take only five or six in his or her whole career. If s/he takes more than this it will be, either because s/he is running a gigantic, global corporation with many divisions around the world, or because s/he is taking too many decisions! These types of decision require much preparation and contemplation. They require the input of multiple sources of data. They are also typical of the kind of decision the success of which may be impossible to judge, until many years after the leader has departed and drawn his final success bonus.

Decisions to exit key markets or areas of interest are also difficult because they frequently involve writing off large amounts of corporate assets. We may not be aware until it is too late that the decision may also bear the danger of destroying corporate wealth.

Mini case study

The leader of a major player in the USA telecommunications industry, decided to enter the global fibre cable entertainment industry, because that is where he deemed the communications businesses of the future were headed. He could contemplate this strategic initiative because he had a free cash flow of approximately $4bn per annum from his mature telephone business. Frankly, the cash was burning a hole in his corporate pocket.

Unfortunately, a few years after entering the new cable market he realized that the emerging industry was so big and demanding of capital investment that he had to face leaving the mature telecommunications industry, to finance entry into the new one. In order to get a head start he sold a wireless telephone business that the corporation owned for $3 billion cash. (Just three years later the new owner sold it on for $25 billion, a very special level of profit. Who was the more far sighted leader?) The $3 billion was used to buy a 25% share of a major Hollywood studio. Unfortunately this leader had never dealt with Hollywood studio owners. They took his cash but supplied none of the services, access to entertainment, share of knowledge or access to the stars, he had assumed would be available to anybody owning 25% of the business. He tried to sue them in the USA courts, but had to withdraw with his cash still locked in. He forgot that, without honour on the part of the company you are investing in, 25% only buys you 'bubkas' (a Hollywood, Yiddish phrase meaning literally, 'peanuts' or 'nothing'). Only 51% buys you control!

He then bought one of the largest cable network businesses in the USA for $9 billion of shares and cash. Most commentators thought this to be a hefty premium. A few weeks after completing the deal, one of the subsidiaries that had just been purchased suddenly showed danger signals all over its financial indicators. When his key accountants went to examine the problem, they found that this international subsidiary (which was situated a long way away from the USA) was bleeding cash at a rate of about $60 million a month. They had to give the shares away and write off $500 million value from the bottom line. There was no legal redress from the auditors who had carried out the 'due diligence' just weeks before. A few months later, all the leaders of the $9 billion business he had bought (about 50 of them) left the business, having collected their share option cheques of between $10 million and $50 million each. I wonder how long it will be before they use the cash they received from this leader to start a competing business?

There are many more stories like this than ever see the light of day. The opportunities for them to happen only come when leaders decide to do big things like enter major new industries or exit apparently mature ones. The moral of the story is that this leader was paid vast bonuses amounting to millions of dollars every time he took each of the decisions outlined above. Yet every single decision he took moved the corporation closer to its final loss of control over its own destiny. However, the shareholders did get richer each time – in the end the business sold for over $50 billion. Yet every decision was mis-guided and wrong; each one failed to achieve its objectives; together these decisions ensured that the shareholders owned a business with-out a viable position on a global or national scale. They eventually had to and did lose control of the business. It's a bizarre world.

Sir Michael Edwardes, when he chaired Chloride Batteries, was fairly ruthless when removing Board executives who were not making things happen fast enough for his 'vision'. This had the unfortunate effect of making the Board Room look like a roundabout with the different ex-ecutives getting on and off continuously. Another effect was upon the authority of those executives when they were appointed to the Board. Because their expected 'life' as a Board director was rarely more than 12 months, upon being appointed, they lost all the authority and respect of their managers. Why? Because these managers (who were vital in running the factories) knew that their newly appointed Director would probably be dismissed long before any decisions he imposed would become operational, whereas, they were very likely to be there much longer, provided they managed to avoid an appointment to the board! Sir Michael later went on to reorganize the British car industry . . .

On the other hand, there are many positive examples. Jan Leschley took over the leadership of SmithKline Beecham (SB) from Bob Bauman, who had done an outstanding job combining Smith Kline and French with a long established pharmaceutical firm, Beechams. He left the business in a healthy condition. Being a wise leader, he left high quality successors in place. Jan Leschley took up where Bob Bauman left off. He made a series of lightning takeovers to place the firm among the forefront of global pharmaceutical businesses. Another leader in a similar mould is Sir Richard Sykes. He is the Executive Chairman of Glaxo Wellcome, although the 'Wellcome' part was a con-sequence of a brilliant takeover he led, making the business one of the leading pharmaceutical organizations in the world.

The leadership wisdom and empathy that goes into successfully merging two large businesses, composed largely of bright, scientifically qualified, highly trained personnel, is of a high order. I participated in developing some of the programmes for the merging of the two cultures. It rarely felt as if the programmes to effect the merger between Smith-Kline and Beecham was being successful, because there was much angst around the managers of the business, worrying whether they would survive the merger process. But it was successfully completed, largely through the determination of Bob Bauman to achieve a culture that encapsulated the best cultures and work habits of both the merging firms. Most mergers fail. When they succeed, it is highly laudable and evidence of great leadership.

Glaxo and SB themselves tried to merge during this period. Unfortunately there was a personality clash between Jan Leschley and Sir Richard Sykes. When Leschley left SB, in 2000, the merger was effected and Glaxo SmithKline became one entity in January 2001.

Optimal and suboptimal decision-making

The concept of decision-making belongs as much in the realm of economics as that of leadership, because defining decisions in terms of optimal and suboptimal is equivalent to judging a decision through the standards of a *time horizon judgment machine*. Today's *suboptimal* may be tomorrow's brilliant investment decision. Vickers, the engineering business which also owns Rolls-Royce cars, has put the car business up for sale. It looks like a crazy decision to sell off, for a few hundred million £'s one of the world's most eminent car brand names. Have the leaders who took that decision done their homework? Perhaps, background analysis has demonstrated to the Vickers' leaders that all prestige car manufacture is going to hit the buffers and this is an optimum time to sell out. That would make the decision to sell look like optimal decision making by geniuses. However, we suspect that it is more likely to turn out to be a suboptimal decision by *nominal leaders*. The purchaser will find the Rolls-Royce brand name, to be a source of gold for many decades. The decision makers at Vickers will continue to collect their pensions long after the suboptimality of their leadership decisions have been revealed in its appropriate light!

Of course suboptimality may be more appearance than reality. History is always written by the victors. If a leader fails to sell a decision to the Board and they are subsequently dismissed, their decision will be described as awful, by the successors. It is incumbent upon leaders to ensure that decisions are widely accepted as the best possible, given all the circumstances. To do that, the leader has to stay in place to defend the decision. Many readers will know the old leadership joke about the outgoing boss leaving three envelopes in his or her desk as a guide for the new incumbent of the desk. Envelope number one contains the advice 'blame everything that goes wrong in the first year upon your predecessor'. A year goes by and business is not good. So s/he opens the second envelope. It says 'restructure the company'. S/he follows this advice and attributes the following year's bad results on the costs of restructuring. But matters don't improve. So s/he opens the third envelope. It reads 'prepare three envelopes ...'

One way to judge whether a particular decision is optimal, is to ask whether it opens new strategic horizons which were not available previously. At the end of the day, the best insurance against poor leaders taking suboptimal decisions is the excellence of the Board of Directors. It is the role of a quality Board to recognize suboptimality early and not to be afraid to act on their findings, even if it means throwing the culprit out. Optimal decisions deliver the best possible result over the longest feasible term that the organization should contemplate, given its size and ambitions.

It is never acceptable to take suboptimal decisions if you know that's what they are, at the time. The difficulty is knowing, in advance, what is suboptimal. Unfortunately, only time can prove a decision to have been unwise. But how can we judge the quality of a decision in the short term? One has to use different criteria:

- intuition (later corroborated by post hoc examination demonstrating the sheer stupidity of a decision);
- the judgment of peer groups (the Board, investors, bankers etc.);
- ask the leader to explain.

Let's examine each in turn.

Intuition

Intuition is a highly underrated source of insight. It can be similar, in its style, to that special quality children have, when they make direct, incisive observations, that cut to the heart of events they observe. We often ascribe this capacity of children to be direct to their having less consciousness cluttering their mind. If that is true, perhaps leaders need to take a leaf from their book. When confronted with a dilemma, good leaders often have intuitive, immediate reactions which indicate the best response to them. It is only after they start to examine the arguments for and against their first idea that they lose touch with their original intuition.

For example, I was advising the leader of an entertainment business which occupied the number two position in its industry. He received a cheeky takeover proposal from the leader of the business in the number five position in the industry. Intuition said 'this is a rotten idea – let's reject immediately'. But caution, and the modern fear of legal action by shareholders, made him consider the offer. The leader of the other business was smooth and skilled at the arts of persuasion. He almost convinced him. These talks went on for 6 months. Of course, they leaked to the market. The morale of people in his organization began to sag. Eventually, he was reminded of his original instincts. He helicoptered above the debate and saw that rejection of the bid was a 'no-brainer'. He threw out the proposal the next day. However, not before it had done real harm to his business. It had always been a bad idea that a company with a third the capital of his business, a third the number of customers, a rotten infrastructure and a bad market situation could contemplate taking over his corporation. However, once he had started to analyse and think about it and allow the other, sweet-talking leader to begin to exploit his powers of persuasion, he had become hypnotized, for a short time. If he had gone with his original intuition he would have been saved a lot of agony and trouble for his employees and himself.

Often, intuition works by drawing the observer's notice to the obvious. For example, we often find that the ordinary workers in the business, have seen clearly the stupidity of some decisions. Consider the example of the building of the Channel Tunnel as a commercial venture. Although it is an admirable achievement to have built it at all, it was always destined to be an all-time great, business blunder. It never had commercial viability. Reflect on the behaviour of British Gas, who used to have a monopoly on gas supply in the UK. Their leadership practically declared war on its industry regulator. The concept of a powerful monopoly attacking its regulator was self-evidently misguided. It will be seen as one of the sillier industrial actions of late twentieth-century industry in the UK. Subsequently, British Gas, then rewarded the Chief Executive, and the Chairman, for the insightfullness of their leadership decisions, with a retirement packages of internationally, generous dimensions.

The judgment of peer groups (the Board, investors, etc.)

When it comes to judging the quality of decisions, there are peer groups who are properly qualified. A well-constituted Board of Directors should be a residual body of collective wisdom. Unfortunately, in the UK, even the best Boards rarely work up the power or aggression to do anything useful before it is too late. Although, individually, they often recognize stupidity, they perceive themselves as a group as powerless to act until the situation is so acute that their intervention is pointless. The Sears Group (a conglomerate of retail businesses in the UK) was led by a man who failed, for 5 years, to deliver promises on strategy, marketing, revenue or profits. Yet, two different Chairmen, both nominal leader types, defended his performance with the plaintive line that 'he has my confidence and needs to be given time'. I assert elsewhere in this book that any quality leader should be able to deliver improved results within a year of taking office, because there are always methods to make this happen. If a leader doesn't know the short-term tricks of profit making, there is little reason to assume he understands properly the skills of long-term strategic investment decision-making.

Ask the leader to explain

It is astonishing how poorly most leaders and their key stakeholders communicate with each other. Frequently we find that an inordinate amount of time is spent speculating about the CEO's latest decision. All too often, colleagues and subordinates simply fail to ask the leader to explain his or her decision. They could question, simply and starkly, 'What factors did you take into account when you decided this? Were you aware of all these other variables that we think are relevant and important?' I have often pondered why they don't! There are some valid reasons. Sometimes, they feel that if they ask and, subsequently, don't like the answers, they might be obliged to do something about it, even take action which might be premature. At other times, it could be because they are afraid that they will look stupid for asking, because the answers might be so obvious that they will feel that they should have known without being told. This fear of looking stupid accounts for a lot of behaviour in corporate boardrooms. Readers may wish to furnish their own explanations for this.

Taking decisions with 'black holes' in the data

Sometimes a decision may look suboptimal because some of the components of the decision include unknown factors, or data which has to be 'guessed at'. Poorer quality leaders might be aware that data is missing and become immobilized about taking any decision. They will usually postpone the decision until it becomes irrelevant or too late.

By comparison, one of the most marked aspects of some of the great leaders I have met, is their ability to take decisions in spite of vast quantities of apparently relevant and important data being missing. Gifted leaders, with superior judgment, somehow 'fill in' the missing data and take a decision anyway. They do not actually *guess* the data. They make prognostications about the nature of what is missing and arrive at a decision which works strategically. They do this no matter what the data turns out to be. It is an uncanny ability and, for me, is the ultimate proof that a leader is great. It is not encountered often. Consider the following example:

Black paint holes

In the days when ICI was chaired by Sir John Harvey-Jones, one of ICI's larger businesses was the manufacture of paint, mainly for industrial use, of which a substantial proportion was sold to the automobile industry. The paints division was led, in those days by Ronnie Hampel, later Sir Ronnie, who also, subsequently, became Chairman of ICI. Sir John and the ICI Board did not want, at that time, to take a decision to step up from being an important UK and European paints manufacturer to becoming a global player in the paint industry. They had too many other, more pressing investment priorities. However, they did not want to lose the opportunity to become a global player later, if the data and strategic analysis indicated that this would be wise. This meant allowing a takeover opportunity for a big paints manufacturer which dominated the US, to pass them by and go to another owner. Because it was in the public sector they knew that they would be able to buy it later if they needed to. Anyway, the American company was very large and buying it would have committed ICI to become a global player by the sheer size of the business resulting from such a takeover.

Simultaneously there was a much smaller French firm available which had received a bid from a competitor of ICI, which was a wholly privately-owned company. If that French business were purchased and taken out of circulation, that could lock ICI out of the European paint trade forever. If ICI were to step in and buy the French business, they could do so without being committed to the global strategy. So, they held an extraordinary Board Meeting on a Sunday, took a decision to buy and bought the French paint organization that week. They let the US opportunity go past. Ronnie Hampel's argument was that the French company, in private hands, might never come back onto the market, but the US company would probably remain in play because it was quoted on the New York Stock Exchange. Fascinatingly, 15 years later, ICI bought the US business and completed its positioning to be a global player in the world paint industry.

Balancing the stakeholders

Herbert Simon, an Economics Nobel Prize winning academic, developed a theory that all decision-making in business organizations had to be suboptimal by definition; all leaders have to take decisions which take account of many different groups' interests. Those groups have contradictory objectives (see above, integration and differentiation). The leader always has to balance the interests and power of the stakeholders within the business. Simon called this phenomenon *satisficing*. Balancing all the stakeholders is a special art that all great leaders must acquire because there is almost never a situation where there are no contradictory stakeholder interests.

The organizational stakeholders range from bankers and other financial institutions, to shareholders, debenture holders, stock holders, trade unions, staff and other employees, customers and suppliers. In short, every group or body of people who need to be taken into account

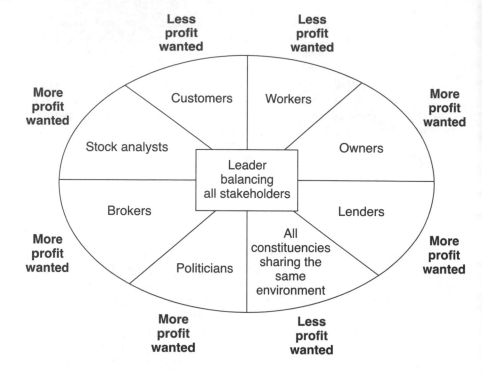

Figure 8 Stakeholders and their attitudes towards profitability. Business stakeholder theory, conceived by the academic Professor Herbert Simon, a Nobel Prize winner, states that a leader always has to take essentially suboptimal decisions, because the many stakeholders in a business have contradicting, preferred outcomes from the results of the organization's activities. In the diagram a set of typical stakeholders is differentiated on the single criterion of which prefers more and which prefers less profit to be made by the business.

when deciding what to do with the organization, when to do it, and how much to aim for (e.g. in profits, investment, number of employees, quantity of buildings, land, other assets).

Consider Figure 8, showing a basic list of stakeholders. Consider which you consider to be the most, and who the least, important, with regard to an assessment of profitability within a business.

Examine the fairly simplistic assessments in the diagram. Both customers and workers might want less profits; customers, because they would consider more profits mean higher prices for the products or services; workers, because higher profits mean less money available for wages. It is astonishing how often we hear company spokespersons mouthing nonsense such as 'everybody wants our business to be healthy and have large profits which demonstrate that health!' On occasion they are doing it on a communications medium being viewed by either their customers or workers and they are thus alienating members of their key stakeholder constituencies. Some leaders make the same mistake. All the other stakeholders in the diagram, want greater profits, but for different reasons. For example, owners wants them because profits should lead, if they are shareholders, to increased dividends. Lenders want increased profits to decrease the risks inherent in the loans they have made to the business, hopefully, without a corresponding decrease in the interest rate they charge (that's how they increase their own profits).

The key theme of stakeholder theory is that stakeholders have conflicting requirements from a business. That goes for much more complex issues than just profitability. Although the employees want the highest possible levels of remuneration, and the shareholders might want lower levels of wages to ensure higher profits and dividends, the different lenders might want completely different approaches. For example, debenture holders (fully secured lenders) might not want the business to be launching too many new products because these are risky and endanger the safe income of the debenture holders. Ordinary shareholders want those product launches because any one great new product adopted by the customers might increase the share price. The business' bankers may prefer a low-risk approach. Senior managers on high bonuses for short-term achievement, might want to take greater risks to achieve their objectives earlier. Should the firm pay higher dividends to underpin the share price or higher wages to attract the best employees? The answer depends on external circumstances and what the balance of the stakeholders will all simultaneously accept. If managers believe that raw materials supply is important at that time, they might negotiate with suppliers in a more conciliatory manner. However, if they pay higher prices to suppliers, should they then keep wages to workers low or product prices high or merely moderate dividends to shareholders? The satisficing problem is ever present.

Stakeholder theory indicates how managers and leaders are always making trade-offs between conflicting demands on how limited resources should be allocated. It requires fine judgment. Ultimately, that is what they are paid for. It is another area where a leader requires delicate balance and precise judgment in an objective, equilibrium condition. They need to juggle more complex elements than any computer could calculate. This points to why it is important for a leader to have a finely balanced emotional condition. The stable background helps their equilibrium when assessing and taking such delicate decisions. It also explains why the ultimate leadership decision-making quality comprises *perspective* and *judgment*. When this is aligned with *determination*, it is an unbeatable combination.

Factors which make decisions right

The key factors in decision making are:

- time;
- power;
- timing;
- quantity of resources;
- number of employees;
- capacity to take complex decisions;
- capacity to explain and communicate it;
- capacity of the organization to implement the decision;
- need to improve skills and core competencies of organization.

Time

Leaders need a keen sense of time, past, present and future. They need totake account of what the organization has done, when it did it, and how. The leader needs to know when and how, in the past, the organization made its most momentous transformations. This knowledge is needed to understand better what to do in the future. A sense of time must also be aligned with our personal situation, not selfishly, but relevantly. Why? Because the decision must be taken in the context of how much longer they intend to work in the organization? Will they be able to see through the consequences of their decisions? If not, are they about to take a decision that their successor will understand sufficiently well to sustain and bring to fruition?

Power

Power is commonly defined in several forms. These are:

- coercive power   the ability to punish;
- expert power   based upon special knowledge or skills;
- legitimate power   based upon the authority bestowed by title;
- referent power   influence reflecting from the leader's charisma;
- reward power   stems from control over pay, bonus, incentives.

Many standard management texts refer to power as a key aspect of leadership. In my personal work with leaders I am often surprised how little power they feel they have. The power that leaders have is mainly due to the quality of their judgment when decision-making. If they are able to communicate the reasons why the decision is the best possible that could be taken, their people will want to implement it. Most of the forms of power described briefly above are, practically, both great and diminutive. The more they are used the less real and the less force they confer upon the user.

For example, whenever any leader promotes a manager to a new level, if that manager then asks him or her to confirm in writing to his or her new subordinates the power and authority that s/he now has, any competent leader will know that s/he has made a mistaken promotion. A manager creates the power s/he is seen to have, it cannot be conferred by memo!

Timing

Bringing any decision to fruition requires an exquisite sense of timing. Is it the right time for the relevant stakeholders? Is the Board ready for this particular key decision? If not now, when will the timing be right? These are key elements of leadership decision-making. Great leaders do it instinctively. But for those who torture themselves and agonize about it, they should note that most leaders find timing a most difficult element of the decision-making process. Observations over many years lead me to believe that hesitancy nearly always works out to be the best policy. If you are still asking yourself questions about whether the timing is right, it is probably your intuition telling you that the timing of the decision is premature. One exception to deliberate and careful use of hesitancy, is when the organization is expecting a change in structure. Restructuring an organization is destabilizing for the people who work for the business, at any level, as well as for the customers. In these cases, my advice is to do it fast and get it over. With that proviso, however, reflect on the following case study, which amply illustrates the value of deliberate waiting for the right moment.

Mini case study Biding his time ...

A leader in the telecommunications industry appeared to be faced with a *fait accompli* by a fellow shareholder who owned 25% of the stock of a large business, which, in earlier times, had a valuation of £2 billion. Over a couple of years, the value had decreased and it was valued at only about £800 million. The other shareholder (whose parent corporation was in cash flow difficulties) wanted to sell his share of the business to a third party, for what looked like too low a price. My client, who tended to take a longer-term point of view, believed that the price the fellow shareholder wanted to accept, did not take sufficient account of the underlying value of the business. In addition, he did not like the other business leader who he didn't know or trust. *He bided his time ...*

He investigated the bidding company and discovered they were not running their business as well as his managers. He also knew that his partner was short of cash and cash flow. *He bided his time* . . .

Eventually his partner tried to force his hand by bringing in lawyers to threaten him with a law suit if he continued to block the bid for his block of shares. But my client pointed out that their agreement meant that they had to give each other a first option to buy each other's shares at the same price any third party offered to pay. He would be willing to do so. *He bided his time* . . .

He offered to buy out his partner. He reminded his partner that he had the right to ask for 60 days to get his capital together ready to pay. The partner wanted cash *today*, from the external buyer, but my client insisted on his rights. *He bided his time* . . .

Meanwhile, the share price went down. The potential bidder disappeared off the scene. *He bided his time* . . .

Eventually, his partner accepted a bid at 30% of the original price of the shares.

The wise leader stopped biding his time . . . Biding our time can sometimes be the best way to an optimal decision!

Quantity of resources

In the business world of the twenty-first century, the quantity of available financial resources should never be a problem. The world abounds with vast, varied and ready sources of capital. There is never a real shortage. Rather there is a profound shortage of *good ideas*. If any business has insufficient resources but great ideas it will find the capital. On occasions, when it can't, the reasons are usually sound. If a bank won't lend to them, it's because the risks are probably too great for a banker's fairly risk averse attitudes. If the venture capitalists won't lend, perhaps the idea is too hairy or you are not taking enough personal risk to convince them you would die for your dream. If you are already a limited company persuade the shareholders to put in more equity? If they won't, is that because they are not pleased with what you have been doing with their equity so far or because this latest idea has less credibility? Perhaps you haven't explained it properly. What about trying a high interest junk bond issue? If the junk bond dealers don't want to touch it, is that because you or the organization have let them down, previously, on other matters? If not, is it because they consider this particular idea a non-runner? Is it the leader whom they distrust. If it's the idea they don't like, give up the idea. If it's the leader, perhaps you should consider resignation, for the sake of the idea and the organization.

The number of employees

The last two decades of the twentieth century saw many businesses indulging in down sizing. This became a synonym for getting rid of human resources. In retrospect many businesses that survived have come to regret letting go of all the know-how that they sacked so unreflectingly for the sake of the short-term profit and loss account. In retrospect, letting human resources go for anything other than a profound change in the long-term market demand for your goods is now considered to be a serious mistake in leadership decision-making.

The number of employees within a business is a function of medium-term demand, history and *organizational slack* (the amount of spare resources around the business). Drastic haste, whether increasing or decreasing the number of people employed, is always dangerous. Fast increases are dangerous because there are hardly ever sufficient trained and ready personnel in the market place and there is rarely sufficient time to ensure the recruits are properly inducted; rapid decreases are undesirable because once you have broken faith with your employees with large-scale redundancy programmes, like a broken piece of china, the organization will never be quite the same again.

Capacity to take complex decisions

This refers to both the leader and the organization. The leader's capacity to take complex decisions is a function of strategic leadership intelligence, in my theoretical terms, the leader's time horizon stratum. If it is beyond their capacity they may not be bright enough to realize they are facing a decision which is too complex for them. But we must also ask whether the organization can cope with a complex decision? Elsewhere we describe research findings on time horizons and decision-making over time. Are there enough people at the top of the firm, with sufficiently long-time horizons, to understand the leader's complex decision and translate it into simple enough messages for the rest of the business to understand and operationalize? Will the people in operations, marketing and sales find a way to explain it to their relevant groups of people? Can the decision be sold to The City or Wall Street?

Capacity to explain and communicate decisions

The capacity to explain and communicate a decision runs parallel with the previous subject. Complex decisions take a lot of explaining. It is always necessary to devise a separate communications strategy to ensure a particularly important decision will be fully understood both within the organization and externally (the storylines will not be the same for each constituency). It can never be assumed that people will accept a decision without explanation. That does not mean they need, or will be able, to understand all the detailed complexity of the decision. The leader will have to judge how to communicate the decision with a clear storyline, which honours integrity while explaining enough to convince people the solution is relevant and optimal.

Capability of the organization to implement decisions

Another fine judgment skill when making decisions, is deciding whether the organization has the capability to successfully implement a great idea. Most organizations have myriad superb schemes floating around. Often people with fine projects think they alone are bright enough to have had the idea and everybody else in the business is essentially uninspired. Not so. Great ideas are common currency. It's the power and skill to implement which is the rare currency. Knowing when and how an idea is implementable is a key leadership skill. They must know what has to be done to make the organization more fit to implement the decision, in the future, if the organization is currently short of the necessary core competencies.

I witnessed a classic example of this problem in the Directors' dining room at a major pharmaceutical business in Switzerland. This organization was immensely rich, although not as successful in the pharmaceutical industry as its competitors. The top finance executive was speculating about all the exciting takeovers he could make with all his reserves of capital. In particular, he imagined how he might take over SmithKline Beecham and rocket his business into the top echelons of the industry. One week later, SmithKline Beecham and Glaxo Wellcome announced their merger, which leapfrogged them above all their competitors to become the leading pharmaceutical business in the world. In years past, the Swiss pharmaceutical had been beaten at the post by one of these two major pharmaceutical businesses at every takeover opportunity. They had the present capacity to implement great ideas, as compared to that FD's capacity merely to conceive them.

The need to improve the skills and core competencies of organization

Leaders should be continuously reviewing the strategic state of the organization and reflecting how to improve its core competencies and skills. Getting the organization fitter for the future is a prime responsibility of leadership. That involves taking small decisions all the time, by default, if not deliberately. For examples the type of people who are being recruited to the organization; the amount of investment in the business' equipment renewal; updating the IT systems; monitoring the people development that creates the attitudes and cultures that prevail in the business; and the receptiveness of the most important stakeholders to change, when it is necessary.

Guarantees of optimal outcomes from decisions

Great leaders know when they have optimized. After that, success is based upon their determination to deliver all the predicted outcomes, no matter what external events arise, even those which could be predicted at the time of the decision. This capacity to determinedly carry a decision through successful implementation is one of the strongest facets of great leaders. To a certain extent, it almost begs the question of whether a decision can be optimal. *A decision will be optimal when a good leader takes it and is determined to ensure it is carried out.*

What about the executives who must implement the decision? They may need to be continuously convinced that the decision is the right and best one. They often have to be taught to trust. However, they, too, must use their intuition to whisper to them whether a decision is turning out as predicted. Are the measures devised to test the correctness of the decision turning out as predicted? Are there sufficient *litmus tests* (see Chapter 10) to measure success along the critical path of the implementation process?

Different forms of decision-making

This book is not meant to be a manual on decision-making, more on leadership. However, it is worth putting in an *aide-mémoire* for leaders on various concepts of decision-making. First, inspect the matrix below to get an overall view of the different forms of decision-making and when they are applicable (see Table 9.1).

Zero-based decision-making

The zero-based budget decision-making method consists of taking decisions as if there were no precedents. It consists of approaching a

Table 9.1 Different decision-making methods and when to use them

Decision-making type	Definition	Situations when most applicable
Zero-based	Taking the budget decisions for a new period as if there had been no previous history.	Market undergoing rapid change; Major new technology in the industry; Competitors making rapid and deep inroads into the market; When the executive in charge appears to be failing; When the leader is considering hiving off the division and wishes to contain costs rigidly until a buyer is found.
Incremental	Taking budget decisions on the basis of a small, step change rather than a radical reappraisal.	In politics, in order to avoid upsetting constituents; In most business decisions, because most of the business does not change much from year to year; When the stakeholders don't mind because you are delivering results within their comfort zone.
Suboptimal	Taking a decision which is not aiming to get a maximum result; rather it is aiming to achieve merely a satisfactory, middle level objective.	When an organization has undergone radical change and needs a period of calm and achievement; When the stakes are not high, nor the rewards; When there is no right answer and it is *not* the moment to 'bet the company'; When the shareholders are more than satisfied with current performance.
Optimal	Taking a decision which is aiming to win the long-term future of the organization. The decision has to be the best possible.	When there is a strategic opportunity to achieve a winning position in an industry; When the businessis in danger of failure and only a major 'breakout' strategy will suffice; When competitors are at a low ebb and could be taken out with the right, optimal strategy.

Maximizing	Taking a decision to go for the highest possible profits or the greatest possible market share.	When a technology breakthrough gives your organization a unique advantage over the competitors; When your competitors are at a particularly low ebb and their cost structure is out of line; When your management structure and development is running especially well; When the leadership of your key competitors is weak or vulnerable.
Time constrained	Taking decisions within limited time corridors.	When time is of the essence and your business has unique opportunities, such as limited patent life on high technology products or when the business has sole access to important ingredients of the supply mix; When competitors are propitiously vulnerable; When potential competitors are considering entering the market and you wish to warn them off; When there has been a technological breakthrough which offers a unique opportunity to win market share.

situation, or division or department, asking 'if your part of the business did not exist, would we start it at all? If the answer is yes, why, how, and with what minimum budget?'. It is particularly useful when examining parts of a business that look as if their market place is undergoing radical change, whether of growth or diminution. When we assume that the business may not exist we have to decide, in the light of as much new and old data we can assemble, what are the minimum resources that we should put in, *if any*. Zero-based decision-making techniques are usually thoroughly disliked by executives and staff alike because the method requires the questioning of every assumption ever made about the budget and business and about the allocation of each part of the corporation's resources. The process makes people feel extremely uncomfortable and fearful. It can be highly disruptive and cause massive instability.

Incremental decision-making

Aaron Wildavsky (1975), a distinguished US academic, in his seminal work, *Budgeting, A Comparative Theory of Budgetary Processes*, wrote on the budgetary process with, mainly, politics in mind. He highlighted the fact that most decisions in government are governed by *incremental* decision-making. That means that most political decisions are taken on the basis of small increments of change at any one time, usually between 5% and 10%. The same rules seem to apply to most business decisions. The majority of managers offer about 5% to 10% better performance than last year. Most bosses only ask for that as well. Too often, both parties to the review process set their annual budget with little reference to the prevailing market conditions and without considering thoroughly enough the true potential of demand for products and services.

This also explains why the zero-based budget process is often full of strife and is politically sensitive. Examining everything is the very opposite of incrementalism. It causes intimidation because managers fear they will lose far more of their budget with a zero-based examination of their part of the business than when they are asked for an incremental increase or decrease.

Incrementalism, on the other hand, can be cosy, lazy, wasteful and ineffectual.

Suboptimal decision-making

This concept was partially discussed earlier. It is worth noting here that suboptimal decisions may offer the best solution after we have taken account of all the available options. For example, the market for Cable Television in the UK has consistently performed below expectations. Leaders in the industry seem unable to decide whether the causes are either that the British just don't like TV enough, or, that the prices are too high. If the latter, the economics of the industry don't work. It could be that the market is just taking longer to evolve. The industry also has problems because its supply chain is imprisoned by the iron grip of a supplier with short-term profit maximizing tendencies (BSkyB). Meanwhile, businesses in the industry have the opportunity to keep themselves above water by exploiting their telephony business where another dominant firm (British Telecom) is controlled by its regulator (and is also more circumspect and long-sighted about exploiting its market dominance). In circumstances like these, there is no perfect or right solution to the strategic questions faced by leaders in the industry. Suboptimality becomes the prevailing wisdom and the safest route to a solution will emerge from the marketplace, some time in the future.

Optimal decision-making

Optimal decision means taking a decision aimed at winning the long-term future of the organization. It means getting everything right, the stakeholders, the economics of the industry, the timing and the opportunity. It requires a high quality team at the peak of its form with the leader working at his or her best. The situations when optimal decision making are required are not frequent but they are important. When decisions go just right there is enormous satisfaction. They will include situations such as when there is a strategic opportunity to achieve a winning position in an industry or when the business is in danger of bankruptcy, see Chapter 11. That is when only a major 'breakout' strategy will enable the organization to escape the liquidator. Occasionally the leader might judge that the competitors are at a low ebb and could be taken out with an optimal strategy decision. This is always a dangerous assumption because competitors are rarely as stupid or as asleep we assume.

Decision-making aiming for a maximum result

Taking a maximizing decision means going for the highest possible profits or the greatest possible market share. It is always a high risk procedure because it leaves no margin for error. It also has the unfortunate side effect of setting up the leader for failure. If they achieve anything less than the maximum they are aiming at, it could be deemed a 'failure'.

Most leaders, wisely, avoid such situations. There are occasions when the maximum may be an appropriate objective. For example, when a technology breakthrough has given an organization a unique advantage over its competitors; or when a competitor is at a particularly low ebb and its cost structure is out of line (they may be locked into a bad contract, for example); or when their leadership is weak or vulnerable. It should always be a key condition of going for the maximum that your management structure and development should be running especially well.

Time constrained

Time constrained decision-making is appropriate when the opportunities and the prizes in the marketplace are especially propitious. There are times when a leader has to go for the main chance. It often seems to be most applicable to industries such as the pharmaceutical industry and, sometimes, high technology industries, such as IT, software and hardware, consumer entertainment systems, and modern, chip-based gadgetry. In these industries the power of profitability is controlled, largely, from ownership of a patent for a particular drug or software or methodology. The period of time that one is able to legally exploit the patent monopoly in the market is limited. That is why a time constrained decision-making methodology is recommended.

We often find that the prime mover in businesses in these industries, under modern conditions of vast levels of necessary investment, wins the day. Usually an aggressive form of decision-making is most appropriate under those circumstances. It should also be speedy decision-making because this is a relevant axiom when the market is developing fast and therefore necessitated the aggressive decision in the first place. There is no point in being aggressive and going for it if we do not also do it fast and try to beat the competition into the shops or wherever the marketplace requires distribution.

Communicating decisions

Great leaders know that taking the decision is just one part of a long leadership process, from recognizing a problem, to researching possible solutions, through data discovery, to selection of final preferred solution, through decision communication to decision implementation. Like strategy analysis itself, the process and the choices are relatively easy. It's the quality of implementation that ruins the outcomes of decisions. The first task after taking a decision is to communicate it to all relevant managers. Of course, much of the communicating should have taken place before the decision is even formally ratified, because the leader should have consulted all the people in the organization who will be responsible for implementing the decision while assembling the data to take the decision. He or she will thus have given them 'ownership' in the decision. They will feel that they played a part in the decision-making process.

Normally, the only exception to this will be when mergers, acquisitions or takeovers are the decision subject matter. Under those conditions secrecy is vitally important both legally and to prevent share prices reacting to the news and the target company's price moving (possible destroying the feasibility of the bid because the news leaks and changes the relative share prices). There are also formal and legal requirements of law on managing the news in such situations.

When it comes to communications, the size of the organization is the key guideline to the required methods and channels. Large businesses with 100,000 or more employees require the use of modern communications techniques. The leader should probably use video film or telecommunications or radio links to all the relevant sites where the employees are massed. In the case of international businesses of that size, a minimum is the use of telephonic video conferencing, although televised telephony conferencing is getting less expensive all the time and can be more effective for communications, if the leader understands and has mastered the techniques of that medium. By and large, it is a good idea to avoid paper and bureaucracy. In general, the less paper that emanates from the office of the Chair or Chief Executive, the better.

For businesses between 50,000 and 100,000 employees it is probably still feasible for leaders to try to retain some personal presence, by going to the physical sites and talking to their people. It is particularly important when major decisions are being taken and need to be communicated. It should be built into the diary as an absolute. There are always spurious reasons why visiting the sites to talk to your employees, seems less important than meeting all the important and 'interesting to talk to' City analysts, bankers, journalists and consultants. However, those external advisers rarely make money for a business. The workers do. Go see them, on site, where they work.

When important decisions are in the process of being taken, it is important not to communicate too soon. Early exposure can ruin a decision, particularly if it is controversial. It may cause too many people to raise their hackles and create enough anger to cause the failure of the decision when you do, eventually, get approval from the Board to implement it. Once a decision is taken, communicating it to the right people, in a clear way, will get it accepted. Going through the correct procedures of etiquette, process and good manners is a great discipline and often helps ensure that you get it right. This will apply equally with regard to your behaviour with your Board of Directors as well as any outside parties such as regulators, bankers (with whom you may have covenant agreements on their loans to the business), merchant bankers and stockbrokers. For the same reasons don't communicate to the wrong people, such as competitors or suppliers (before workers).

Give the right message, try to imagine hearing, seeing or reading the words you are using and how they will be perceived, to ensure that the words you use express what you intend them to mean. Although this sounds simplistic, it is astonishing how frequently even excellent communicators fail to think about how to transmit their message clearly. It is always advisable to rehearse well (no matter how long you've been doing it). People hearing messages always manage to find incredibly creative ways of misunderstanding your meaning. They will see something in the communication which contradicts utterly what it is intended to communicate. Different peoples' capacity for multiple interpretations of the same set of words is vast. Wise leaders never underestimate the problem and always check to see how their messages have been received and what, exactly, people understood. It can be a salutary exercise.

Monitoring the consequences of decisions

All good leaders make strong assertions (at least to themselves) and set up litmus tests of their predictions about the future. They will do the same about any decision they make about the organization and how it will cope with and react to their decisions. They will know how to react if a decision's consequences don't turn out as they predict. Taking remedial action early enough is as important as trying to get the right decisions in the first place. They will also carefully monitor the external environment, to check whether their predictions about the future come out as forecast. Great quality leaders accept when they are wrong about predictions or subsequently discovered facts (when the environment refuses to cooperate). They change their decision to match changed circumstances. Sometimes they may even have to admit that the original decision was just plain wrong and needs to be changed or improved upon.

Leaders need to get their decisions right most of the time, but not all the time. Demanding perfection in a leader is too formidable a requirement! However, when they do get it wrong they must know how to recognize it, be prepared to accept it and put it right as quickly as possible. This also means that an overgrown ego is definitely NOT a leadership quality, nor arrogance, nor a lack of humility. The organization's interests should always remain paramount. If they are not, both the leader and the business are in danger.

When leaders fail to offer strong predictions about the outcomes of their larger scale decisions, their Board has to insist. If the leader still manages to avoid offering 'litmus test' type predictions to the Board, the Directors should put in their own predictions instead. However, when they do, they must monitor with data, truth and facts, not politics, rumour, and gossip. The Board should also ensure that the rewards and bonuses it offers the leader are aimed at fulfilling the decisions and outcomes they have backed. Only too often, sly managers subtly adapt their predictions and promises into other measures and objectives which resemble more closely what is being achieved rather than what was promised. When leaders do not deliver, bonuses should not be paid. Furthermore, appropriate reactions should be installed and implemented instead.

Summary

This chapter has examined different forms of decision-making and under what circumstances each might be appropriately employed. These forms are not just for leaders at the top of a business but for every aspiring leader to learn to exploit and select when they find themselves in the different situations. Although most leadership decision-making should be about the longer-term, there will be many occasions for the rising executive, who is destined to become a leader, to have to take short-term decisions with long-term effects. A brief outline of stake-holder theory, as originally examined by Professor Herbert Simon is set out and its implications for retaining perspective, helicoptering and learning to make balanced decisions has been discussed. The next chapter will develop further some of the qualities it takes to rise to the heights of organizational leadership.

10. Creativity in Leaders

Is a leader's creativity different?

What are the first images that come to mind when we think about creativity? Most of us conjure up images of the brilliant scientist with his unkempt hair dashing around frantically creating experiments in a laboratory or the artist in his lonely garret designing and painting their latest creation. Creativity in a leader has a different form from those classical images. It is also a different kind of creativity that we might expect from the managers and executives who work for them.

This chapter examines the balance a leader must tread between using his or her own innovative or lateral strategic thinking skills rather than those of their managers. The creativity of leaders is directly related to their role as the creator of the mission of the organization. Even in this regard, the classical clichés of creativity are inappropriate. The creativity of the leader is based upon his judgment about the collective potential of the total mix of human competencies and capital wealth of the whole organization s/he leads. Undoubtedly, the best long-term organizational growth can only come as a combination of the profoundest use of both Emotional Intelligence Quotient (EIQ) feeling and IQ thinking. Later in the chapter I will suggest ways of maintaining or increasing your powers of creativity and how to use other peoples' imagination to best advantage for the organization.

Normal creativity and leadership

A standard definition of creative thinking is 'the ability to think out of the box'. People who are able to do this autonomously generate genuinely fresh and new ideas from within themselves. In terms of the Belbin Team Skills Test, discussed elsewhere, they are the '*plants*' of a team, because when you *plant* somebody with these skills in a team, the whole team becomes more creative. That is *not* the creativity that leaders usually have or need. People with the 'plant' skill often lack both interpersonal skills and judgment about how well other peoples' ideas compare to their own. They are not, usually, skilled team players. They often need help to communicate their ideas. They need a Chairperson who knows how to exploit them and maintain their self-esteem and flow of ideas when others reject what they think are their best insights. The Chair is more likely to be the leader who ensures the plant gets a hearing in the team.

The leader's special creativity comes from the ability to take the best ideas from the team, analyse the external market situation, judge the attitudes of all the stakeholders and then take an optimal decision on behalf of everybody involved. That is the special skill that I believe it is right to call the *creativity of leadership*.

What is leadership creativity?

The creativity of leaders is different from that of other employees in an organization because it's concerned with strategy and vision. They have to create a corporate mission statement that is perceived as smart by all the stakeholders. This will include such diverse sets of eyes as the brightest people in the City, other investing shareholders, customers, right down to every ordinary member of staff who will use the mission statement as a guide to where the company is going and when.

The leader's creativity has to scan the total external environment, often around the globe, and find the essential parts which offer exciting growth opportunities. A leader has to intuit fresh dangers, when others cannot imagine any hazards at all; they need the creative ability to decide which opportunities to take advantage of and when; then, how to avoid the dangers and embrace the opportunities with the minimum risk to the business. Top leaders have to scrutinize the inner workings of the organization to understand how to exploit the internal strengths and culture of the firm and the best and fastest way to repair any weaknesses. They will appreciate the *core competencies* of the business and know how to conjure up whatever additional skills will be necessary to complete the necessary set to achieve the future strategy, at a profitable price. When all this data is assembled, the great leader can only then begin the process of *innovative strategic creative leadership into the dark chasms of the unknowable future of the organization*.

After deciding, creatively, what to do, the leader then has to find ways of communicating it in a digestible form to the full range of recipients, both bright and obtuse. This, in itself, requires a special kind of creativity. I always used to allow my MBA students to write any length for their first paper for a few minimal marks. The next paper, which carried most marks, was always limited to just three sides of double spaced typing. Why? Because comprehensive brevity is the hardest thing to accomplish and takes creative genius to do successfully. Great leaders do it and don't show the strain.

What form does leadership creativity take?

The creativity we are describing here is not defined in most current text-books. It is a special form of creativity that great leaders need. They have to be creative about all strategic aspects of the organization. What is included?

- the way they spend their time;
- the expenditure they authorize;
- the attitudes they display to staff;
- the definition of the mission statement;
- the attitudes they display to customers;
- the human resources they select and appoint;
- the development and evolution of the budget process;
- the manner in which they develop the strategy and structure;
- the communication of the strategy to staff, customers and stake holders;
- the ways they symbolize the culture and values of the business through behaviour.

The examples leaders set are the consequence of creative, strategic thought, applied to setting a safe, profitable and long-lasting future for the organization. Their creativity manifests itself as a continuous stream of thought, behaviour and actions which are always focused on the strategic health and future well-being of the business. Leaders need to be creative continuously when thinking and doing their work for the business. Their behaviour always creates exemplars for their people, it is important that they demonstrate how to behave and what to do to achieve the organization's purposes. That requires imagination. The way leaders react to news of corporate results requires continuous creative processing in their minds. Possibly the most difficult creative effort is required when they adjust the organization's administrative processes to any new social values which evolve. They have to judge and react continuously to decide what is important and which news are merely passing 'journalistic fashions'. All this requires creative juices of the highest order.

Leaders' creativity emanates from dynamics

The key ingredients to great leaders' 'creativity' seems to be based upon a series of paradoxes or counterbalancing dynamics. Consider the fol-lowing paradoxes which summarize how many leaders behave mentally:

- utterly lateral but firmly based and grounded;
- creative but mundane;

- complex yet simple in their aggregation of the data;
- lucidity emerging from mental brightness;
- customer focused yet with careful regard to workers;
- individualistic while grounded in everybody's generalized thinking;
- conclusions obvious after the event, yet cannot be seen coming;
- cover the short and the long term in one sweep;
- although based on complexity, their ideas can be explained simply.

Leaders rarely seem to know where their inspiration comes from. We must be aware how easy it is to imitate the creativity of leadership. There are many who don't have it but have the appearance of it, therefore one needs to beware when facing the imitation rather than the real thing. The difference is hard to perceive. Some leaders know how to create value because they understand how to manipulate investment criteria and stock markets. Others know how to imitate the sounds and appearances of a creative strategy-led missionary leadership. But too often they are not the real thing.

How can you tell you are confronting an sterile fool rather than a ingenious genius? The signals are subtle and barely visible. A foolish leader's strategy appears to be sensible but never quite takes shape or achieves reality. When they enact symbolic leadership behaviour their subordinates are never quite sure how to interpret what is being indicated. When these leaders devise a new mission statement their people cannot understand what they have to do to implement its concepts. Visionary Leadership Imitators appear strong and decisive but are really people who do not know what to do after they take their derivative decisions. Then they are timid and do not care to do it. Their mundanity appears creative, but only for a brief moment. Their apparent complexity is actually simple. They are customer focused in appearance but they approve company rules which prevent people from looking after the customer. Their individuality is based upon selfish self-absorption.

They appear to be thinking strategically and long-term but everything they do is tactical, mediocre and short-term. They rarely do anything interesting; but if they do people think 'that is so obvious it has no merit at all'. Their ideas can be explained simply because they have no complexity, subtlety or devious cleverness behind them.

How can leaders ensure they have sufficient and appropriate creativity?

This begs the question 'can creativity be created or is it just there?' Is a leader born with creativity or can it be developed in business schools or by consultants with training programmes? Ultimately it is a vital

Table 10.1 The balanced dynamics of leadership creativity (a first set of balances and trade-offs)

The creative leadership dynamic	Creative effect
Rounded and balanced	Sees all sides of the strategic picture
Objective rather than subjective	Takes objectively optimal balanced decisions
Capable of dispassion yet biased in what they believe	While remaining humane, they take decisions in the best interests of the business
Sees the bigger picture and then condenses it	Self confidently best suited to take decisions, with humility and self questioning, able to draw the strategic picture for all those around him to understand and join in
Emotionally mature and naive	Understands the human aspects but sees clearly what is important and ignores the rest
Wise and clever	Uses the whole range of intelligence and emotional maturity rather than IQ alone
Both an individual and a team player	Having served management time as a good team player, as a leader their individuality is the premium that makes the difference
Enough 'character' to impose and enough personality to impress	While endowed with the gravitas of character, they have enough ephemeral personality to persuade those who need the more superficial touch

part of the leadership role, that a leader must be able to make the right decisions for the organization. If they cannot summon or assemble the special type of creativity of leaders, whether they use others in a team or particular individuals, then they cannot be said to be fit for the purposes of leadership. A great or good leader must have the necessary strategic creativity, or know how to assemble the creative elements to enable him or her to exercise his or her judgment to take full responsibility for the ultimate decisions his or her role demands (Table 10.1).

Every leader has different qualities which make up their unique set of attributes. Some will find they lack the capacity to create original thoughts when working out their strategy. This is not a problem. As I state in my work on strategy (Levicki, 1996) there are not too many ideas that could possibly work in any strategic situation. Choosing a new strategy does not require creativity but judgment of a high order. It is not *what* to do that is difficult but *how* to do it.

Rounded and balanced

A rounded person sees the world around them, 'with balance and circumspection'. They understand that, when people and events are going well, there is likely to be a compensating downturn. They know that most aspects of life have balancing factors. The rounded person is neither optimistic, nor pessimistic; neither a party pooper, nor a person who has to occupy the centre stage. They are 'grounded' and stable, while still being capable of joy. They prepare for the downturn way before the bull market tops. And they never enter the depths of depression when others believe the recession will never end.

Roundedness describes the kind of maturity needed by leaders. To be rounded, a leader will have reached a point in their life where they see things as part of the whole cycle, with circumspection. Leaders need to be rounded to ensure that they can use their sense of balance to helicopter above both the people and the data, which envelop and surround important decisions. They know that although they still have to align themselves, eventually, somewhere on the decision-making spectrum, when they do, it must be in a position which still allows the maximum avenues of future strategy and possibilities of flexibility if the future does not turn out as predicted.

Objective and subjective

Although the leader must be thoroughly human and retain the subjectivity of their humanity, they also need to be able, at the moment of final decision taking, to be totally objective in their decision. They cannot be influenced by personal interests or idiosyncratic likes and dislikes. A certain leader I admired appointed one of his people who was a delightful, although alcohol dependent, strategically blind, no-hoper to an important job. But they played golf together and liked each other too much. It was a terrible mistake. He put him in charge of the best performing division. It soon became the worst. It took just two short years.

Dispassionate and biased

A leader must be able to feel bias and partiality, like all other humans, sometimes in spite of the arguments and against rationality. But, having felt the feelings and gone with the flow of what popular opinion might prefer, s/he has to measure the arguments for a decision dispassionately. This is different from the concept of plain old objectivity, because it encompasses the idea that leaders must have a cold centre, a capacity for cutting off totally from the emotional hurly burly of the organization. It is a *capacity of not belonging*, an ability to *not be there*. Many of the most creative and successful leaders at times stand so completely apart from everything around them, that their dispassion is tangible and fearsome. But it counterbalances bias and passion and offers a safety harness against stupid irrationality. For example, consider John Major dealing with the IRA, when he was trying to forge a peace settlement for Ireland. His personal distaste for the people who had carried out the murders of some of his political friends and colleagues was overcome for the sake of the greater interests of the United Kingdom's long-term peace and security.

Sees the bigger picture and then condenses it

The leader has to retain the ability, when the chips are down, to see the bigger picture. It is something all great leaders have in common. It is a trick that enables them to imagine situational outcomes whereby their organization must win, whatever the quandary or the twisting of fate. Having seen the large picture, they must be able to see the small frame and the micro effects. Sometimes it will be the reverberations of smaller aspects of the decision upon the customers or the staff or the public which bring forth the worst damage that could not be foreseen in the overall, optimistic, big picture. For example, in the rush for third generation mobile telephone licences in the UK government-led auction, the bidders in aggregate bid a total price for the five licences of £30 billion. Nobody, including the leaders of the industries concerned, forecast at the time, that this would open every other government's eyes to the possibility of a bonanza. This, in turn, would change the valuations of *all* mobile telephony businesses throughout the world, for it was now seen that they would all have to hand over a considerable quantity of future profits to pay for their licences. Every company then had to be rated downwards in any appraisal of potential future growth and profitability.

Emotionally mature and naive

Maturity and naiveté are a strange and contrasting set of qualities a leader needs, to ensure that their creativity is retained. Emotional maturity is about being grown up and accepting of all aspects of ourselves. Berne (1968) wrote about the three aspects of personal evolution in humans – child, parent, and adult. What many people do not understand is that it is legitimate to retain aspects of all three throughout a life. In other words, there are times when it is appropriate for a grown up person to be a child, a parent and an adult.

Grown up children often find this difficult to accept. They often want their parents to remain the parents who brought them up. But mature people want their children to grow up, accept them as adults and allow their relationship to grow into an adult to adult relationship. Other children want their parents to remain in the parent role, against which they can rebel or conform forever. Many are often not sure which they really prefer or want. Possibly, a parent when they need help and an adult when they don't. A mature person also knows they have the right to sometimes be a child, too. They can let their hair down and be child-ish and not take everything too seriously. They can permit themselves an occasional fun evening or drink at the pub with their people.

Unfortunately, to be a leader you need to be an adult most of the time because your people need to be treated as mature adults in their own right. When you are playing out the child fun part of yourself you will see the world with fresh and naive eyes. That can be useful for a leader. Children always ask 'why' and 'why not?' – great leaders do the same. Leaders have to ask the vital breakthrough questions, which create, in others, the inspiration to come up with the new product or see a hitherto disguised new market. Akio Morita, an early leader of Sony, the global electronics business, used to say 'I don't do market re-search to find out what the public might want. It is my job to imagine things they can never dream of, create them and then delight them with a product they wondered how they ever managed without'.

Wisdom, cleverness and genius

We have discussed elsewhere the difference between wisdom and cle-verness. Wisdom is the profound insight; cleverness refers to the quick wits of straight IQ. Cleverness allows a leader to cope with the enor-mous quantities of data s/he must ingest and understand when contem-plating taking decisions on behalf of a corporation spanning billions of £'s of value, many continents and states, and a multitude of differently developed economies and nations. A classic example of cleverness might be said to have been displayed by John Birt (now Lord John Birt) while he was leader at the BBC. He and his consultant friends analysed the BBC to a level of minute detail to maximize cost effective-ness. Unfortunately, he lost sight completely of what his creative people wanted to do and what the public wanted to view. He was very clever, but quite lacking in wisdom.

Wisdom represents the ability to have insights into multiple agendas, to understand with the heart and the head at the same time. It enables a leader to permit human weakness and failure in subordinates and still not lose an appreciation of their qualities and value. When it comes to creativity, wisdom is vital, because it informs the leader how to be both the adult and the child, how to be objective and subjective, how to be both creative and analytical, and ultimately, to know how to decide the optimum solution.

Where does genius come into it? A great leader of a corporation may demonstrate genius like anybody in any other sphere, music, sport, politics, the military or philosophy. We all believe we know genius when we are near it, although some people are prone to overuse the word. However, there are some people who the world accepts in an objective judgment as genius'. It is always applied in terms of a particular skill or talent. Jacqueline du Pre was a genius at cello playing; but it stopped when she had MS. Mozart was a genius at musical composition; but his lack of political skills lost him his places at court. Churchill was a genius at political leadership during a military period; but the people didn't trust him in peace. Einstein was a genius in theoretical physics; but his personal life was relatively fraught (see Folsing, 1997). Bobby Fischer was a genius at chess; but held utterly weird views about life.

The point about genius is that it a genetically endowed accidental talent. The genius can destroy it by failing to have a minimum of self control and life skills. But it comes we know not where from and, if one is lucky, it is nurtured by unusual environmental conditions. The nurturing of genius is an unknown science. It seems to rely on luck and accidents. However, the keynote is that it is apart from and entirely unconnected with life skills, decency, morality (consider Wagner's views on race), niceness, gentility, frailty (consider Stephen Hawking's appalling physical condition), or strength. If the genius' life skills are truly inept they can destroy their own genius (note Bobby Fischer above).

This short discourse about genius is intended to draw your attention to two features about genius in the sphere of leadership.

First, it can exist in a leader. Some leaders have a happy knack of always finding brilliant and winning solutions to all strategic problems. They always launch their corporations into the first rank of everything they try. Jack Welch, the leader of GE in the USA may be such a person. In the UK Arnold Weinstock, the leader of GEC, the power and electrical giant was similar. Alfred Sloan at General Motors in the USA was another who exhibited genuine signs of genius in a leadership capacity.

Secondly, the presence of genius in any area of expertise does *not* guarantee the same level of skill in life management. In other words, people who are gifted in special ways and who are able to accomplish things which leave ordinary mortals speechless and in awe when they demonstrate their genius in their special area, are just ordinary human beings in every other area of their life. It is rare that they will have special gifts in life management itself. They will struggle, like the rest of us, in trying to do the right thing, be a little unselfish, give a little to charity, be kind to their parents, partners and children. Indeed, there appears to be some evidence that gifted people are less endowed with life skills than other more mortal beings. This may be because the development of their special gift leaves little time in their development for the evolution of ordinary life skills.

The only difference in leadership as a form of genius from other forms, whether music, sport or literature is that a corporate leader must be moral, ethical and decent. If a leader does not have moral fibre, they are dangerous to themselves and to their employing corporation. Hitler would have been one of the world's greatest ever genius' in leadership if he had not had the fatal flaw of a complete lack of morality. We should all be thankful. That was what separated him from the otherwise equally flawed leader genius who vanquished him, Churchill.

An individual and a team player

It is a feature of most leaders that they know how to join in teamwork and how to be both a leader and a follower in a team. They will have had a normal management career, during which the teamwork of management would have been a vital skill. Ultimately, when they become leaders, the loneliness and solitude of the leadership role has to takeover. Consequently, many great leaders lose their commitment to teamwork. Upon becoming a leader, they have to separate themselves from the team and become more independent in their thinking and feeling.

It is also a quality of leaders that they need to retain a detached quality (see above) and that they retain a part of them that is free from teams and associations. That is also the part of them that ensures they become a leader rather than a team player or manager. In politics, in the UK, there was always the famous example of R A Butler, who was a great supporting minister to two Prime Ministers, Sir Anthony Eden and Harold MacMillan, and was considered to be the 'greatest prime minister Britain *never* had'. He was the ultimate team player, not a leader. And when it came to the special need, desire, and ambition for the top job, he just did not 'have what it takes' to grasp the prize.

A melange of 'character' and personality

This was discussed in Chapter 4. Suffice to remark here that when it comes to creativity, character is much more important than personality. The latter gets in the way of the creative purpose. It distorts because it looks for the casual and superficial. Leaders with character bide their time, let others make their inputs, and then catalyse the decision-making process to a successful outcome.

Yet, personality is sometimes needed to put across the mission and the objectives. It may be called upon to convince doubters that they can achieve what is required and the leader will make it fun while they do. This is done with personality rather than character, although it can depend on the nature of the recipient of the message. Some will prefer the effect of personality. Others will respond to character and the longer-term type profundity of a person's nature and belief.

Natural creativity in leaders

A leader has to be natural. That is to say, at one with him or herself in what they do and who they are. Excessive false *reconstruction* of ourselves causes failure in our capacity to be creative. It is well known that in brainstorming situations one is always advised to suspend all criticism and assessment during the 'solution creation' session. This is done in order to avoid the sterility caused when criticism stifles creativity. In a leadership situation a person's creativity is diminished if the leader is continuously acting out a style which is an artificial rather than a natural style.

Maintaining an artificial 'presence' can prevent the leader from being balanced and rounded, because s/he has to focus on the artificial act rather than their natural demeanour. Leaders cannot afford to waste energy constraining their natural selves. The necessary freedom to be creative and intuitive is destroyed too easily.

Intuition is a source of creativity; that demands equilibrium and neutrality as a background to the ability to let ideas flow over the full range of 'scenarios' that a leader must contemplate. This allows their minds to find the optimal course they wish to design for the organization's future. Intuition allows a leader to be relatively objective in judgment because it will automatically take account of built-in prejudices and preferences while it works. Intuition facilitates insight and imaginative leaps into the unknown. It induces the ability to conjoin ideas which do not naturally belong together, but, once conjoined, create concepts for new products or services that their customers will appreciate and buy at profit making prices.

Leaders need to know when and how to take the organization into new industries and to ever greater heights of achievement than its constituent members thought possible. The leader needs to be strategic, visionary, attractive and fun to work for. Part of the creative process for leaders is also to pull out the best inputs from everybody around them. Above all, the leader needs to be creative, in the special sense being described here and throughout the book, because creativity is the vital catalyst for the creation of wealth, excitement and fun. Creativity is a special and necessary attribute in a leader.

A leader also needs a subtle understanding of how people *hear* communications. Leaders know they need to say the same thing a thousand times. They have to give their message in many different ways, at every level of the organization, to varying types of people. Every time the message must be thoroughly communicated, especially when it contains important ideas for the organization's future. To avoid the risk of boring both themselves and the people around them they have to learn to say the same thing in different ways. Each different mode in which a leader chooses to communicate the mission of the organization must maintain the same consistent message given to those who are hearing it for a second time. Furthermore, every time the leader has to express the idea with slightly different words they may also be understanding their own concepts in a more profound way.

In addition to verbal ability, the leader also requires a facility with numbers (in the modern era all businesses measure themselves and are measured by others numerically). Most great strategic ideas need to be tested arithmetically for their impact on the market and their value on the bottom line for the business. Numbers are often a creative medium for those leaders who think mathematically rather than verbally.

The ability to assess people accurately is important and also relies upon creativity. We need to be able to focus upon and imagine a person's best qualities and how they could be best employed. A leader must make people realize that s/he cares about them. Each person will respond to different strokes. It is sometimes said, cynically, that the ability to *imitate sincerity* is one of the highest leadership art forms. Perhaps the ability of leaders to appear to be close and yet remain distant creates this impression, while still caring for their people all the time.

Managing the creative juices

Leaders who inspire people to strive for and make achievements beyond their imagination are also creators of immense job satisfaction. They do it for themselves and for others. Great leaders need the ability to undertake highly concentrated activity, under intense pressure. In the modern era, with vast communication capacity and the ability to swing large quantities of capital around the world almost instantaneously, crises and opportunities arise with little warning. It could be a takeover bid or an opportunity to gain a licence to develop the business' products in a vast market like China. It might be one of the businesses going into a sudden meltdown (following currency problems or a rumour on the Stock Exchange, for example). Whatever the cause, on occasion sudden needs inevitably arise that force one to react fast and devote ourselves intensively to a particular problem for a period. At these times we have to be able to draw upon the necessary concentration powers and stamina or one will fail at the first hurdle. Crises can make or break a leadership career. Great leaders must always be ready to meet their 'Waterloo'.

By the way, if you find you are having too many 'Waterloos' each year, you ought to be thinking about whether this is related to your leadership skills or the need for a deputy to be fielding some of the flak.

You also need to know when and how to relax. That will be necessary between the crises and even during the crises. If you cannot control yourself enough to relax some time every day, you are not going to remain fit for the important battles and wars. One *nominal leader* boasted to me that he spent nearly $10,000 on telephony charges while on a 10-day cruise on a liner, with his wife. It was meant to be a holiday. He believed it was impressive that he had stayed in touch with his businesses, while on holiday. In fact his boss was profoundly unimpressed by his behaviour. The boss decided there was little that could be done to help a man to improve his leadership skills when he was unable to relax at a non-crucial time, while away on holiday. The boss gave up on him!

Last, but equally important, every leader needs multilevel listening skills. This refers to the ability that many leaders' have to listen to the multitudinous messages, carrying a host of potentially different meanings, both profound and simple, from large numbers of variegated people at every level in the organization. This skill is also employed to function on the multiple agendas, from the same set of messages, that are often being delivered to leaders, whenever people communicate with them.

Skills and traits leaders don't need

Leaders need a capability to understand the essence of every part of the business without a corresponding technical competence. For example they need to grasp how IT can be exploited to do things for the organization, without needing to speak the language of gigabits. They have to demonstrate the technical ability to take the decisions without trading techo-speak with experts. Some of this ability comes from the natural authority that leaders learn to exude. Another part comes from the ability to comprehend a multitude of complex subjects without needing to understand them technically or scientifically. That skill is part of the creativity capacity of great leaders. It is needed because there isn't time for them to become expert in every area of every business they might command. It is their judgment which is being called upon, not their expertise.

What about classical creativity? I noticed, many years ago, that classical creativity is often missing in leaders. Do leaders need it? My answer is an emphatic 'No'. Most leaders do not need imagination. It might actually get in the way. Why? Interestingly, neither imagination nor creativity is a necessary trait or skill for leaders because they usually have more than enough bright younger managers who are at their peak of imagination and creativity virility. Pure creative imagination is usually associated with younger people. It nearly always dies down or subsides in later life (almost all the great scientific innovators make their Nobel Prize level breakthroughs in the third decade of life, long before most leaders get to the top).

Being the originator of an idea can actually get in the way of the leader's ability to decide which is the best from among several contrasting solutions to a problem. It is remarkable how few leaders or senior managers have the creative *plant* skill, as defined by Belbin (1991). In summary, the key reasons why imagination is not a necessary prerequisite to leadership are:

- Imagination skills tend to be associated with passion while leadership requires dispassion and objective judgment to choose the best idea. It is much harder to achieve that if one of the many ideas from which you are choosing is your own.
- Very few people have imagination and leaders cannot be disqualified because they lack it.
- Compared to even the low number of people with imagination there are even fewer good leaders with high quality judgment.

Thus, imagination is unnecessary in a leader. They have to know how to exploit the imaginative ideas of others, to turn them into wealth for their corporation. Consider the case study below. It demonstrates one of the sources of my belief that leaders don't need ideas. High quality judgment is a much more desirable quality.

Mini case study 'no ideas' is good

One of the few sad aspects of the high quality leadership career of Sir Peter Thompson was his resignation. He resigned at the age of 60 from his Chairmanship of the National Freight Consortium. He was a very youthful 60-year-old with a young wife and two young children below the age of 10 at the time. The company went downhill after he left.

Over dinner, some years later, I asked why he had resigned, prematurely, as I saw it. He replied 'Well, Cyril, I had run out of fresh ideas. I thought that if I didn't have any ideas of my own for the business, I had a duty to move out of the way and let somebody else do the job'.

I then realized what a terrible mistake that had been. Once he had no new ideas he would make an even better leader than before (and he was formidable before!). He could then concentrate on dispassionately using his best judgment to select which of the many ideas his young executives were putting forward, was truly the best. There was far less chance of a mistake when none of the ideas he had to choose from belonged to him and he could exercise only his tremendous judgment skills.

Another aspect of leaders which appears strange is that they frequently lack a passionate *need to know things*. That desire for data appears to be superfluous. It may be attributed to the fact that data comes at the leader all the time, particularly with regard to people and their personal problems. Often they don't have time to deal with all these problems which can actually get in the way of the leader's real work. This does not contradict earlier advice where we said people and ethics are important (especially when reducing numbers of people in the organization). This is different. The leader cannot get involved in excessive detail about individuals. This won't stop them focusing on those individuals who are essential to the excellence of the leader's own performance. Leaders don't need detail and they usually do not seek out data. I hypothesize that they rely on receiving so much information that they will get all they need to know, when they want to take any important decisions.

I have also noticed that leaders don't need to be good at detail, especially *finishing and checking*. Again, this is explained because these skills, as a personal attribute, become increasingly unnecessary as they move up the corporate ladder. They accumulate people around them to do the finishing and checking for them. It is more important to exploit their immense ability to create wealth than to make them finish off detail and dot *i*'s and cross *t*'s. Leaders usually have enough people in the organization around them to do the completion work.

Some years ago, when Cable and Wireless plc, then a leading, UK based, international, networks and cable entertainment business, was attempting a cultural revolution at its UK telephony subsidiary, Mercury Communications, they dismissed many higher level executives' personal assistants, saying that they expected their managers to use modern technology to manage their own office. This created the astonishing phenomenon of highly paid senior managers doing their own typing, when that work could have been more effectively accomplished, in half the time, by secretaries who could be purchased at 20% of the price of an executive! Cable and Wireless got itself, eventually, into quite a mess. The mistaken policy of not allowing executives their personal *finishers*, which is the function that many personal assistants fulfil for their bosses, was probably created by a senior leader who failed to realize that s/he personally still had his or her normal retinue of people looking after the detail and finishing things behind him or her. His executives needed the same. By abolishing their secretarial support he removed from them their capacity to be effective at what they were paid to do. It was their executive work that suffered.

In his seminal work, *The Living Company*, de Geus (1999) described a study he was asked to do for the chairman of Shell plc (the oil business) who aimed to discover what made businesses live a long time. The four factors he isolated were:

(1) harmony with the world (long-lived companies kept within the broad rules of society);
(2) cohesion (people felt they belonged to one company);
(3) tolerance (they let people try new things); and
(4) conservatism in financing (they always kept spare cash in the kitty).

Above all, they seemed to have enduring values, often dating back to their founders, who ensured that the business was more a social than an economic entity. These businesses received extraordinary loyalty from their people in the good times (when they might have earned more income elsewhere) in return for the loyalty of the business to them in the bad times (when the business could justify removing staff based upon short-term considerations).

The power of de Geus' study is that great leaders need great companies and that great companies are based upon solid values as much as sound judgment from the leader. In these circumstances a great leader must exercise judgment about what accommodates the greater good of the organization. S/he must allow disseminated power to take the day-to-day decisions. Creativity, from a leader in a business like that, stems from being environmentally sensitive to the organizations' style, values and long-term future, from a belief in the idea of the business' autonomous life. de Geus points out that businesses have a duty to stay alive to retain employment and be a source of living for their people. Again, this demonstrates that a leader need not be creative. de Geus sets out the principle that the organization learns by disseminating its decisions throughout the business, not by concentrating knowledge and decision-making at the top. The leader's job is to be the guide and, occasionally, the arbitrator, ensuring the values are complied with and that good people are recruited who also adhere to the idea that loyalty to the organization is more valuable than personal aggrandisement or power accumulation.

Characteristics leaders should not have

Anger is the primordial characteristic that leaders should either not start with or should certainly lose, before they get to any position of influence or power. Besides the fact that it is a useless emotion that achieves little, it certainly gets in the way of dispassionate and objective judgment. Furthermore, it tends to intimidate and frighten people, removing their courage, neutralizing their imagination, and distorting their ability to think straight. Leaders always need to remember that their title and office exude much power in their subordinates' eyes. Their interests are better served by staying calm and trying to remove the effects of power and status to get the best out of people. Anger only gets in the way. The same applies to all *excessive emotionality* which causes tension and creates strain for everybody in and around the business.

A fascinating, seeming contradiction to the *anger rule* is the example of the construction and exploitation of the Channel Tunnel, led by Sir Alastair Morton. This massive project, which never had much chance of being commercially viable, needed a very special type of corporate entrepreneur. They found their man in Sir Alastair Morton. He was one of the fiercest corporate jungle warriors to ever carry out such a huge project. He battled with governments, bankers (a bountiful number), two competitive nationalities (French and British) and finally competition from the likes of P & O, the largest ferry company having an interest in the Channel Tunnel's failure. He made anger into an extra working leadership tool. The competitor ferry company, P & O, led by Lord Sterling, knew exactly how to influence banks and governments to maximize the problems for the Tunnel. Sir Alastair had to retain his fiercest qualities and his aggression to complete his task. More sophisticated behaviour would have been inappropriate. A less fierce and angry person would not have made it. It took just his eternally driven spirit to complete the task of building the tunnel itself. He is a classical example of the use of anger, not temper, as a driving force. His anger was always about the situation and never against the individual.

It is vital that a leader should not be *indecisive*, although this is primarily a characteristic of *nominal leaders*. It can be immense damaging when executives suffer from such a leader. Sometimes the indecisiveness manifests itself in an inability to stop collecting data before taking decisions (often referred to as *analysis paralysis*).

Leaders are also better fitted to do their job if they have no irrational prejudices and are open to the maximum number of inputs from any source. It also helps if the leader does not need to be a dominant personality. Any lack of personal balance or equilibrium not only makes it harder for them to make balanced judgments but also destabilizes the people who work for them. *Nominal leaders* are often obsessive about detail. *Strategic leaders* do not see the need. They consider it a waste of time, because there should usually be people around to deal with detail. Excessive attention to detail removes the quality leader's capacity to focus on the big picture and make judgments about the large strategic issues. It is terrifying that so many Board meetings of multi-billion pound revenue businesses indulge in endless discussions about car policies or minute quantities of expenditure, while investments worth much more go through 'on the nod'.

What skills and characteristics are essential?

Great leadership requires a capacity to make quality decisions using judgement about complex sets of data. It has to combine this with an insight into the human psyche because strategic decision-making has to be implemented by people. Leaders need to be able to predict the future accurately and to intuit what their customers will want and what they will be able to afford. They have to be able to persuade their relevant stakeholders, that their decisions are right. They have to believe in their choices in order to persuade anybody else to want to implement them. Then they will need moral fibre and backbone to see it through, because they will have to continue to believe in their policies, long after others have decided their ideas were not really so good, after all!

Leaders must be clever enough to command the respect of the greatest brains in their organization. But they must also retain enough appearance of 'ordinariness' to be able to communicate effectively, with every employee, at any level in the organization. They need the empathy of a saint while retaining the ability to be cold hearted and totally dispassionate when deciding the best, objective, course for the future of the organization. They have to be effective, visually and verbally, at every level of stakeholder to listen, see and understand. They must be ordinary and extraordinary. They must be both clever and wise. Above all, they must be capable of inspiring followership, that special ability to create in their employees, the desire to do the leader's bidding and fulfil their vision for the organization.

It's a formidable list of qualities!

The brain of a leader

The key brain characteristics of the best leaders work in a series of balanced paradoxes. Their brain works differently to others and seems to use a range of motors, exercises and spectra to arrive at conclusions. Let's list the range:

- fast and slow;
- simultaneously questioning and decisive;
- communicating clearly;
- ponderous while still capable of lateral thinking.

They are both *fast* and *slow*, depending whether they wish to grind data or arrive at conclusions. They can approach problems with a heavy duty grinding machine, yet, become swiftly decisive with a light touch when the moment of decision is right. They are both darting and accurate in their honing in on relevant data. They can be *simultaneously questioning* and *decisive*, while still *communicating clearly* to their subordinates. At other times, I have observed the same leaders being *ponderous while still capable of lateral thinking*. I have seen their accurate but general search for knowledge and information, sifting many contradictory inputs. Then their mind swoops and incisively poses the relevant question which, without losing the accuracy of the rifle, invites a blunderbuss of information. This may then be used to generate the general policy which will facilitate the exploitation of valuable markets which previously were hidden from all concerned.

Watching individual leaders use their unceasing mental energy, exploiting their high quality subconscious skills is fascinating (their very best thinking is often done by these people while asleep). When they look at problems whose answers seem impossible to fathom, they work their brain and come to conclusions that are obviously right once they have made up their mind.

Entrepreneurs

It is surprising to most people to learn that few entrepreneurs are imaginative or creative. They are often the reverse, even dull. Why? Because an entrepreneur needs very few original ideas to make profits. Often, too many ideas can get in the way. Great entrepreneurs usually make their fortunes by implementing a few good ideas ruthlessly, brilliantly, and repetitiously, with quality. Consider, for example, Bill Gates at Microsoft. Essentially he built the world's biggest fortune on one big idea and one major product, ruthlessly exploited and implemented. Unusually, Richard Branson has had a few more ideas, but the same comment of single-minded exploitation of the few ideas applies.

Few entrepreneurs are inventive. Rather they are more organizational and determined. Leaders have to fit their particular skills into the types of organization available. Entrepreneurs, by and large, are not usually even employable within the corporate context. Organizations have life cycles. First they are conceived and born, usually with the aid of an entrepreneur. After, when they grow, they are often still led by the entrepreneur, but, if they are wise, they engage the assistance of professional managers. Eventually the organization becomes 'corporate', gets floated on a stock market and its shares are distributed among many owners. By then it has become corporate or managerial and the entrepreneurial origins need to be removed for the organization to thrive.

'Litmus tests'

Many leaders use some form of what I describe as a 'litmus test'. In chemistry, litmus paper is used to indicate clearly, red or blue, when a liquid is acid or alkali. Litmus tests by leaders are rarely so clear-cut. However, they have to theorize about everything around them. This includes people's personal development potential, future economic and political events, outcomes from strategic decisions or predicted results from installations of new technology. Although their litmus tests do not usually give as clear a red or blue indication as a test for acidity or alkalinity in a laboratory experiment using litmus paper, competent leaders still get excellent signals, from both small and large tests, when they create hurdles for their managers. How? They set deadlines, budgets and implementation dates which test the full range of their managers' limits. When their people give appropriate indications on these litmus tests, sensible leaders heighten the hurdles, to test them further. If somebody fails, the leader will quietly draw the necessary conclusions. That will not mean that the person is unworthy or a failure. It will indicate to the leader that the last barrier, the one they failed to surpass, marks the limit of that subordinate's *current* capacity and skills as a leader. That is what a quality *litmus test* does.

One leader I worked with had almost no skills in strategy, although, he was astonishingly inspired in using people strategically. He did this by setting 'litmus tests' about their personal development, with a rough timetable in his own mind, predicting when they would reach particular peaks. When his people achieved those skill levels (he never told them his expectations, that's how he kept the litmus test valid) he would promote them and make his next prediction. Although this leader was useless at strategy, he was so good at exploiting clever subordinates and maximizing the use of their strategic skills, that he had a successful career up to a level of an £80 million revenue business.

Getting into the habit of making these predictions about the development of the capacities and skills of the people around and below the leader also develops the quality of the leader's own judgment. They should also use *litmus tests* to assess their personal progress. Wise leaders use their predictions about the future of individuals and events, not only to find successors and promotees but also to freeze somebody at their discovered level of competence. Much more damage is done to individuals when they are promoted above their skill capacity than is ever done by not promoting them early enough.

Litmus tests require care if one is going to employ them successfully. First, when setting imagined targets of behaviour for people and waiting for them to fulfil the predictions, it is important *not to tell the person concerned of the expectations for them*. That would distort the power of the litmus test method. You could never evaluate whether they were doing what you said because you told them, or, because they think it's the right thing to do.

Secondly, it is essential to *keep a careful tab on the original predictions*. We all have a tendency to ignore results which contradict our expectations and forecasts. Many people change their views and memories to fit the data which arise. They are not comfortable with results which contradict their predictions. Good leaders have no trouble with this because they differentiate between what is truly predictable and what must be accepted as haphazard outcomes. They also know that judgment only improves if properly tested and investigated, when wrong, in order to get it more right next time.

The helicopter tool and the time horizon machine

A useful mental tool is *helicoptering* above problems. What does it mean? It is a device to get things into perspective. Earlier this book covered concepts relating to emotional maturity and their relative importance to pure intelligence. Helicoptering, is one of the ways one can learn to use emotional maturity and perspective to avoid inappropriate reactions to events. Events where fear or anger are aroused easily, cause wrong, bad and emotional reactions when calmer balanced reflection is needed. That's when you should *helicopter*.

The best *helicoptering method* I have developed, is to place everything into a *time horizon machine*. How do you use your *time machine*? First, whenever some catastrophe or apparent disaster befalls you, you must ask yourself, 'how important will this be in, possibly, 3 months time?' If it still feels painful, ask 'will it be relevant and still hurt in one year's time?' If that still feels distressing, try a 3-year time horizon. Will you even remember the incident without looking it up in your diary in 3 years' time? If the 3-year time machine test fails, go to 10 years. It is amazing how few incidents or events really rate as important, in the 10-year perspective. If it still ranks high when placed in the 10-year perspective, I suggest you become seriously anxious. You are going to need all the adrenaline you can muster!

The power of stupidity

One of the phenomena I have always found utterly weird is the amazing effectiveness of fools. People who are self-evidently stupid, sometimes do the most amazingly effective things. Wise leaders should always be ready to learn from everybody, including fools. But they should also fear the *power of stupidity*. Fools can achieve wonderful and terrible things. This is because less bright people (fools) pursue their goals single mindedly, because they are not clever enough to think of more than one goal at a time. For the intellectual leader, with a multitude of agendas and the power of conceptual thinking on many levels, the capacity of the single minded fool to defeat them or divert them from achieving their goals, is strong. Intellectually gifted people are particularly vulnerable to the *power of stupidity*.

One leader I worked with defined himself as a specialist in 'turning around sick organizations'. This was based upon the fact that one boss, many years ago, asked him to sort out a seriously haemorrhaging business. He entirely failed to solve the business problems although he did some beautiful work on the logo, the branding and the image of the company. For the rest of his career, through at least four appointments at managing director or chief executive level, he took over successful businesses and made them unsuccessful. It was only then that he could try to fulfil his self-image of being a turnaround specialist. His latest exploit was to become the boss of a major airport. It took just three months to cause the first strike by the airport staff in the history of that particular airport.

Excessive use of personal PR can prevent leaders from achieving their purposes

An advantage of the large corporate setting is that it often gives you opportunities to get into the media. The press, radio and television are omnipresent and easily available. It is tempting to use them. Apparently good reasons often present themselves – the best marketing books emphasize that PR is more effective than advertising. It is easy to decide that an opportunity for self promotion is also for the good of the business.

There are dangers associated with the use of publicity and the media that few textbooks will inform you of. Firstly, journalists love to build and then destroy. In many ways, they are like stockbrokers, they only make money out of turnover. So, although they love good stories, they love bad ones even more. They will happily make you into a hero. The press will tell the world that 'your vision is unique, your executives love you, and profits are enormous because you are a genius'. Just as soon as they can they will return to the story when your luck turns and tell the world 'you are a villain, your goods have killed children, your trucks ran over an old lady, your debts are mounting and yesterday's genius is today's idiot'. It is not a conspiracy. It is how they sell newspapers. Their job is always to return to haunt you.

How does the seduction process take place? First, they invite you to remodel, what is often your instinctive business insight, into a set of clichés to enable them to recount to the readers what you do, in language which the readers use but which you do not normally employ as business parlance. That forces you to express yourself in their thinking mode, not your own. In addition, they can easily spark off an addiction in you which takes the form of needing to hear people start dinner party conversations with 'I saw you on television last week'. When the thrill of media recognition dies down after a few months, you begin to obsessively need another PR/media adrenaline kick.

By now you will have learned the trick of achieving media coverage. You have to issue any press release with a story which is the *first* or the *last* time something happens, the *largest* or the *smallest* of anything or any other story a journalist can sell to his editor. You wrap up another of your ideas into a cliché. Pretty soon you are running your business along the lines of the clichés, instead of with your original instinct and intuition. Thus, you lose touch with your own business. You begin to believe your own mythology. Then you are on the slippery slope.

Rule: *Never believe your own publicity*

The same argument applies to awards for 'Business Person of the Year or Decade'. Why? Because they have the same effect as described above caused by attention from the media. You have to turn your instinctive skills into clichés for the news agencies. You'll end up taking decisions according to the slants of your clichés, not your instincts. Remember also that admiration from your peers soon turns to envy. It is advisable to continuously ask yourself whether your business will benefit from the award? Can it help your career? Awards like 'Business Person of the Year' serve little purpose other than to sell the media which promote them.

There are real benefits to keeping a low media profile. Bad luck and unfortunate incidents in your career will have far less means of following you around. By the way, never give credence or discuss any unfortunate incidents in your career. That way, nobody will find it easy to use them against you. Your enemies will always find good ammunition. A lack of publicity makes it much easier for people to forget them. If, however, you do make an enemy inadvertently, don't ever fool yourself that they will have forgotten the incident. People rarely do. It is far wiser not to make the enemy in the first place. Similarly, avoid crooks and immoral people. They always corrupt people who associate with them and their dirt rubs off. Unlike journalists, who follow a relatively honourable profession, the corruption in the soul of crooks is always contagious. It will damage the people who associate with them.

In general, personal publicity is most useful to others, as an exemplar, at the close of a career, when we have no corporate goals to achieve but when we can pass wisdom on to the rising stars. It is probably the best time to theorize about what methods really worked for you, as a leader. It will also then be safe to admit your mistakes and what others might want to avoid.

Changing your mind

Good leaders change their minds! That is an absolute. But under what circumstances is it appropriate? There are four identifiable situations when leaders might appropriately change their minds:

(1) When external events turn out differently to their predictions or forecasts.
(2) When the human resources of the organization prove unfit to implement the decisions (which would, of course mean that the original decision-making was of dubious quality and judgment).
(3) When unpredictable trauma and events change the data. For example a competitor may mount a takeover bid, or make a technological breakthrough. There may be a major stock market crash reducing the general availability of capital through the stock markets.
(4) Sometimes competitors behave unreasonably, unpredictably or even stupidly (although 'stupidity' in a competitor often turns out to mean that they were cleverer than you!).

Some things cannot be easily predicted, such as the leader or an important executive becoming unwell. It may be decided to change a decision to give the organization more chance of success, in the light of a leader's poor health. Sometimes, key people leave a business or fall ill, although no strategy for a medium or large business should ever be too dependent on any one individual. New technology or innovations sometimes change the given data of the industry. Other events which just cannot be predicted might be political interference; unpredictable action(s) from regulators who change the 'rules of the game'; or, just bad or good weather, which has large effects upon the annual sales of drinks, food, and fuel businesses, on a regular basis.

The one area where leaders should rarely change their minds is on ethical or moral issues, where somebody has broken agreed ethical codes or an organizational process has led the business into behaving unjustly to an individual. These rules should only be changed when the leader finds he has failed to think through all the consequences of an ethical code or a new situation forces him to realize they had not understood its principles properly.

Persuading short-term stakeholders to get things into perspective

A few years ago a managing director received the following letter from one of his regional directors, who was due to attend his annual performance and bonus review. It read as follows:

Letter to the Boss

Dear Boss,

I am writing this letter from a hospital ward. I am waiting for the Transport Minister and local Member of Parliament, who was knocked down by our truck, to recover consciousness. I should be able to attend next week's performance review, but that depends whether the Industrial Tribunal closes in time, you will remember we are defending a sexual harassment hearing of that secretary who had twins. I may have to leave the review early because the local bank has asked to see me. There appears to be a discrepancy between the figures our accountant has sent Head Office and the actual cash banked.

No other worries at present, although I hope you don't mind if I stay overnight, a head-hunter wants to speak to me. I'm only going because I'm not sure if it's about me or another of the senior team, but it's always best to go along and find out, I'm sure you'd agree. I look forward to seeing you,

Yours sincerely
Fred

PS *Actually, boss, I just missed one budget target (I overspent on training by 1%). I achieved all other objectives. I feel the team have performed tremendously and deserve their full bonus, which I am coming to the meeting to discuss. **I just wanted to help you get things into perspective.***

Good leaders keep things in perspective in their organization, both for themselves and their key personnel. No single manager is so important that his or her departure can damage the corporation. Very few single events can actually bring down the whole pack of tricks of the corporate state. Ensuring that everybody realizes this and gets each event and happening into perspective, is an ability that all good leaders need.

We have to particularly admire leaders who also manage to persuade shareholders to 'keep things in perspective', often for years on end. I especially admire leaders of quoted companies who persuade shareholders to forgo dividends. In the long run it usually makes the shareholders much richer, although it also renders them less able to judge the performance of the organization. Few people are able to see clearly how much of the apparent capital gain is made at the expense of the foregone dividends! (This is also the key 'trick' of the life insurance industry, too.)

The short-term considerations of leaders

It was stated above that there is no excuse for any leader not to deliver short-term as well as long-term results. Young managers, on their way to the top, never know how long they will be in any particular job. They should always try to make a difference early, based on long-term principles of good management, which will be a precursor to their eventual leadership style. Choosing how to economize in an ailing business in the immediate and short run is a creative art because economizing unsatisfactorily can destroy opportunities for many years to come. Below are set out the type of controls to which any competent young manager and potential leader should give their attention in the short term, to ensure that positive results come through early. They have to examine the control of short-term costs. These should include, at least, everything on the following list:

- ceasing the use of temporary staff;
- cutting any wasteful use of company cars and the fuel that goes in them;
- reducing the excessive use of hire vehicles and taxis;
- examining any invoices for fast messenger and parcel delivery services;
- selling any excess property that is not being exploited or rented out;
- stopping any property lease renewal projects that may be unnecessary;
- cancel any new IT being installed without immediately justifiable commercial returns;
- removing all excess numbers of secretaries and personal assistants;
- stop all regular payments of fees to outside consultants;
- examine the costs of all company canteens;
- cancel subsidized or regular supplies of food and beverages for staff and workers;
- examine all standing orders or direct debits;
- cancel all subscriptions for newspaper or magazine subscriptions;
- any other subscription services that may not have been reviewed for some time.

A ruthless review of all the items mentioned above will guarantee, in any large business, the possibility of finding considerable savings, possibly returning to short-term profits. At least it avoids waste. It is always worthwhile examining attitudes towards human resources.

This is an area where the greatest laxness prevails because it is human nature not to confront people issues.

One concern of leaders, in the short term, should be to continuously monitor any matters arising from current fashion and short-term trends. A leader should always be assessing whether something represents a passing fad or a genuine long-term trend. Similar considerations apply to short-term changes in demographics (more working women available, subsidies for employing youths, etc.). Leaders need to differentiate between passing fashions which may give opportunities to make some short-term profits and other 'fads' which are irrelevant as a business opportunity.

Leaders' long-term considerations

There appear to be certain subjects that most leaders keep to the forefront of their minds, as key indicators, and potential scenario material for their thinking about the leadership decisions they have to make. Often one such key factor is the trend in long-term interest rates. These affect everything to do with the cost structure of any business, whether it is managing its own investment funds or investing in capital for future manufacturing. Similarly, the rate of inflation can be a leading trend indicator, but for different reasons. Inflation is a potent distorter of financial information. Poorly performing companies often use inflationary figures to cover up their failure to produce real profits. This phenomenon was prevalent towards the end of the highly inflationary 1980s. During that period, businesses which had not traded profitably for years and which had been dressing up their inflated revenues to look like profits, suddenly saw all their chickens come home to roost, their apparent profits disappeared as the inflation rate returned to normal levels and their businesses died.

Leaders need to pay careful attention to the long-term economics of the industries and organizations they are leading. *In the long run, no matter how clever they may be, nor how brilliant their chosen strategy, no leader can beat the objective facts of economics and the demand curve.* If customers won't buy the service you are offering, at the prices you need to charge to make a profit, you cannot remain in the business. We mentioned the cable television industry earlier in this chapter. That is exactly their problem. The people in that industry face a different demand curve in the UK compared to that in the USA, where the demand for the service is guaranteed by the grant of a genuine local television monopoly in many cases. In the UK the case is unproven because the industry competitors in cable television face competition from a subsidized and effective public sector BBC TV and radio network and News Corporation's B Sky B satellite network.

The long-term trends of the products and services of any organization will need to be monitored and continuously evaluated to judge where the long-term direction of the demand curves are headed. This will be the prime indicator to judge potential long-term profitability.

Good leaders also take time to install analytical tools to test the nature of the long-term economic demand curve. That is more important than just grabbing short-term profits, year-on-year. Although we argue above, that good leaders will know how to produce immediate, short-term profits, as well as long-term economic value, they should always take steps to ensure that not too many short-term profit-appearance or profit-creating tricks are being played on them. These might include managers failing to spend marketing budgets, not using their budget allocations of human resource training, failures to repair buildings properly (thus developing long-term legal liabilities), over extending the company car leasing arrangements to save taking 'hits' on residual vehicle values and the many other ploys that managers exploit to assure their bonuses and promotions.

Good leaders focus upon the long-term development of people, particularly development programmes for future leaders, graduate entry programs and the development of middle management. Wise leaders also never neglect plain skills enhancement for other workers and staff. Noel Tichy, a University of Michigan professor and consultant, has found that really successful organizations concentrate on producing a 'leadership engine', which produces high quality leadership skills in all the junior, middle and senior managers of a business. Organizations should not rely on having one of the few great leaders around. They can overcome the need for 'one great leader' by creating high quality *leadership* throughout the organization. How? By creating an appropriate people development and mentoring system throughout the business. All the leaders in the business should take responsibility for developing people proactively. With leadership as a culture, the business creates a resilience which safeguards the organization during those times when new, top leaders are settling in or when they are just not the best there could be.

Another factor in good leadership is the choice of quality subordinates. There is probably no other explanatory variable that can make or break a leader's career than the ability to select, appoint and retain quality people. Many successful people have claimed 'I don't need to be good. I just surround myself with good people!'

Alongside good people, it is always advisable to install a mentoring system, whereby the best amongst the leadership group choose subordinates in the organization to mentor, teach and look after. This ensures that the best people are being brought on and succession is being prepared. Of course, there is a supplementary advantage to mentoring systems, they keep leaders in touch with live projects going on around the business, and ensure that any necessary warning signals about the quality of succession planning, are being monitored and reacted to. Great leaders also pay heed to the problem of succession to themselves. A good leader succeeded, by an idiot, becomes, retrospectively, a poor leader. If the business is going to fall to pieces as soon as they leave because they were too 'great' to have good people around them ready to succeed, they have no right to the title of 'greatness' at all.

This also raises the question how we might expect a good leader to deal with rivals for their own position. If a rival is worthy, some choose to encourage them *at a distance.* However, the wisest leaders I know, often choose a different reaction and keep their rivals close to hand. That way, they can measure their rival's ambition compared to their knowledge and wisdom. If the rival is really good, they will not endanger their leader. If they are better, a truly wise person would put them in charge and take an appropriate bonus for doing so. Before that they will give them testing responsibilities. As they succeed, they can promote them fast. You won't want a high quality personal rival working for the competitor and you need to discover just how good they are. Prepare them for succession. You might find they are just too good for your organization because the business does not have enough potential for their talent. In that case, send then to another organization to give them the future they deserve. Of course, if, upon testing, they prove unworthy, there are other choices. They may be unworthy but nice, most leaders I know keep them around somewhere useful. If they are nevertheless of value to the organization, albeit, not as a potential successor, then they need to be developed to make the best use of their skills for the business. If they have few redeeming features, dismiss them. If they are really nasty, give them a superb résumé and send them to work for the competition!

Good leaders always pay attention to the ratio between fixed and variable costs. The former are always dangerous because they cannot be managed away easily. With the latter, the more variable the costs of the business, the more the organization can react to its markets. Wise leaders always try to minimize fixed costs or render them more variable. Variable costs are always a preferable form of overhead because these maximize the flexibility of the organization's capacity to adapt to any external circumstances. Redrawing the lines between fixed and variable costs is a major work of art. Great leaders do it creatively, efficiently and fast.

Finally, in my experience, leaders monitor long-run demographic trends because these provide the vital indicators about potential, future employees and customers. In other words, all the opportunities that the future, with imagination added, can offer. If we understand what people truly want in the long run, we have the necessary information on how to survive and thrive. These data will link closely to the classical marketing information which all leaders monitor, such as long-run consumer tastes, technological breakthroughs in associated and non associated industries, and the long-run nature of consumer trends themselves. If you do not know what the consumers of the twenty-first century are going to want, no matter what sector your business is in, you will, sooner or later, lose touch with their potential effects upon your business.

How leaders move ideas from creativity to executive implementation

There appears, in most businesses of size, to be a fairly predictable pattern of action. It goes, normally, in three stages:

- Stage 1. In normal corporations, ideas come from the Research and Development or New Product Development departments.
- Stage 2. Ideas move from NPD departments into marketing for analysis of potential sales and their sustainability.
- Stage 3. They then move into operational analysis and thence production.

What should the leader be doing at each of these stages?

- Stage 1. Ensure corporation is making an appropriate level of investment in R&D and NPD.
- Stage 2. Ensure organization is marketing oriented and that marketing is keenly monitoring and stands ready to grab best ideas almost before they are ready.
- Stage 3. Ensure that operations care about the success of products and use their knowledge of practical market and consumer usage considerations to enhance the eventual market product.

AT&T offers an interesting insight which is fairly typical of the telecommunications industry. Traditionally, they have had a research centre continuously preparing ideas which nobody has tested against any criteria such as, 'will anybody out there be interested in this concept or product if it ever gets to the market?' They only need a small percentage of their ideas to become successful to justify their existence, while the business remains so profitable. As soon as AT&T has a downturn in its performance, we must anticipate the research department being among the first to be cut back, to force them to be more selective about what they choose to research and develop. They overcame this problem, partially, by floating off their research arm as Lucent Technology towards the end of the 1990s.

ICI displayed similar characteristics before Sir John Harvey-Jones, as Chairman, forced the research people to justify their existence with predictions and prognostications about the market for their research. If they couldn't, he forced them to stop spending the money.

While the above-described stages are taking place, the leader must keep the overall portfolio of company products and services within view. S/he must also simultaneously consider a whole range of other options:

- the average age of the product and services portfolio;
- whether the balance of products is in primary, secondary or final (mature) stages of their product life cycle;
- whether the general portfolios of the organization are becoming obsolete;
- whether the corporation should be moving strategically into newer areas of investment and development which offer greater capacity for long-term survival and succour to the body of the organization;
- which combination of the mature portfolio should be invested in new development to keep the balance of the stakeholders in equilibrium.

It's a fairly formidable list. It probably enforces the concept that leaders without creativity are probably as useful as cars without fuel or people without food.

Summary

This chapter has debated the concept that leadership creativity is fundamentally different from that of the generally acknowledged inventiveness of normal managers and strategic thinkers. It has described the creative and dynamic balances and qualities that leaders need, as well as the traits they need genetically and the skills they have to acquire. It also sets out some qualities they should suppress and do not require, such as technical ability and classical innovative imagination. It explains that leaders should avoid anger and detail. Leaders often use litmus tests to manage their people creatively, as well as the 'helicopter tool' and a 'time machine' to keep things in perspective. After a warning about the 'power of stupidity' and the use of PR, the chapter tells leaders to have the courage to change their minds if circumstances require it. Finally, leaders are reminded that they must move on from creativity to implementation at the right moment. The timing of the process requires creativity in itself.

11. Self-appraisal

Can it be done?

The capacity to be objective about ourselves is probably the hardest thing to achieve in life. If, as a leader, you are not able to do it, it is highly unlikely that you will also be able to be objective and impartial when forming judgments on behalf of the organization you are leading. Most relatively intelligent people know themselves quite well. What they often find hard to do is acknowledge their weaknesses consciously. The truth is that most of us prefer not to face up to our worst short-comings or failings. It makes us uncomfortable and most people assume that they cannot do anything about many of them.

In this chapter I will review all the important issues which will enable you to understand whether you are cut out to be the leader of an organization. As we have described in previous chapters, there are many different types of organization and as many sizes of business as there are people. Even if you are unfit to be the leader of a giant corporation, you may see yourself as leader of something smaller. There are many things left to lead besides the giants. There is a multitude of small and medium firms as well as many social, charitable and other organizations that are crying out for people who are prepared to accept some of the responsibility of leadership. If that is how you perceive yourself there will be many opportunities to implement your vision. But if you assess yourself as not fit to run a large corporation then the organization and yourself may both be much better off.

Personal birth circumstances

The circumstances surrounding your birth are probably the most impor-tant influences that you have no control over that play a leading part in your capacity to be a leader or, indeed, upon the whole of the rest of your life. First, there will be a genetic inheritance that parents have given. That is the first indication of who we are and what we are likely to grow up into. That would seem to indicate a relatively brief and easy analysis of our parents. Unfortunately, that is easier said than done. Otherwise, there would be very little reason for the amount of mutual discomfort that so many parents and children experience. Similarly, it explains why so many parents whose children have grown up, fail to have a good relationship.

The relationship between a child and its parents, in most circumstances, is naturally close. We probably live more closely and intimately with parents than with any other person except a spouse or partner in later life. The problem is that the relationship is not one of equals. Your parents job is meant to fulfill a teaching role, giving you your moral paradigms as well as how to look after yourself and survive physically when you will eventually have grown up. It is extremely difficult to value our parent's and assess their effect upon our personality in an objective manner.

Later in the chapter is laid out a questionnaire which, if you answer it frankly and honestly, will help you gain a deeper insight into the formative make-up of yourself and what makes you tick. It is labelled 'An enquiry into your emotional horizon'. Those questions will guide you to the subjects and relationships you need to examine and think about in order to try and understand as objectively as possible the aspects of your evolutionary years between birth and, perhaps, 25 years of age, when almost all the major inputs which created your 'emotional values and character' took place and which control and guide your actions through the rest of your life.

If the reader completes any normal questionnaire on emotional intelligence s/he would find that many of the questions remind them of the questions in my 'emotional horizon inquiry'. However, in too many emotional intelligence questionnaires you are asked to focus on recent events. That means that it is studying your short-term behaviour to look for patterns of emotional behaviour today. The questions in my 'Inquiry into your emotional horizon' are designed to help you interrogate where your values emanate from. This, in turn, will allow you to understand the causes of the behaviour you enact. The questions are, therefore, much more fundamental and important than those in an emotional intelligence questionnaire. I hope you will be able to be honest with yourself. I suggest that all your answers should be written down in order for you to test them against friends, siblings and possibly a spouse. They may help you to see the significance and effect of some of the things you will have written about yourself, your values and your behaviour. They may also be able to help you see things in a new light and more objectively. Sometimes they will help you refocus your interpretation of what has happened to you. That can assist you get things into perspective.

The use of psychometric analyses

We listed in Chapter 4 a whole range of psychometric exercises. These are exercises based upon questionnaires which enable their responses to be compared to norms. These are established from all the previous answers to the questionnaire by other respondents. When an individual is compared to the many others who have previously completed the exercise, their similarities and differences can be revealed. Psychometric analytical tools can be most efficacious when trying to analyse our own or others peoples' personality or character.

Some are more profound than others. The Belbin team skills test, for example, is useful but gives little profound long-term insight into character. Rather it informs the user about the current preferences of the recipient in what they contribute to a group's team needs at the point in time when the test is administered. One great value of psychometric testing is to test what intuition is telling you about the people around you or about yourself. They can be used to confirm impressions given during interviews or when working alongside somebody. They are particularly useful if there are behaviours which we cannot find an explanation for but which give cause for doubt or worry.

Psychometric tests are also useful as a means to initiate a discussion on topics which most individuals find awkward, whether in a work or domestic setting. They can liberate both the respondent and the facilitator and 'create' the right atmosphere to talk about sometimes difficult and intimate subjects. Their use can get one into interesting and revealing discussions faster than any other development or teaching technique.

We must always remember that psychometric testing sometimes gives warnings or indications about the sadder and more difficult aspects of people's psychological make-up. It is vital that adequate provision is always made in both time and resource for these major problems to be followed up with counsellors and other advisers who have the time and skills to help those who have uncovered more than they can deal with alone.

Psychometric tests can be used to facilitate the creation of a balanced executive team or a board of directors. When the test results are shared among key players in the organization, they can give everybody a common vocabulary with which to express their feelings, their thinking style and their behaviour. This can be important, later, when working together in emergencies or even on mundane organizational processes. When used sensitively, psychometric tests can provide major indicators to handling gifted but difficult executives. They give the essential clue how to maximize their individual contribution.

Some careers advisers base much of their advice on psychometric testing as a means of helping people decide their choice of employer. Similarly, many employers use them to get a basic understanding of the type of temperament, style, preferences and the inhibitions a person may be bringing with them into a job.

A few people have themselves tested every few years to keep track of their personal progress in emotional maturity, to control any less desirable qualities and to ensure that they are still keeping to the sensible career path dictated by their consciousness and their inner needs.

I began using an emotional intelligence test evolved from the work of Goleman (1996) in *Emotional Intelligence* and others, such as Cooper and Sawaf (1997) in their *Executive EQ*. This type of test is not yet fully evolved but already helps those completing it to gain interesting insights into aspects of their emotional 'wear and tear'. These effects can play havoc with a person's emotional energy and reduce their capacity to be effective in both their private and business lives. The questions listed are typical of those used in emotional intelligence tests, although I prefer to focus more on the long-term causes of profound behavioural imbalance rather than on the shorter-term causes of current turmoil which seems to be the methodology of many emotional intelligence tests.

Below are described in more detail a few of the psychometric exercises most frequently used (in the UK).

1: Myers–Briggs Types Indicator

The Myers–Briggs Types Indicator is one of the most commonly applied tests in the business world. It describes a respondent's personality on four axes. They are:

- introversion/extroversion;
- sensing/intuition;
- thinking/feeling;
- judgment/perception.

It is based upon the fundamental work of the psychologist Jung. It was developed by Isabel Myers and her mother Katharine Briggs. It is designed to make a fundamental examination of the effect of psychology upon personality. Common sense will tell the reader that there can be up to 16 different settings of the four axes given above. They are shown on Table 11.1.

The Myers–Briggs Type Indicator is highly esteemed by its many practitioners. I have seen it used to great effect by leaders to gain insights into some of their key executives. Many use it as part of their selection criteria for new employees at senior level. However, I have some reservations about it which do not diminish its general merit.

First, its practitioners tend to use too much mumbo-jumbo when they talk to each other and their respondents. Occasionally it is used in too technical a manner, so you cannot see the wood from the trees. It can be confusing to some respondents because it has so many types they find it hard to see what is, and what is not useful, when they examine their results or those of their people. Nevertheless, it does help respondents to understand the full range of human behaviour and to have

Table 11.1 The Myers–Briggs types

Introvert (people who renew their mental strength internally and alone)

Sensing types		*Intuitive types*	
Thinking	*Feeling*	*Feeling*	*Thinking*
ISTJ	ISFJ	INFJ	INTJ
sensing, thinking and judging	sensing, feeling and judging	intuition, feeling and judging	intuition, thinking, and judging
ISTP	ISFP	INFP	INTP
thinking, sensing and perceiving	feeling, sensing and perceiving	intuition, feeling and perceiving	intuition, thinking and perceiving

Extrovert (people who renew their mental strength from interaction with people)

ESTP	ESFP	ENFP	ENTP
sensing, thinking and perceiving	sensing, feeling and perceiving	intuition, feeling and perceiving	intuition, thinking and perceiving
ESTJ	ESFJ	ENFJ	ENTJ
sensing, thinking and judging	sensing, feeling and judging	intuition, feeling and judging	intuition, thinking and judging

greater sympathy with people who have entirely different temperaments to themselves.

2: The FIRO-B: introduction and explanation

The Behaviour Questionnaire is closely based upon the work of Jung and was developed by W. C. Schultz (1955). FIRO-B stands for *F*undamental *I*nter-personal *R*elations *O*rientation-*B*ehaviour. It examines the way people typically interact with others. It is helpful in any work setting, especially when we combine this knowledge with information about people's interests, skills, values, and desires. When we work in situations where our natural tendencies are in harmony with the job, the employee is happier, does better work and has more of a competitive edge.

The FIRO-B questionnaire helps people become more aware of their interpersonal behaviours and habits. They can then adjust their behaviour where it might cause distortions in people's reactions to them. The FIRO-B gives information about individual on three aspects of work behaviour:

(1) inclusion;
(2) control;
(3) affection.

Each dimension has two poles, which are:

(1) how much you express to others;
(2) how much you need from others.

Control may be better expressed as:

(1) how much control you want over others;
(2) how much control you will accept from others.

Inclusion

The *Inclusion* dimension refers to a person's social skills. *Inclusion Expressed* refers to the social skill whereby one makes people feel they are being included in the social and business life of the department. *Inclusion Wanted* refers to how much you *really* want to spend social time with those people other than the necessary minimum. *The two measures of Inclusion together* indicate whether a person has too large a differential between the social skills of giving an intimation of sociability and their actual preference to be alone. Too low a score on *inclusion* expressed also indicates that they may lack some of the social skills necessary for leadership.

The second dimension of FIRO-B is *Control*. *Control Expressed* describes *how much control a person likes to exert over others*. *Control Wanted* describes how much control a person is willing to accept from others. This dimension can indicate when a leader resembles what I have called a *nominal leader*. Such leaders often exhibit an excessive need to control others, accompanied by an inability to accept control from anybody else. High *control* expressed people tend to attempt excessively high objectives. They then either fail to deliver results or they deliver them at excessive cost to the organization (in people and resource terms), thus making it harder to deliver reasonable expectations in the future. They also annoy the more rational thinkers among their subordinates who understand the goals they aim for are excessive.

The third dimension of the FIRO-B is *Affection*. This relates to deep, rather than superficial, personal relationships. *Affection Expressed* describes how much affection a person expresses to other people. *Affection Wanted* describes how much affection they want from others. Some leaders, who exhibit a low need for affection, may have an unbalanced attitude to their private life. If the test indicates an excessive need for affection from others, it could indicate a degree of insecurity and dependency which is problematic for a leader. Significantly, on this scale, very low scores on both affection wanted and given could be a signal of an emotionally isolated or stranded lost soul. I always try to investigate these cases when I discover them. There is nearly always a serious problem underlying such results.

FIRO-B also gives another indicator which is relevant and important to leadership practice. It is the Expression of Anger Score (EAS), which can sometimes be more easily understood as the 'frustration score'. It indicates how much frustration or anger you show people. People who display low anger fail to give appropriate signals to people about the effects of their behaviour. When anger scores are too high it usually means that person's anger is causing people around them to avoid them. Eventually, they become isolated, get little feedback from their staff and render themselves ineffective. When anger scores are too low, it indicates that a person fails to give sufficient feedback to their subordinates (because they are uncomfortable when giving clear signals of dissatisfaction to people).

FIRO-B is a remarkably accurate gauge of how people behave at work. When used by skilled practitioners, it can give a powerful insight into how a person is perceived at work. I find it astonishingly perceptive about people's entire emotional and management vocabulary. It is particularly useful when analysing social skills, people's need to control and their anger scores.

3: The Belbin Team Skills Test

For the greater part of a leadership career, leaders lead teams. Sometimes the leader's capacity for individuality will not only be superfluous but could even get in the way of the team's need to achieve its objectives. A leader must know, under these circumstances, what their own team skills may be. One of the best questionnaires on team skills is the Belbin Self Perception Inventory. It is available freely from Dr Belbin's book (1991), *Management Teams.*

The essence of Dr Belbin's work is that no individual can combine all the qualities it takes to accomplish a total team effort. This is why it is the team that is the instrument of sustained and enduring success in business. The implication is that we should devote far more thought to teams, their selection, development, psychology, motivation, composition and behaviour. The problem is that our knowledge of what makes teams successful, is tiny.

Dr Meredith Belbin's crucial contribution is that all members of a management team have a dual role. The first role is that of fulfilling our functional specialty; a manager belongs to the team because s/he is an accountant or production engineer or whatever. However, people working in a team tend also make a general contribution to the whole team's achievement of the task. Furthermore, people tend to deliver similar types of contribution to the team effort besides providing their functional role. Some always come up with bright ideas, or move the team towards a final decision or insist on checking the team has completed the task as requested. These people are likely to show the same characteristics whatever team they belong to.

Dr Belbin has found eight characteristic roles that all teams seem to display and are needed in a team to achieve balance. They are:

(1) chairperson;
(2) company worker;
(3) plant;
(4) resource investigator;
(5) shaper;
(6) monitor evaluator;
(7) team worker;
(8) complete finisher.

If we think about the process of a team accomplishing a task all the roles fall into place. A chairperson organizes the team's task. The company worker schedules all the subparts that must be done to accomplish the task. The plant comes up with ideas how to solve the problems. The resource investigator finds out how other teams have done it in the past in cases where the team cannot 'create' an original solution. The team worker soothes the ruffled feathers and looks after peoples' feelings when the shaper (who tends to be maniacally task driven) has upset them. The monitor evaluator tells the team when it is half way through whether and how it is going wrong and that it should consider changing direction or method. And the completer finisher ensures that everything is done correctly and thus does nor incur wasteful costs.

Below is a very brief summary of the traits and meaning of each of these:

(1) *The chair*: The chair is a person who clarifies the group's objectives and sets its agenda. They are stable, dominant, extrovert and tend to preside over the team and coordinate its efforts to meet goals and targets.
(2) *The company worker*: The company worker is a person who, once given a decision will produce a list or schedule.
(3) *The plant*: This person is usually the team's source of original ideas, suggestions and proposals. They tend to be dominant with a high IQ. They are usually introvert.
(4) *The resource investigator*: These people make friends easily and have masses of outside contacts. They are stable, dominant and extrovert. The person who usually 'knows someone who has one of the things we need'.
(5) *The shaper*: The shaper is only reassured by the task and by results. Their results driven behaviour has a compulsive quality.
(6) *The monitor evaluator*: These people mull things over and give objective judgments. They usually have a high IQ, as well as being stable and introvert. They often appear to be a bit of a cold fish.
(7) *The team worker*: The team worker may be better thought of as the

team friend. This person promotes unity and harmony and counter-balances friction and discord.

(8) *The completer finisher*: The completer finisher is a compulsive meeter of deadlines and fulfiller of schedules. They tend to be anxious and introvert, worrying constantly about what might go wrong.

Belbin finds just eight team roles. What happens if you have fewer than eight people? Everybody has 'secondary' team skills. Thus they can double up when necessary and perform more than just one function.

Balancing the team is not of the same importance in every kind of operation. For instance, a group whose principal role is to supervise steady and continuous process without much change over the years with no great need for alteration or innovation, will have little use for the plant role.

Teams are important. But great leaders get things right, in spite of sometimes being stuck with poor teams. They tend to work on improving their team from the start. The case below tries to put things into perspective This man had the training, he even had the brains; but he didn't have the insight into his own strengths and weaknesses to know what he needed his team to be – to make him what he needed to become.

Mini case study: Teams can lose businesses as well as win them

A senior executive worked for many years as a bright and extremely intellectual leader. He was sent on a Managing Director's programme by his employer to prepare him for leadership at that level. This man had a tendency to intellectualize most business problems.

Unfortunately, this skill was not accompanied with a capacity to relate to his colleagues at a human level at work. This doubt was recorded in the programme and explained why his promotion to Managing Director status came many years later than he expected. But, at last it came.

When he had been in the post about a year he ran into difficulties because the new Board of Directors he had formed was not really knitting as a team. Unfortunately, by the time he asked for help, he had already changed most members of his team. He had new Directors of Marketing, Information Technology and Finance.

When asked what criteria he had used to compose his team, he responded 'They are the most thoroughly intellectual group of people I could have wanted. Every one of them has a high IQ.' It was pointed out that he, as MD, had enough brain power and IQ for any team. What he needed from his people was empathy and emotional insight into the feelings running around the firm and its customers to cover his personal lack of these skills.

But it was too late; the new people were in position. A year later he and his Board decided to change the firm's technology. It was an intellectually daring and exciting challenge. The change went catastrophically wrong when the workers in the company proved unable to change their work habits. The firm started to lose money at the rate of 10% of total revenue. He and his Board were all asked to leave the firm.

Emotional quotient tests

The following questions (see Questionnaire 11.1) do *not* form an emotional intelligence test as such. Those tests tend to be rather more formal and to focus on events which take place at intervals and episodes between 1 month and 1 year prior to the test. My questions are more designed to enable you to examine the landscape and horizons of the important events in which went into the formation of your emotional profile. It is designed to guide you into asking yourself the most important questions about all the matters likely to be relevant. It will also remind you how you received your social, ethical and emotional values from the people who are usually important to anybody in their formative years.

I have not weighted the questions and answers because each person's individual responses will dictate the importance of any data that the questions are intended to remind you to take into account.

Examine the following list of questions and reminders about significant aspects of almost everybody's life. Reflecting on each will help you see yourself in an objective light. When a particular question does not seem to apply to you, think how what it describes might have affected you anyway, if you had experienced it. For example, a lack of siblings or a father missing from most of your childhood. What effective difference did that make to your life compared to other people?

Questionnaire 11.1 An inquiry into your emotional horizon

This questionnaire is a guide to understanding emotional predispositions and behavioural styles. Please reflect upon each of the relationships referred to, line by line. If any does not apply to you, think about the effect that missing relationship(s) had upon you compared to the effect it had upon other children (e.g. having siblings or an absent-from-home father). We advise you to write down your answers and consider them again on a regular basis.

Parental circumstances

Father   Was born to low income or unemployed parents?
       (your parental grandparents)
       Mixed (one poor and the other comfortable)?
       both comfortable?
       One comfortable and the other wealthy?
       Both wealthy?

Mother	Was born to low income or unemployed parents? (your maternal grandparents)
	Mixed (one poor and the other comfortable)?
	Both comfortable?
	One comfortable and the other wealthy?
	Both wealthy?
	Did either parent deliberately rebel against the values they received from their parents? Why?
Father	What job does/did he have?
	Was it a recognized profession?
	Was he proud of his work?
	Did he work long hours?
	Did he read to you in the evening?
	Did he play sport with you?
	What did you speak about when you spoke?
	Was it about emotions or solid facts?
Mother	What job does/did she have?
	Was it a recognized profession?
	Was she proud of her work?
	Did she work long hours?
	Did she read to you in the evening?
	Did she play sport with you?
	What did you speak about when you spoke?
	Was it about emotions or solid facts?
Parents	Did they stay together?
	Were they loving or 'hands off' in their behaviour to each other?
	Did you receive pocket money?
	Did they make you earn it? How?
	If your parents divorced, do you remember the process?
	Does the memory hurt? How?
Step-parents	Did your natural parent die or were your parents divorced/separated?
	What effect did this have upon you?
	Did you have a step-parent?
	Mother or father?
	Did you feel they cared for you like a parent?
	What differences?
	Did your parent and step-parent have children of their own?
	How did that affect the family equilibrium?
	Did the step-parent favour their natural child/children over you?

Childhood circumstances

Did you live in a poor, middle class or prosperous neighbourhood?

Did you like where you grew up?

Did your parents move home rarely, if at all?

Did they move home frequently?

Did you feel stable as a child?

Did your parents take you on holiday regularly?

Did you go away to the same place or somewhere different every year?

Did your parents practice any religion?

Were you included?

What effect did that religion have upon your childhood?

Does it still have effects and what are they?

Orphans/ Adopted

Were you brought up in an orphanage?

What effect did this have on your self-esteem?

At what age were you adopted?

Did/do you know your natural parents?

What are the long-term consequences of adoption upon you?

Education

What are your most profound and affecting memories about your primary school? Secondary school?

Sixth form or pre-university school?

Did you go to university? If not, tell yourself the most honest reasons why not.

If you went to university what are your most profound memories about your undergraduate life?

Your time as a graduate student?

Family

Do you have siblings? (weaker indicator for leadership)

Are you the eldest? (strong indicator for leadership)

Are you the eldest male? (strong indicator for leadership)

Are you a middle child? (weak indicator for leadership)

Were you an only male child? (strong indicator for leadership)

Do you perceive yourself as your mother's favourite child? (strong indicator for leadership)

Were you your father's favourite? (positive indicator for leadership)

Did you have any strong relationships with any aunts or uncles?

What was the effect of those relationships upon you?

Personal circumstances

Have you married or lived with a partner longer than one year?

How many times?

Have you divorced or separated from a long-term partner?

What were the circumstances?

What residual effect has that left upon your attitude to relationships?

If you have had more than one long-term relationship, what were the similarities between the partners?

And the key differences?

Friends   Do you retain any friends from your childhood?

From where exactly?

Do you have many or few friends?

If you have lost all your friends from childhood days, who let who go? Why?

Do you make new friends easily?

Do you lose friends easily?

Why, in both cases?

How do you make new friends now? From what parts of your life (private? business? family? school? social? other?)

Economic circumstances

Do you feel yourself to be poor or rich?

How do your family consider your circumstances?

Are your friends richer or poorer than yourself?

Do you live in a substantially better quality home than your parents?

Do you live in a similar home to your parents?

Was that poor or middle class?

Friends   Do you have many or few friends?

Are they from your business or private life?

Do you go to regular and similar events or spontaneous and different events?

Would you like more or less friends? (honestly?)

How do you lose friends?

Mentors   Were you mentored at your first employment?

What level was your mentor?

Do you or they stay in touch?

Are any mentors from other employments?

Are you still in touch?

Do you mentor others?

Who and at what level?

Associates   Who do you associate with at work (if anybody)?

Do you have casual associates in your personal life?

What do you do with them?

Why have they or you not evolved it to friendship?

Is that a regular pattern of behaviour?

First employer   Were they a top quality employer?

Did they treat you as a high-flyer?

How long did you stay?

Is that length of time now a pattern?

Post university development	Have you done any other personal development work?
	Are you maintaining your knowledge increase rate?
	If not, why not?
	What have you planned in the next 12 months?
	If nothing, why?
Health	
	Are you in general good health?
	Were you sick as a child?
	Did you miss schooling as a consequence of any long illness?
	Did any illness as a child cut you off from other children?
	How did any illness affect your relationships with your siblings?
	Were any siblings permanently disabled?
	How did it affect family life?
	Are you permanently disabled?
	How did it affect your parents' behaviour towards you?
	Are you fully recovered from any childhood illness?
	What long-term effects has it left?
	Do you still suffer from any regular illness or physical discomfort?
	What effect does it have upon you?
	Have any 'middle age' physical symptoms begun yet?
	If so, how do they affect your temperament?
	Do you eat healthily or without reflection upon health?
	Do you drink moderately or excessively?
	If the latter, how often?
	Are you visibly overweight? Why?
	Do you know how to get your weight back to what it should be?
	If yes, why are you not doing it?
	If no, why don't you take the trouble to find out?
	Are your parents still alive?
	Are they healthy?
	Do you live a similar lifestyle?
	If your parents have died, how old were they when they died?
	Mother? Father?
	What did they die of?
	Are you avoiding all the contributory factors that caused their deaths?
	If not, why not?

If you have managed to be relatively honest with yourself and if you are lucky enough to have had few trauma which have distorted the transparency of your memory, then it is possible that, by asking yourself and thinking about your answers to all the questions in the preceding pages carefully, you will have reminded yourself of almost all the important events that have created the type of person with the precise emotional characteristics that control how you behave in your private and business life on a daily basis. You will also find that the power of the exercise is increased if you write all the answers down and review what you have written on a regular basis. This will serve two purposes. It will enable you to amplify your memory on issues as you think more about what you wrote last time. Secondly it will enable you to change those answers which you realize, in retrospect, you had recorded inaccurately.

You should measure the type of changes you make. Consider how many of the changes are amplifications of what you wrote last time. How many changes are really more contradictions or just utterly different interpretations of the same events? The more amplifications you make the more likely it is to mean you suffered few traumas. You are increasing the accuracy and depth of your memory as you work it harder. If you find yourself making profound changes and adjustments of interpretation treat this as a measure of your adjustment towards a more honest and meaningful insight into your own true make-up.

Can you help yourself?

How can you know if any imbalances, incorrect instincts or inappropriate automatic responses exist in your own range of behaviours? Study the way people react to you. You can tell, by and large, because most people can feel when they are behaving irrationally. We all tend to tolerate our worst behaviour too easily. We delude ourselves that we cannot do anything about it. It is necessary to force ourselves to ask what can be done to repair and rebuild all the imbalances, incorrect instincts or irrational responses, in one's profile. There are always solutions.

Read as much as possible of the literature on emotional intelligence and balance as you can; see the references in Chapter 6 and at the end of the book. When thinking about how you grew up, investigate your childhood deeply and carefully from your own memory but also from family members, such as siblings. Ask those who observed your upbringing. Although, they can never give you completely neutral views on your childhood nor your parents' strengths and weaknesses (neutrality doesn't exist in these matters), they can be informative. You can question close childhood friends, friends' parents, neighbours and others relations of the family.

Try to achieve a sense of neutrality about everybody's various observations of events. Then work hard to make fresh interpretations of any events and actions from your past that may have caused any irrational, automated responses in your behaviour patterns. Most of us have some. Remember that it is likely that they were not caused by any bad or wrong purpose or intention on the part of parents or guardians. They may just be the result of your own accidental and wrong interpretation of events by yourself (for which you will, of course, forgive yourself, when you sort it out).

If you are really unable to get new perspectives and change behaviours which you know are irrational and deleterious to your life, you may need to consider going to get help from a professional therapist.

Having a balanced emotional life is the most important aspect to having a happy life of any sort. You owe it to yourself to be happy. It is the right thing to do. There are no arguments against. None.

I have met some leaders who had particularly miserable business and personal lives. They thought they would never know happiness and had grown accustomed to thinking that they, somehow, had missed out on the *happiness gene*. When I insisted that everybody has a right to be happy and that they owed it to themselves to find out what stops them from enjoying their lives they were enormously buoyed up. In many cases those people managed to change their lives and, as I would put it, start living a full life of satisfaction at work and contentment at home.

What should you do about your personality (based on findings from tests)?

What do you do when the results of one of these psychometric tests demonstrate to you that you are not as perfect as you first perceived yourself to be? First, breathe a sigh of relief. The perfect human being is somebody we are all ready to hate! But then realize rationally that these tests are there to help you get an insight into yourself and the effect of your behaviour upon other people. It's rare that you discover something about yourself that is completely new. Rather the tests should be reminding you of behaviours that you have stopped paying attention and to remind you how others see you. That's often a salutary lesson.

Finally, psychometric tests can give you an agenda for change, especially when you are reminded that you and your family and friends may be paying severe prices for the leadership life you have chosen.

You need to ask yourself whether the price is too high for the rewards you are getting. I often think that the most valuable use of psychometric exercises is to tell you *what you cannot do* and *what you lack*. This tells you what you need from others, in a dependent way, to become a truly great leader.

A challenge

Using the information about the two tests described in detail in this book, complete Questionnaire 11.2. It is an amalgam of the concepts of the Belbin Team Skills Test and the FIRO-B questionnaire (Questionnaire 11.1). When you have completed it think about the implications of the questions and your score. What do they tell you about your own personality and traits? What are the best and worst features of your own behavioural habits? What should you do about them? Try to draw up a plan to obviate the worst effects of your key three weaknesses. Set yourself a target date by which you will have made some headway in combating their worst effects. Keep a timetable. When you achieve the first three goals, set three more. Make it a habit of self-improvement.

Questionnaire 11.2 Self-assessment: Using concepts from the FIRO-B, Belbin and Myers–Briggs questionnaires

Study the statements and then assess yourself on a scale between 1 and 10

1–2   means you do it very little;

3–4   means that you do it a little;

5–6   means you do it moderately;

7–8   means you do it a lot;

9–10 means you do it a great deal.

Then apply the multiplier and put the final score in the last column.

Number	Statement	Your score	Multiplier	Final score
1	When confronted with a problem or a decision your first instinct is to produce a list or a schedule		×4	
2	When you attend a meeting with a group of people, you tend to be the person who clarifies the group's objectives and sets its agenda.		×7	

	You enjoy coordinating the team's efforts to meet goals and targets.			
3	You tend to focus strongly on achieving each of your tasks and you are reassured only by results. That is a strong driver of what motivates you to work.		×3	
4	When meeting with a group of people, trying to solve a problem, you tend to be the person who comes up with original ideas, suggestions and proposals. However, you sometimes find it hard to get your ideas across.		×1	
5	You make friends easily and have masses of outside contacts. You like people and find it easy to get them to give you information.		×3	
6	You like to mull things over and give people objective truth. You usually get it right but find, quite often, that you are not appreciated by people when you do.		×7	
7	You enjoy being a friend to all members of your team. You believe it is your duty to promote unity and harmony and counterbalance the atmosphere caused when others are driving the team very hard.		×1	
8	When the rest of the team is pleased that it has completed a task you feel it is your duty to remind them they have failed to complete important details. Then you nag them to finish the job properly.		×2	

9	Your social skills come relatively easily and you get on well with people. They want to be in your team.		×5	
10	Having given your time to people at work, when you've completed your day, you prefer to keep further social interaction to a minimum.		×2	
11	As a leader you feel a strong need, because of your ability, to be in charge of others.		×5	
12	Although you are the leader, you feel no problem in letting others guide you whether they are above, below or at the same level as you in the organization.		×3	
13	You find it easy to express genuine, close friendship to people both within and outside the organization.		×3	
14	You like people to express their genuine close feelings of friendship to you both within or outside the business.		×2	
15	Most weeks you need a fair proportion of time on your own to recharge your batteries.		×2	
16	You find all types of people easy and interesting to work with, no matter what their skills or style.		×4	
Add your final total score				

Evaluation	
0–99	Possibly not destined for leadership
100–199	Potential competence but needs a lot of work
200–249	Competence beginning
250–299	High level of competence or, possibly, high drive with medium competence
300–349	Potential to be a fine leader
350–399	Probably always a fine leader
400–449	Moving close to top levels in major corporation
450–499	Destined for top levels in major corporation
Over 500	Should already be leading a large organization

Now, who are you?

If the reader has diligently completed all the questionnaires and guidelines so far in the book s/he should, by now, have a much clearer idea of their psychological make-up. Most people will be saying that they find it interesting but they have not discovered anything that they did not already know. A few others, possibly a significant minority, will have uncovered aspects of their life and consequent values and behaviours which surprise or disturb them. I suggest, humbly, that those who discovered few or no surprises should be asking themselves whether they have been honest enough or possibly whether they may be just a tinge complacent.

Some high achieving leaders are naturally more reflective. However, many are not. I am reminded of a general practitioner who used to be my medical doctor. He later became a professor of general practice. He told me that he expected all doctors who worked in his surgery to undergo a thorough course of psychotherapy. The objective of this was to ensure that the doctors in his large practice were treating the illnesses of the patients and not their own mental disturbances. The same could be required of leaders. They are in charge of the general body of the organization. The business will largely reflect their opinions, objectives, desires and values. If any of these are based on bad trauma or an unusually distorted childhood which has given them inappropriate, dangerous or unhealthy behaviours or ethics then it is likely that these would also become a contagious force within the organization that they lead, unless they are dealt with and modified.

This is not to imply that every leader should lay down on the psychiatrist's chair and put himself or herself through a total analysis. All leaders, however, should bear in mind that they are people who have the incredible drive and ambition to force themselves up the hierarchy of an organization via the greasy pole of ambition. They are, almost by definition, unusual and abnormal, even if they don't realize how much so. If they are good quality leaders their abnormality will stem from having an unusual and different intelligence from most other people. If they are poor quality leaders it is likely that their drive stems from an unhealthy and distorted personal background. Their drive may come from the manipulations of unhealthy parents or from the effects of unfortunate but bad experiences during their formative years. Whatever the cause of their ambitious drive, a leader owes it to themselves and the organizations that they lead, to investigate the source of any unhealthy abnormality. We repeat, some abnormality is normal and necessary to generate the drive to the leadership position. It is only the sick and dangerous aspects of unhealthy personal ambition that need to be adjusted.

What should you do about who you are?

In order to decide whether you need to do anything about your inner psychological make-up or values, you have to first find what needs adjustment. Everybody will have some inner view of themselves that is distorted or out of kilter from the way others would interpret any particular event and its potential effect. Everybody has their own idiosyncrasies or modes of distorted communication. It is a duty of all leaders to formulate and communicate their vision of what the organization should aim to be. If there is anything off balance or unusual about the way that they communicate; if the way they use language is distorted; if they misunderstand themselves or the world because their vision is mal-adjusted because of their childhood development; or, if their ambitions for top job are based upon distorted personal needs rather than genuine leadership aptitude, they have a duty to themselves and their organiza-tion to adjust their behaviour.

Leaders need to ask themselves what needs de-emphasizing and, in other areas, emphasizing more. Are there any areas in their emotional make-up which require revolutionary change? As with all important and difficult aspects of life, asking the questions is easier than making the changes and ensuring that the changes are real, meaningful, pur-posive and permanent. It is only too easy to make a superficial change in behaviour for a few days and fool ourselves that the 'makeover' has been successful. I have witnessed many leaders and senior executives on development programmes. Often we get their colleagues and subordinates to report back on them and tell us if they have really ad-justed their behaviour. Their behaviour stays changed as long as we are on the case. When we return after 6 months or a year and check again, we nearly always find they have reverted to type and readopted their previous inappropriate and unhelpful behaviours.

Why is it so hard to change? Because the behaviour we learn during our childhood and the traumatic experiences of our lives are deeply em-bedded into the electrical circuits of our brain. It has become automatic and ingrained. We frequently find that people have built up massive post hoc rationalizations to explain and excuse what they know could be interpreted as harmful, foolish or even crazy behaviour.

For example, one executive I worked with expressed some strongly right wing and anti-Semitic political opinions while on a senior pro-gramme I was conducting. I pointed out to him that both his boss and I were Jewish and his opinions were likely to be at least self defeating while he stayed in this particular business. They would also be consid-ered, by most normal people, as highly undesirable. Many organiza-tions would regard his values as distorted and dangerous. I invited him to ask himself why he held them. His response was to adopt an alienated attitude for the rest of the programme. Needless to say, his career did not progress much in that company. He did, however, manage to find a major global car manufacturer which shared his dis-torted anti-Semitic and racist value system. He continues to flourish there today. That particular manufacturer has recently been accused by trade unions of conducting a racist policy towards its black workers, even to the extent of removing them from photographs of their staff used for publicity purposes.

What this brief story indicates is that a leader has choices. He may choose to try to change and adjust his values and behaviour by adopting more socially acceptable norms. He may decide that perhaps society has got a better fix on how we should treat minorities, underprivileged groups, or, indeed, workers in general. On the other hand, he could choose to do nothing about his attitudes but merely to find an organization that conforms to his maladjusted values and opinions. There are many legitimate businesses which welcome such people. Anybody who has ever been taught by me will know that I always recommend people like that to join industries like tobacco which sell a dangerous product to people it puts into an addicted condition, thus enslaving them to what should be the eternal profit ridden shame of the shareholders.

I believe that most readers will try to change themselves. After all, it is simpler than trying to find maladjusted organizations to match what is wrong with their psyche! What advice can be given about change? First, like dieting to lose weight, it should be done slowly and surely. It can also only be done successfully and permanently if it is based upon a radical appraisal of the causes of the problem. That may not necessarily require help from external sources. It will require profound hard work on deciding what caused any wrong values, what values we would wish to replace them with and what behaviour will represent the new values properly. Then you have to decide how to monitor your success in achieving the desired change.

Most people who are sent on company development programmes go back to work after the course and immediately try to apply the lessons they have learnt. It is a well-known syndrome sometimes called by their subordinates the 'I've been on a programme phenomenon'. Naturally, most people around managers with this syndrome know that the phenomenon will not endure. For similar reasons you are advised not to change the way you behave in any radical way in the short term. Go at it slowly, letting people gently and imperceptibly observe your new ways of thinking and behaving. Let them adjust gently as you find out what it is that profoundly troubles you and what you find unsatisfactory about your current psychological make-up and the values which stem from it. You will not find it easy to decide on the changes you wish to make in your mind nor to actually make them. When you have done so, the behaviour with which you communicate your changed value system will evolve easily and autonomously. Take it slowly and gently in case you have to change your mind.

It is certainly not an objective of this book to persuade people to give up their ambitions to become as big a leader as possible. However, some people might decide, after carefully filling in and deciding upon the results of the questionnaires, that they do not really want to be a leader at all.

Mini case study: The deputy director

Some years ago I was teaching a programme to senior executives of local government in the United Kingdom. At the end of the 2-week programme, participants were invited to select any of the university faculty they wished to get advice from or help on any subject they might desire. The deputy director of a large authority walked into my office. He looked as if he had the weight of the world upon his shoulders. I asked him what he wanted to discuss. He responded that he was the deputy director of _____ . He wanted my help to formulate a plan to become the director.

I asked him to discuss his life in general first. It is hard to give advice without some background. He described his family life with his wife, daughter and son to me. He told me that they held strong religious values and their greatest love was going to the church choir to sing together. They spent most weekends either rehearsing or performing around the country. It was the thing that gave the most meaning to his soul and made his family life cohesive and united.

As he spoke about his family and the enjoyment they all took from their obviously wonderful life together, his whole body language and demeanor changed. It was as if the weight of the world was lifting itself. His face began to smile, the worry lines disappeared, his back straightened and he seemed to emit almost a glow of happiness as he described the family's private happiness.

It was not difficult to formulate my advice. I told him that he had just described one of the most beautiful family lives I could imagine anybody could have. I asked him why he wanted to become the director? He responded that he didn't want it. He just thought it was expected of him. I told him he would be foolish to take any risk with the fabulous family life that he had. He would be far wiser to remain as deputy director and not allow the appalling weight of responsibility of the director's job to intrude into his lovely personal life. That man walked out of my office as if he were walking on air. I may have deprived his authority of a great leader but I feel sure I had helped safeguard for his family the most wonderful husband and father that they could ever want.

Do you have a career leadership plan?

If you refer back to Chapter 5 on the development of a leadership career much of that material will also be relevant to what this chapter covers. Most great leaders do have an intuitive working leadership-career plan. That does not mean that they know what will happen from year to year or what jobs they will be offered or will be doing next. However, they do know, quite early on in their career, what level they believe they could achieve and approximately how they intend to get there. In this chapter you will have discovered a great deal more about the dynamics and drives of your personal family circumstances, if you have answered the questions we have invited you to answer honestly. Possibly you have discovered new aspects about yourself that you did not know. I hope that you realize it may take you many years to adjust to and overcome any negative effects. However, I earnestly wish that you do set out on the journey and that you reach your goal of emotional intelligence coupled with strategic and visionary leadership. That, together with your leadership intelligence, will combine to give you both a happy and prosperous working and private life, too.

Everybody knows the old joke that nobody lay on their deathbed saying 'I wish I had spent more time at the office'. That same epitaph could apply to most people who do not get down to sorting out the unsatisfactory aspects of their emotional profile. As a leader it affects many other people. As a human being it may only affect ourselves. But that is the only self that you have, surely it's a waste of life itself to reduce your potential happiness for the sake of a one-off effort in adjusting your psychological make-up or interpretation of events that happened to you before you had power over your own destiny.

Economists always assert that business exists to maximize profitability. Of course they never define over what period of time that maximization is to take place. When it comes to running and maximizing our personal life then it seems to me that the main objective must be to maximize our happiness. Most people reading that would consider it a cliché that cannot be operationalized. It is the thesis of this chapter that it certainly can. I believe that a person's duty is to optimize their lifetime happiness. So, let's discuss what we can mean by happiness.

What is happiness?

We always feel an aura of trepidation at the prospect of another of those attempts to define happiness. The reason is that everybody's definition is the right one for them, individually. If you are lucky enough to have the right job, enough hobbies and sufficient friends who make you happy, then you are a very lucky person indeed. Perhaps it is easier to define what unhappiness is. Some of the leaders I have worked with tell me they do not know what makes them happy. But they do know that they don't want to stop working manically for as many hours as they can every day to avoid the possibility that they may feel unhappy when they stop running. That is not a satisfactory interpretation of the meaning of happiness. Rather, it is a formula to keep so busy that you never get to ask yourself whether you are happy or not.

Most people are happy when they are busy. However, they are happier when they are doing things they want to do rather than just doing things because it prevents them from finding out they may be unhappy.

There is an important difference between the two. In the mini case on p. 243, that man knew he was happy when he was singing in the choir with his family. Most people will define their happiness in terms of doing things with people they love, usually a spouse or their children. However, if you ask them to think about it further they will usually say that happiness is maximized by having a healthy mixture of giving and receiving love, having good health, enjoying a pleasant and fulfilling job at a level which is demanding but not excessively difficult and having interesting hobbies and pursuits that offer a contrast from the many things they feel they have to do by duty.

For those people who have a special personal drive (some would call it a pathology) and a need to achieve, their happiness may depend more than the average person upon fulfillment at work at a senior level. They will feel a need to look after those who depend upon them at work as much as in their private life. However, even they will need to reflect upon their personal needs, what makes them happy over the whole horizon of a total life. After all, like many people who were lucky enough to be born in the privileged top 20 or 30 materially advanced nations of the world, the wealth, accumulated goods, retirement packages and family protection that they can surround themselves with may well fulfill all their sociobiological needs but leave them feeling unfulfilled spiritually. We may all be lucky to be born where we were. That does not remove nor diminish the right to maximize happiness in the lucky place we are born even if we are lucky compared to those less fortunate than ourselves.

Like everybody else, you have to ask yourself whether everything you are currently doing in your business and in private family life is getting you to where you want to go. Does your answer apply equally to your non-business non-family social life? If your answers are all affirmative, congratulations. If not, answer the questionnaires and start work on the most important goal of them all, the pursuit of happiness. I hope this chapter has helped show you the path.

Summary

This chapter has guided the potential and actual leader along the paths of self analysis. It urges objectivity, as far as it is possible. It recommends using psychometric tests as well as the author's own 'Enquiry into Your Emotional Horizon'. It explains the details of a few preferred tests, particularly the FIRO-B and the Belbin team skills tests. The former gives insights into the balance between a person's needs to exert and accept inclusion, control and affection, as well as levels of anger and social activity in general. The latter (the Belbin) indicates a person's contribution to any team they work with. Those qualities are distinct from their technical ability which is what the business is primarily employing them to deliver.

12. The Politics of Leadership Roles

Let's define

'Politics' is defined as 'the art or science of government' in the *Longman Dictionary of the English Language*. That is exactly what a leader does when s/he practises the political arts in a business. Organizational politics refers to both the informal and the formal processes by means of which all organizational and corporate executives work alongside each other. This definition is deliberately couched in a non-pejorative and objective form. That is because politics is a perfectly normal part of organizational behaviour. Good politics is equivalent to a high-quality process and is just the best means of getting things done. Bad politics is the way that some people get the wrong things done using political methods to beat either better quality ideas or to defeat higher qualified and more appropriate leaders.

I believe it is important to accept this relatively innocuous and neutral definition. It will be demonstrated throughout this chapter that many people who fear the actuality of a job at the top of an organization express that fear as 'a dislike of the politics in the job at that level'. That is really being unfair to the concept of politics as normal senior level organizational process. It is not the politics that they are really frightened of. Rather it is the job they are terrified of and believe they will be unable to cope with. Many people who get promoted beyond their level of competence become intimidated, racked with nerves and display many dysfunctional behaviours. These will include high levels of aggression, petulant anger, nervous fear, physical illness, irrational stress and inappropriate reactivity. A proportion of these people will turn to behaving politically (in the pejorative sense) in order to avoid responsibility for their inability to perform their job. That is what gets politics a bad name and the derogatory slant that make most people believe that all politics in organizations is bad.

One person's politics ...

Politics at the top of organizations is that part of organizational decision-making which facilitates and eases the process of getting things done. This is neither a trivial, nor trite, statement. It could sound like it to those who 'can't stand politics' or imagine that politics at the top of organizations are internecine and nasty and that all Board Rooms are a den of vipers and fit only for the criminals of corporate evil-doing. Actually, life at the top of almost all the organizations I have been close to, is pleasant, most of the time. This will ring eminently true for leaders who know how to get things done.

Most Board Rooms are free of the nasty pictures of politics that are painted in television dramas, or falsely rehearsed in Sunday newspapers by journalists when they are short of information and long on imagination. Naturally, there are times when the temperature rises and leaders need to summon all their concentration, guile and cunning to deal with crises of people or process. But those moments are relatively ephemeral and pass quickly. The general ambience is quiet and, when led by quality leaders, has the quiet hum of 'things happening smoothly and inexorably'.

What appears to be politics is, mostly, *organizational process*. It is the way that leaders persuade the stakeholders to consent to and approve their strategic ideas and vision. Senior echelon work has an etiquette that needs to be understood and followed by anybody seriously wishing to play in the top league in industry. It is usually well-mannered and relatively straightforward. But it has to be done right. If it isn't, the other parties become suspicious and assume there may be dangers lurking or the person they are dealing with cannot be trusted. Part of the etiquette requires the leader to know what to do, and how to do it, without actually having it explained in so many words. This is not because it's all some code learned at Ivy League universities or the top ten business schools. Nobody is totally sure, all the time, of quite what one is supposed to do or when. They are all guessing much of the time. Let me give an example.

Mini case study: Getting the process right

The Chairman of a large engineering business had been misled by some merchant banker 'friends' into taking an easy non-executive appointment after an illustrious career in the City. They told him it would be, practically, semi retirement.

Unfortunately, it did not turn out like that. Shortly after he was appointed, within a month or two, the Finance Director came to the Chairman to tell him of his discovery that the CEO appeared to be exploiting his position a little too ruthlessly. The CEO was ordering crates of wine every month. It was being charged to the company but was being delivered to his personal cellar. Furthermore, he appeared to be keeping, at the company's expense, an apartment in New York and another in Australia. He also seemed to have a mistress installed in each apartment, each on the company payroll as a personal assistant at inflated salaries. They did not seem to be reporting for work. At least, not at the office.

What did the Chairman want the FD do about it? For this highly ethical Chairman there could be no doubt. The CEO had to go and the sooner the better. But the FD had told him in confidence. And the FD was really a subordinate of the CEO, and should not, strictly speaking, have been speaking to the Chairman other than through the CEO, at all. The Chairman also had to take account of the fact that this CEO had grown the business 500% in five years and deserved better than an ignominious end to his career. Anyway, it could damage the company share price which was languishing at that time. It could even make the company a takeover target at a time when it would be in no position to defend itself, without a CEO.

The Chairman spent the next few months selecting new non-executive directors who were his personal appointees, to the Board. He then spoke to each privately, once they were installed, and told them of the problem. They agreed to authorize him to offer the CEO a package that would pay him off, on condition he went immediately. It set conditions of mutual secrecy. He then asked the CEO to resign with immediate effect, which he did. The episode was over. But it had taken 6 months and many more bottles of wine and wages to mistresses than most leaders like to donate to a lost cause.

That is a typical 'political' story from a Board Room. It would never normally see the light of day. Even now, of course, no names are being revealed. The players have long since retired from the field of battle. But it is a true story. Can such episodes ever be stopped? The simple answer is *no*. Even with the best governance in the world there will always be crooks and cheats at every level in some organizations. Sometimes, unfortunately, these villains are good business people too. The decision to remove them may be against the short-term interests of the shareholders. In the long-run crooks always damage the organization because, sooner or later, employees see what they do and copy them. Then the sickness becomes an epidemic throughout the organization.

Can the process of removal be made more efficient or be done faster? Again, probably not. There is some merit in the tardy etiquette of the Board Room. If it became too simple to organize top level removals, there would be many more false accusations and precipitate dismissals. It would begin to resemble the stories on the television rather than the rare event it tends to be, in the real world. That is not to deny that there is something fundamentally wrong with the way that non-executive directors intervene under current circumstances. Their power may be excessively circumvented. They rarely have control of a budget to enable them to obtain advice from lawyers or auditors. Too many of them are 'professional non-executive directors' who depend on a series of similar appointments to earn their living. They know that if they get a reputation for being too ready to get rid of chief executives, then it is likely that few chair people or chief executives will want to appoint them. More relevant still is that they only accumulate enough power to intervene in situations where the key problem is the chief executive after a considerable lapse of time and after his or her work has been proven categorically to be substandard and ineffective. Unfortunately, that is frequently too late for a successor to successfully nurse the organization back to health.

Politics at senior levels in organizations, varies by organization. It tends to be a function of the culture of each business, which, in turn, tends to be correlated to the nature and preferences of the leaders themselves. The amount of politics, as 'corporate etiquette', is also a direct function of the size of the organization. The larger the business, the more likely the Board is to contain members of the 'great and good' and other people who have spent lifetimes developing their career and their reputation. These people are usually reluctant to get themselves and their good names, caught up in unnecessary melodrama, or unpleasant newspaper headlines, if a matter can be dealt with without these disturbances. At the same time, they are highly sensitive to any danger to the investment they have built in their personal reputation over a lifetime career.

The *politics of organizational process*, the normal 'way things are done at top levels' is relatively benign. It usually requires the leader to spend time removing the psychological and other obstacles, that might prevent the Board from approving the leader's proposals. The purpose is always to neutralize the power of those who are able to stop any decision being taken, unless they have good business and strategic reasons for doing so. They must also ensure that those who approve, do so vigorously. In other words, the leader spends time, as would any member of a Church committee or governor of a local school, organizing all the people involved to agree a 'yes' before they are formally asked at the appropriate, conventional meeting (normally a Board).

Why call it politics?

We call these matters 'politics' for want of a better word. Politics is, really, just another name for *organizational process*. Unfortunately, the word is often used pejoratively, by those who do not know how to cope with them or who fail to learn the etiquette of the politics at senior levels in the organization. When an executive says 'he is tired of the politics in his job' or 'I wouldn't want the job above this present one because of all the politics at that level', he is really saying that he fears he will be incompetent at the next level. At every stratum in the hierarchy of any organization, politics can be described as 'just the process by which one gets things done'.

Sometimes another mistake is made, to believe that when all the top people are being pleasant to each other, it is just the bosses scratching each others' backs and playing politics. Frequently, being nice to each other and being political are just happy coincidences. They are the way that things get done. If it looks and is agreeable as well, that is a bonus. It also helps in the overall management process. If the procedure of an organization is normally enjoyable and the ambience easy going, when a leader has to 'crack the whip' the point is emphasized more than it might be if there was always a critical and angry tone prevailing.

Mini case study: Subterfuge target

Take, for example, the Divisional MD who also sat on the Board which governed his Group. He was asked to prepare a strategy review of his division for the Group Board. He had never done one before. Why did the chairman ask him to do it? Well, the review was really a means for the Group Chairman to transfer attention from the under performance of the Group led by that Chairman. The owners of the business were beginning to notice.

Meanwhile, the Division led by my client was doing well. But its results were being distorted by unjustified property charges, being made by the Group FD against the Division, upon the instructions of the Group Chairman. My client, the Divisional MD, was advised not to call the Group Chairman's unfairness to book. Instead he offered to make a private presentation to each of the members of the Board (especially the non-executive directors) prior to the main Board meeting when the strategy was due to be presented.

At these private presentations, he ensured that they understood how well the business was really doing if only the property were to be charged properly and fairly. By the time the strategy was delivered to the Board meeting, all the MD's ideas were accepted. They even voted several million pounds of extra capital to sort out the apparent property problems! The non-executive directors also found time to ask the Group Chairman questions about the under performance in the rest of the business. Strangely, the Group Chairman forgot to record the item in the minutes which voted the extra capital for property to the divisional MD presenting the strategy. The Board had to be reminded about it at the next Board meeting. The Group Chair grudgingly had to rewrite the minutes and hand over the money! Was this politics or just the way you do things at Board level?

Many readers will respond it is politics. It is hard to disagree. The sequel of the story is that the Divisional MD being advised eventually lost his job because he was unable to deliver the strategy he had devised. During that period he had been helped to survive and avoid every political bullet that was fired at him. Eventually he was just sacked with a large amount of compensation. I often wondered whether I had failed because I helped him devise a strategy he lacked the skills to deliver or had I let down the corporation in helping a less than able leader to survive too long through my devising 'survival politics' for him. The strange sequel of the story was that he was replaced by another person from another business who, many years before, had been trained in the arts and science of leadership and management by me. So, you see, that Chairman could not get away from a Levicki-trained leader!

Politics can be a bad rather than a good process

If politics is mainly 'managing the processes of corporate governance to achieve the strategic intent of the leader' that must be considered a good and necessary part of the leader's range of skills. Is there any time when politics may be considered a bad thing? They may be considered to be illegitimately used when they are employed to frustrate the implementation of a decision or to achieve mean or personal goals. In the example given above, there are some who might suggest that politics were being played. Some might say that the actions of the chief executive should have been denounced outright and his bluff called. But what rights had the MD to do that? The Chairman had actually done a fine job for the business, for over a decade. If the Board were to decide that his useful period in office was finished, they should make up their own minds and do something about it. That was not the Divisional leader's remit and it would have been invidious to interfere or try in any way to poison the minds of the rest of the Board against the Chairman. The main objective was to ensure that his Division received fair treatment.

Most managers start to use politics in the pejorative sense, when they are overwhelmed by their job and are not up to it. At the end of the day, there will always be some managers who are more skilled than average at getting on with people. This does not indicate whether they do or do not have any leadership ability. But when they have this human quality of being nice to everybody around and never ruffling feathers, they will certainly be able to maximize the use of any leadership skills they do have. Like the individual I described above, they can create a career from their 'political' or 'human' skills. If that is all they have, again, who can blame the individual for exploiting their assets. It is the corporation's job to ensure that people are effective rather than merely 'nice'. 'Niceness' is a pleasant bonus, when it is available.

Unfortunately, wrong-minded 'nominal leaders' will always be using politics to get their way against the wishes or good of the organization. It is important that good leaders ensure that political processes are kept to a minimum and are only used for the good of the organization.

The politics of the Board of directors

Boards of Directors exist to give guidance and direction to the leader and to act as a final buffer against bad decision-making by the leader. This is a contradiction, of course, because it is difficult to serve both purposes at once. If you are there to help, it is difficult to retain a critical and appraising eye on what the leader is doing. On the other hand, if you retain only a critical eye on everything the leader does, it won't be long before you find some, or many, faults. That is just the nature of the process of searching for fault. If you seek them you will always find things going wrong in any human endeavour, you can always find a problem!

The Board also exists to help the leader manage change. If the leadership of the firm proves inadequate, then the Board has to manage leadership change. We have discussed elsewhere in this book that this is a function they find very hard to implement. It is nearly always the case, that the situation has to be dire indeed before the Board usually manages to assemble the necessary power to do something about a deep and important problem. Often, by that time, it is almost certainly too late to do anything constructive about the problem. Profoundly difficult, strategic quandaries in an organization often have to start with a change of the leadership that created the problems. Unfortunately, by the time the Board summons the courage and means to resolve the problem in that radical way, it will have become extremely difficult for the successor to put things right.

The Board also exists to legally represent the owners and the shareholders' interests. This applies whether there is direct representation of the owners or shareholders on the Board or not (Figure 9).

The variables of politics

If we can agree to use the word 'politics' without the pejorative overtones, let's consider the variables, which govern the quantity of politics to be found in the average Board of Directors. The variables are set out in Table 12.1 (see p.258).

Each of these variables has a subtle influence and should not be underestimated in importance merely because it looks and seems innocuous. They have rarely been examined in the literature or isolated in this simple way. Yet they cover the gamut of the multifarious causes of variability of and need for politics at the senior levels of the Board and among top executives in modern corporations. Let's examine each of the variables in turn.

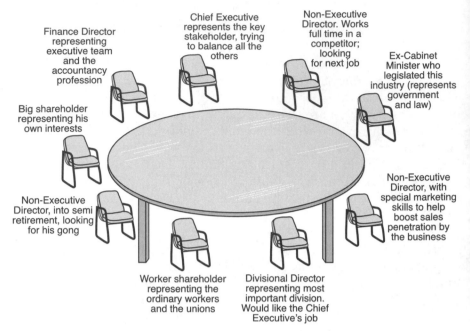

Finance Director representing executive team and the accountancy profession

Chief Executive represents the key stakeholder, trying to balance all the others

Non-Executive Director. Works full time in a competitor; looking for next job

Ex-Cabinet Minister who legislated this industry (represents government and law)

Big shareholder representing his own interests

Non-Executive Director, with special marketing skills to help boost sales penetration by the business

Non-Executive Director, into semi retirement, looking for his gong

Worker shareholder representing the ordinary workers and the unions

Divisional Director representing most important division. Would like the Chief Executive's job

Figure 9 Supping at the Board Table, a classic scene.

The size of the business

It is an emphatic absolute that the *larger the organization, the more the politics.* This is a consequence of decisions tending to be larger in magnitude. When the business is larger, necessarily, there will be a greater number of more complex barriers that decisions have to pass through to get to the top of the business. Large organizations tend to have, and need, more filtering systems than smaller businesses.

The number of persons who appoint people to membership

The more people nominating or appointing people to membership of the Board, the more politics. This is a function of the probability, that when only one or two people have nominated people to the Board, they are likely to have had an integrated concept about the strategic reasons for their nominations or appointments. It may have been to beef up the marketing skills, or consolidate the auditing skills, or control top salaries, by assembling a better Remuneration Committee. A diminishing variable on this rule is that the longer the period since people were appointed, the less united (and relevant) the Board will be. Also, there will tend to be more politics because the unifying vision will have receded over the years.

If the leader does the nominating

Usually, with good leaders, if they nominate the Board members, there are fewer politics. Obviously, if a leader were stupid enough to nominate people who were likely to vote against their ideas, by and large, they are probably too naive to make a good leader. This is not to say a great leader should nominate a set of toadies. Rather, it is asserting that a good leader will appoint people who, while capable of vigorous debate, will, in the end, coalesce around a single vision, with the leader, agreeing the direction for the business.

The befriending skills of the leader

Generally, the better the leader is at befriending the non-executive directors, the less politics there will be. This will result from the leader ensuring that they receive explanations about the policies, in private, before Board meetings, to ensure unity and approval, in advance, of formal Board meetings. If the leader finds the Board members unwilling or unhappy about any proposals, then s/he would be well advised to change or explain them before bringing them before the Board. When they have been changed, they should be checked, again, to see if they meet with approval. Boards are not meant to be rubber stamps, but neither are they the best place to sort out problems confrontationally. Better to solve big problems outside the Board room.

The quality of the leader

Usually, the better the leader, the less politics, because great leaders never present surprises to their board. It is surprises, which shock and worry other Board members, particularly the non-executive directors. They usually see their function as representing the shareholders (sometimes themselves), ensuring the smooth management of the business and guaranteeing that the executive managers and leaders carry out their responsibilities properly. All surprises, whether in the form of new strategic proposals (as Robert Ayling, former CEO of British Airways, did to his Board) or in the form of unexpected poor results, represent bad leadership. It means that the managers are not anticipating events, and acting with prescience, in advance of difficulties. That is poor leadership and needs to be scrutinized carefully.

Table 12.1 The variables of organizational politics

The political variable	Comment	Importance and frequency of politics
The size of the business	The arithmetic is the most compelling factor in politics in organizations*	< 100 staff: politics should be non-existent > 100 but < 1,000 staff: very low levels of politics > 1,000 but < 10,000 staff: managerial level skills required – politics small but can be dirty > 10,000 but < 50,000 staff: understanding of sophisticated processes of politics starts to be important, occupies 25% of time > 50,000 but < 100,000 staff: Subtle understanding, sharp instincts and capacity to proactively cope when attacked are vital > 100,000 staff: You cannot get to this level if you don't understand and know how to cope with every subtlety of organizational politics
The number of persons who appoint people to membership	Different Boards are nominated in various ways. Some have many people with nominating power; others have few or just one.	The more people who have the right to nominate or appoint, the less unified the Board and the greater the politics. The less people nominating or appointing, the greater the unity and the lesser the politics.
If the leader does the nominating . . .	The leader is usually, in this instance, the Chair. This can be problematic if the Chair and CEO fall out	If only one nominator or appointing person, the politics are minimized but there is a greater danger of the Board being railroaded to a poor decision. Can be useful when attempting to decrease boardroom dissent.

The befriending skills of the leader	These work both in finding good Board members and in maintaining relationships	Because befriending is a key leadership skill, this can usually be assumed. It is therefore not a key factor, but, nevertheless, important.
The quality of the leader	The better the leader, the less need for high quality non-executive directors	There are not many quality leaders, so this is a frequent cause of problems. Politics greater while they learn the leadership job.
The quantity and quality of meetings prior to Board meeting	This tends to be a factor of precedent and culture	Boards which meet less frequently often acquire a habit of dining together. This can be an indicator of less political intervention from the Board. Usually, one can assume, the more frequent the Board meetings, the more politics there will be.
The competence of the leader	A leader's best skills should not be in politics, but it helps if they have them	Competence in a leader is a function of their total leadership skills. However, in general, the more competent the leader in their strategic duties and ability to make profits, the less politics they will need to do

* See Gibrat R., *Les Inégalités Economiques*, Recueil Sirey, Paris, 1931.

The quantity and quality of meetings *prior* to the Board meeting

If there is an established habit of holding meetings prior to the actual Board meeting, it usually indicates that problems and objections are being looked for and solved before the meeting itself. This is usually different to the pre-Board dinner or elaborate lunch that some Boards indulge in. Those are far less useful, and sometimes positively dangerous, for the health of the older directors!

In essence, all good leaders try to ensure that they are going to get a *yes* to anything they intend to present to the Board, well before the actual meeting itself. If there is a chance of the Board voting against any policy that the leader is advocating, any good leader just wouldn't present it, for the excellent reason that they would never want their Board to develop the habit of saying No. Once they have learned to do so, there is always the danger they will continue to do so. Better never to let them get the taste of blood! A sensible Chief Executive or Chairman would always find out what it would take, in terms of changing their intended presentation and content, to adapt it to the requirements of the Board. Even then, they would test it again with those board members who had raised objections previously, before another Board meeting. Thus they would ensure that they could expect a favourable reaction, the next time they present it.

Some readers may be thinking at this stage that surely means that Board meetings are just a charade, a rigmarole of procedure with no substance. That is not true. In most businesses, the Board can still represent the best thinking and judging power within the whole organization. Indeed, in some, vigorous debates do take place at the actual Board meetings themselves. In my experience, however, this is not the best place for the hard and rough debates to take place. Those debates and arguments are best conducted prior to, and outside, the formal Board meetings. Such meetings are not the best forums to improve the quality of the decision. The Board should conduct, at best, discussions, to ensure that no key or vital points have been missed in the preparation for the decision. If the process of debate, rather than discussion, takes over at the Board meeting, the arguments tend to go with the people who are better at debating, rather than those who have the best ideas. Often the truly innovative and insightful business people on the Board are less articulate than the tough debaters. They may lose the debate, but the business will lose their good ideas!

One old campaigner I knew, an ex-academic who later worked in politics as a 'thinker' for a prime minister, was highly skilled at political debate, although less than useful at anything to do with business. He'd never truly experienced commercial life. His influence on many Boards was highly unbalanced because his debating skills were as excellent as his business knowledge was absent. He caused inordinate and pointless disruption on many Boards where he sat. His prestige and his title kept him there, even when many Board members had realized he added no value at all.

The competence of the leader

Competent leaders dominate their boards. It is part of their skill set. Of course, if it is the only skill they have, the business is in trouble, because a poor, but politically adept, leader will be able to persuade the Board to allow them to retain their leadership position, long after any quality Board would have discovered their incompetence. This is the type of situation where it helps when other City institutions, such as Pension Funds managers, or Bankers, exercise their influence, and intervene, when they become dissatisfied with the leadership and the business results it is delivering.

Similarly, because good leaders dominate their Boards with their character, they should never receive surprises from their Board. If they are using their befriending skills, they should know what's going on in the mind of the individual players on the Board, whether executive or non-executive, directors. That should enable them to anticipate whenever trouble looms. A good leader should always then, be able to exercise their will, because they will always have the force of *being right*. Likewise, they should be able to inspire confidence in the correctness of their decision because they ooze leadership competence.

Why is it hard to remove 'nominal' leaders?

It is sometimes difficult for a leader to organize a change of *nominal leader*. This can be terribly frustrating when an MD is a genuine *strategic leader* of a business but he has, as Non-Executive Chairman, a *nominal leader*. The nominal Chair level leader with a competent CEO strategic leader, will usually cause little trouble, particularly if they realize that they are meant to be *nominal* only. They are there in case of emergencies or to act as 'grand regulator' on behalf of the owners, institutions, or stock market investors. However, sometimes, they get a taste for interfering or meddling. This can become difficult for the real *strategic leader* and life can become somewhat strained in these conditions. The nominal leader can become a nuisance when he starts to flex his muscles and tries to capture power. It is probable that he understands power and how to use it if he is in the position of nominal leader, anyway. What should the real leader do?

This is when the benefits of the advice given above, about maintaining excellent relationships with the other members of the Board, particularly the non-executive directors, becomes most fruitful. It is vital to bring these Board members in as allies, to either warn the nominal leader to desist from meddling, or to help to remove him. In all cases it is preferable to instigate the least action possible. Thus, persuading him to back off is better than removing him. Removal is public. He will be induced to fight harder and the organization may be more damaged. Simply getting him back into his box is better for his self-esteem and for the organization's well-being. Ensuring that he knows what you are doing, and getting him to agree, requires diplomacy and tact of a special nature. Good leaders know how to do these things. It is probably better if the nominal leader (in the Chair position) never even knows that it was the MD, who organized the people who finally have the conversation with the Chair, over a quiet dinner at a fine restaurant . . .

One nominal leader I once had the misfortune to work with did the opposite. He was brought in as a nominal leader, with the title 'Non-Executive Chairman', to manage an excellent young MD who was highly rated by the City. However, this cunning and highly political old dog (he had to be because he was useless as a strategic leader) could not cope with the bright young MD, who made him feel as inadequate as he really was. Within months the chairperson had managed to manoeuvre the incumbent MD into resigning. He then replaced him with an idiot who made him, the chairman, feel comparatively intelligent. He then went further and removed the 'non-executive' part of his title. He now runs the corporation as its Executive Chairman. He rapidly ran the business into massive debt on a growth programme, which had not even a remote possibility of making business profits. Eventually he forced the investors to take over the company with terrible losses of their capital and the workers' jobs. The only good news on this particular horizon is that he is now too old to get another job, and so, this will be the last organization he ruins. He finally resigned – the company was left in big trouble and a shadow of its former self. It's the second good company this man led into ruin!

Mini case study: The Board is the power

I once worked with a leader who exuded a lack of confidence and utter incompetence. Although his decisions were sometimes strategically correct, he was a poor leader, who could never decide how best to inspire his subordinates to adopt his decisions, or keep to one budgetary path. Nor could he ever convince his Board that his strategic ideas had value. After a short time in office, whenever he tried to sell them an idea, they would throw it out, on principle. Ultimately, using the politics variables described above to analyse what went wrong, he was a poor leader who lacked charisma and character, who had no befriending skills, who failed to inform and get the Board's agreement in advance of meetings, and, whose Board was composed solely of the nominations of his Chairman (who had set it up in order to dominate whatever was going on himself). *This poor individual never did get another job when, eventually, they threw him out.*

Visible versus invisible politics

If we take politics to mean, in the broader sense, 'the process employed to get things done at senior levels in the organization', it is sensible to differentiate between, *visible* and *invisible, politics*. The latter means the type of politics described above, getting things done smoothly, with meetings and background discussions taking place well before the Board meeting, ensuring a smooth path for decisions, when they do finally come before the official Board for formal processing. Board meetings are nearly always called to ratify decisions already informally agreed behind the scenes before the meeting. This is merely the constitutional process of the organization, no different from what Walter Bagehot (2001) described as 'the formal parts of *The English Constitution*' in the nineteenth century. Other formal meetings performing similar functions will include such meetings as those of the remuneration committee; the new products development team; the large projects review board; the finance monitoring subcommittee; and, the Board's annual budget review.

I contend that, usually, the politics of these formal organizational systems are best done invisibly, because that is the most effective way to achieve optimal inputs from the humans involved in them and to enhance the best thinking and decision-making by the business. Political processes are generally not well viewed by those below in the organization. Often subordinates do not understand politics. They therefore form a poor impression of those who practice the art of politics within the organization, even when they think of them as a fine leader in every other aspect of their skill range.

Using invisible politics has the advantage of never teaching new tricks to any idiots the politics are meant to be either dealing with or circumventing! Furthermore, good leaders, because they are unselfish, sometimes get into situations where they are not being adequately rewarded for their labour. In these circumstances invisible politics are vital to get their just rewards. Above all, invisibility in the political process is preferable, because it is much more efficacious than visible politics.

Visible politics can be used by the leader of a business to consciously demonstrate principles or any other important values to the general body of the organization they lead. In these cases the leader has to employ the opposite features of invisible politics. In general we should adopt the principle that it is always better to do politics invisibly. This gives few or no chances to those we may be acting against to retaliate or take revenge. If however, you wish to overtly demonstrate or teach particular lessons to individuals or groups in the organization you may well decide to use *visible politics*. Indeed, if you are going to use politics visibly, then it is best to do them in high Technicolor.

You should only exploit *visible politics* when the person they are being directed at, has no power or means to retaliate or take revenge. They should be in a position where they can do nothing but accept the politics you are applying to them, for the learning purposes of the organization. Examples would be: a public admonition to a manager, because s/he treated an employee rudely or unjustly; an open rejection of a poor budget forecast for next year's achievement, to let the other managers know they must be more ambitious; a public apology in the newspapers for bad service to customers, when this has been demonstrated, and the public is angry; a public praising for extraordinary performance, to encourage others to try harder. There are many other positive and negative lessons you may wish to demonstrate through visible politics. I would only urge caution and moderation. *Visible politics*, like the French say of revenge itself, 'is a plate best eaten cold and rarely'.

We should certainly use visible politics to teach an unethical manager a lesson (after trying every other method to change his ways) or to demonstrate to up-and-coming leaders how to actually conduct politics or processes.

We may, on occasion, use them to demonstrate to a recalcitrant Board that it is wrong minded and must change its attitude. Occasionally we just need to remove a fool from the scene and visible politics is the only way.

In summary, though, always remember the following principles:

- invisible politics beats visible politics for almost all organizational purposes; and
- the less frequently visible politics are used, the more powerful they are as a teaching device; and
- the less frequently politics in general are used, the more powerful they are as a tool of trade of leadership.

Other occasions when good leaders use politics to further their careers

A leader may arrive in the top post to find themselves saddled with a particularly unappreciative board which forms part of the problem rather than the solution to the organization's issues. To demonstrate a boss' own effectiveness to the Board and to begin the process of mastery thereof, s/he may need to use the arts of politics to ensure the Board understands better how matters will be conducted and the sort of 'help' required from them in the future. Oftentimes a leader needs to achieve a one-off breakthrough in strategy. Visible politics may be a way to demonstrate or convince the Board that the leader is on the right path. Such times call for the powerful use of every political trick the leader can summon.

There are other times, when a career is at a fulcrum change point. These may be occasions when the leader has achieved a breakthrough in terms of personal skill levels; or has developed the power to conceptualize at a higher level; or, possibly, in his or her income needs, due to increased family commitments. If it is necessary to demonstrate or prove to the Board that a leader has reached such a point in their career it may be necessary to exploit overt political skills to focus the appropriate audience's attention on the situation.

Other occasions when visible politics are appropriate may apply are when one has created a winning strategy, or an unbeatable product, or a masterly follow-through to a takeover. The open use of politics may be the best way to intimidate the competition or announce to the market, that you have achieved a winning position!

Stakeholders and the political spider at the centre of the web

We refer in other chapters to stakeholder theory. It is worth mentioning that politics and stakeholder theory are quite intimately linked. If we regard the leader as the spider at the centre of the web and the stakeholders all around the web, one gets a fairly accurate view of the way many leaders perceive the job as managing the stakeholders. The crucial judgment skill of the leader, as the spider in the middle of the web, of all the contradictory requirements of all stakeholders, is quite apposite and predictive, especially if one thinks of the tension of the web itself. The stakeholders usually represent most of those with key interests in the business, whether they are large shareholders, the founder or members of the founder family, bankers who have made large investments, or eminent representatives within the industry. The politics of the boardroom are often about managing those stakeholders when they are members of the board. It can be complex. Consider the following case study.

TeleWest is a quoted UK cable company. It had 40% of its shares in the general public's hands with several international cable firms owning the rest. It used to be controlled equally by US West Media Group (third largest in the USA cable industry) and TCI (largest in the USA cable industry) which had 26.75% each, with an agreement to vote together for majority control (this information is in the public arena). When they could not agree how to vote, their agreement states they would vote according to the last Board policy.

One of the CEO's biggest problems is that US West Media origin-ated as a Baby Bell telephony business. They were traditionally mainly interested in the telephony revenue and the owning company used to be judged on the USA stock markets by that revenue. The other controlling shareholder, TCI, is more interested in the enter-tainment side of the business. That type of business is commonly judged, on the stock markets, on the basis of how many homes are buying entertainment from them because that usually represents the levels of advertising revenue they can command.

The attempt to maximize telephony revenue at the same time as increase the number of homes taking entertainment channels always created contradictions in the marketing and sales policies of the company. The CEO could never please both parties! TCI was worth over $50 billion in the USA in January 2001.

Imagine the subtleties required of a Chief Executive Officer of a business like this. He had to bring all major contracts before the Board, for approval before signing them. Some used to relate to deals with a subsidiary of TCI, which supplied some of his programming. TCI also has strong links with Rupert Murdoch's News International Corporation (his holding company) and its entertainment interests in the USA, where they both sell programmes and channels to each other. But BSkyB (a UK satellite TV, Rupert Murdoch controlled, business) is the main supplier of entertainment channels to the UK cable business. TeleWest used to have a contract with Sky for the supply of many of its entertainment channels, accounting for a major percentage of its total annual costs. This contract enabled TeleWest to make only rather poor levels of profits.

The CEO of TeleWest was always trying to get the Board to help apply influence on Rupert Murdoch and his Sky employees to write a better contract, which would give him a chance to deliver more profits to the shareholders. But the stakeholders on the Board seemed to have greater economic interests elsewhere (the boss of TCI, now renamed Liberty Media, recently made a substantial investment in Rupert Murdoch's News Corporation).

With a mixture of interests like that, what premium would the reader place upon the CEO's political skills? Interestingly, TeleWest changed its CEO approximately every 18 months for the first 7 years of its existence. It had a similar burn rate with its Chief Operating Officers.

Fads or trends?

Politics can often be a useful means for the leader to signal, on behalf of the organization, that the organization is responding to public opinion or new long-term social trends. This can be especially applicable in times of media aggression on sensitive aspects of a business or industry (e.g. pollution in the oil industry; safety in automobiles, good health promotion in food products or overcharging by pharmaceuticals). At such times, it is crucial and imperative that the public sees that responsible leaders and their businesses, are recognizing and responding to public opinion. It is another task of leadership to understand and make judgments on these matters. What does the media pressure represent? Is it mere passing comment and 'ideas of the day from the chattering classes'? Or, rather, does it give an early indication of something which is becoming profoundly important, reflecting deeply felt public opinion? The answers are dependent upon a combination of the leader's common sense and intuition. Leaders have to ask themselves the question 'Is this situation or event representative of a real problem or is it more likely to disappear after a short wave of hot air?' Sometimes the answers are indicated by examining what type of people are championing the problem and its suggested solutions. They may be the best indicator whether there is any need to take the issue seriously? The answers to questions such as these will guide the leader on what type of action they have to take.

The tool of silence

The tool of silence is a special skill, which many leaders use with tremendous results. Most people have a need to speak, to fill gaps in conversation when there is a silence; they feel psychologically constrained to fill voids. Most people find it hard to sit in silence when they are in a room, or an office, with another person, if the other party stops speaking. Wise leaders learn to use this awkwardness in the face of silence, to good effect. They ask questions about important subjects they need information about. Often, they know that the respondent may not want to give them the information they are seeking. When the other person has given what they hope is a sufficient but not totally honest or full explanation, a judicious use of the tool of silence will extract, at the end, all the deeper data and information they really need to solve the problem. When we use silence in research work with managers and leaders it is astonishing how much quality information comes, especially in the last minute or two, of any meeting.

Of course, when you try to use the silence tool on quality leaders, it just leads to long periods of silence. You're both using the same tool!

The tool of silence is particularly apt for use when there are organizational politics to process. Often, it is wise to *not* meet trouble half way. In other words, if the leader does not feed speculation, and does not give information where there is no need to do so, the outcomes are facilitated and hastened. The judicious use of silence under such circumstances will be immensely useful. By and large, if we can manage it, the less information given, the less data you are fuelling to problem makers. The main exception to this rule is when there are genuine catastrophes or accidents or statistics about the business spilling out in a public arena. In those cases the opposite of silence is advised. Share the facts as known, adopt an open front whereby it is demonstrated that the company does not wish to cover anything up and state publicly the firm's preparedness to accept blame, if and when any guilt or blame is established.

Closing caution

Wise leaders never underestimate politics and its importance. When you hear yourself say, 'I'm fed up with the politics in this organization', it probably indicates you are tired of your career and you have lost control anyway. Remember that if you don't use politics, somebody may use politics on you. It is not wise to be a *second mover* in the game of politics. It keeps you on the back foot. When you do use politics, you should use them with the absolute minimum of force and power, and then, only when it is vitally necessary. The more politics you use, the less valuable they will be. This will, in turn, reduce the power of any politics you need to use in the future. A great metaphor is to consider politics like the bullets in the barrel of a revolver. Once you have spent the bullets in a battle, you need plenty of time to reload, if you are not going to be shot in the heat of battle! If you run out of bullets, you become a sitting duck. Almost all politics are best done secretly (see the exceptions listed above). Finally, always ask yourself whether a piece of political behaviour is necessary, or just fun? If the latter, don't do it. As a final reminder, ponder on the lessons of the case study below.

Mini case study: Don't waste bullets

I earlier described an intelligent CEO who was competent at intellectually correct solutions but terrible at implementation. There was a time when he was trying to do two important things simultaneously in his business. He wanted to persuade the Board to accept a new, revolutionary strategy to save the business from being a potential takeover target. Simultaneously, he needed to get the Board to approve the dismissal of one of his Divisional Director's, who was failing to deliver results. He was advised not to do both at once. The Chairman was being 'worked on' by several advisers and the non-executive directors were also appraised of the need to remove the recalcitrant Director. All these separate actions would do the job and get this executive removed for the Chief Executive, within a few weeks.

But the CEO could not contain himself. He had allowed this Divisional Director to get under his skin and by now he was thoroughly irritated merely by the man's membership of the organization at all. So, against all advice, he marched into the Chairman's office and demanded his DD's head on a platter. The Chairman asked for time to consult the rest of the Board. But the CEO insisted. The Chairman only gave in once his hand was forced in this way. The executive was dismissed, albeit, with a large lump of compensation.

Unfortunately, what this really meant was that the CEO had expended (metaphorically) at least two of the six bullets he had in his revolver. When the CEO tried to force through his revolutionary strategy at the next Board meeting, he really needed all six bullets. He had wasted some on previous attempts at turnaround. He had wasted two on removing his recalcitrant executive. He had insufficient left for this last great strategy turnaround concept. The Board turned down his proposals. He had no where to go. They dismissed him, peremptorily, three months later.

Summary

Politics are defined as the process of organizational process or governance in business. As such they are normal, just 'the way things get done at particular levels in the organization'. Bad politics are those where people do things for mean or personal reasons rather than the good of the business. The variables which increase or diminish politics are defined as the size of the business, the number of nominators to Board positions, whether leaders nominate for themselves, the level of interpersonal skills of the leader, the quality and quantity of pre-Board meetings and the general competence of the leader. The chapter points out that nominal leaders are often great at politics because it's how they survive. Politics may be invisible or visible, with the former being recommended for most occasions. After a brief excursion on 'the tool of silence', leaders are urged to use the minimum politics while never underestimating their importance.

13. Leadership and Life

How important is it?

The manager of an important football club was asked once how important was football in his life. His response was 'It's far more important than life!' For too many people their leadership career becomes more important than anything else in their life. It doesn't merely overshadow everything else, it crowds out all other aspects of life. If that leader's spouse or children suffer that's just too bad for them. Such leaders are usually clever or lucky enough to choose a partner who will accept that fate for the pleasure of the short amount of attention and time received from him or her. These are private deals between consenting adults and it is their private business and value system that they have to live by.

This chapter will discuss how to balance a leadership career and a full private life. It emphasizes that we should try to achieve a balance between time allocated to business and that assigned to personal life in order to give the best use of an overall lifespan. Necessarily, the values discussed are my personal value system. However, I believe they are so generally acceptable that any rational leader trying to maximize his or her total life happiness would share a majority of them. Further, it is a thesis of this chapter that only a balanced personal and business life can deliver a leader of the best quality. That is a person who keeps their whole life in perspective and who maintains relationships and interests outside their commercial life. Such people are not only richer and more balanced mentally but they are also more likely to understand the context of their business decision-making in a normal environment.

Every individual's equilibrium will be different. For a start, some people have high energy and a very low need for sleep. It was said of Margaret Thatcher that she only ever slept 4 hours a night. Compared to most normal people, this gave her 4 additional conscious hours over the average person to use as she wished. Unfortunately, she used her extra 4 hours to work even more instead of live a normal life! Thus she became more and more unbalanced. Eventually, she was winning all her debates against her ministers because she had read all the briefing papers. But they had been living a life and had their political views in perspective. She had all the facts at her disposal but missed, increasingly, a life perspective. In due time it led to the poll tax, a politically indefensible standpoint. Her demise followed soon after! Leaders often have high energy because that is one of the qualities that distinguish leaders from ordinary mortals. When we are in a position of power and importance it often releases even more energy and acts as a catalyst for getting things done.

Most leaders need a good partner who should be chosen carefully. The criteria for choice are discussed later in this chapter. Many readers have reacted to this idea and suggest that it is slightly immoral or distasteful. Please read carefully what I say there, considering the argument in relation to what I say in the rest of this book, then decide for yourself.

Links between physical and mental health

Physical and mental health are linked and are mutually interdependent. Physical health facilitates quality and speedy thinking (see Covey, 1989). Your mind is your main working tool as a leader. You must keep it fit with regular physical as well as mental exercises. If we just think in common-sense terms, the brain works by the mechanics of oxygen, carried through your blood flow. Your body and especially your brain are dependent on these flows. It must make sense to ensure that the machine (of your body) is in the best possible working order.

A further reason for keeping yourself physically fit is that it is pointless to be so physically unfit that you cannot enjoy the fruits of your labour with the pursuit of pleasurable hobbies? In many ways, both physical and mental health require the same discipline of self-control and good habits. Why not apply the same rules to all aspects of your life? Ultimately an unfit mind will be seen for what it is. I remember a CEO I worked with. We all knew he could never remember any details or even the main substance of what he had said even a half hour ago. He lost the respect of his executives because he could never hold them to account for any verbal commitment. The language of leadership is verbal, not written. Later, he needed major heart surgery. It was discovered that the lack of oxygen in his bloodstream had been reducing his concentration powers for many years. He recovered some of his memory but never really worked properly again.

Of course, being fit cannot safeguard you against the bad luck of ill health. But it ensures that you enjoy any good health you are blessed with. It could also prevent some of the sicknesses (such as heart disease, ulcers, alcohol dependency and depression) that befall many leaders, as a consequence of the demands and lifestyle of their work.

This chapter will discuss the balance between having a leadership career and managing a full private life. Achieving a fulfilled overall life requires a balance between time allocated to business and personal life (although every individual's point of equilibrium will be different). And most leaders need a good 'partner', so choose carefully!

Mini case study: Failure disguised as success

A much admired individual headed a major corporation with £7 billion revenue per annum and about £2 billion profit. I was asked to meet him by one of his subordinates, with whom I had worked for many years. We met over dinner and passed what was, for me, a dull evening. He told me nothing of substance about himself. He boasted a lot about his achievements. He never mentioned his private life, or anything that could make him sound human, or interesting, or a man who had succeeded in his life, at anything other than being a famous and important leader. Just one month later he was taken ill with massive cancers all over his body. He was off sick for 6 months. Even then, he returned prematurely to work, with drugs still needing to be pumped into him, day and night.

He asked to see me and wondered whether he could talk 'his life' over with me. I agreed, although I had no idea what he wanted to discuss. He told me he was dreadfully unhappy. He and his wife had not liked each other since they married. I asked why? He told me that he had made an appalling business decision in his previous job. He had become personally liable for many millions of £'s and had spent the past decade paying all his spare income to the creditors and lawyers, to stave off adverse publicity and ignominy. His wife blamed him for subjecting their lives to such terrible pressure.

Another consequence of that mistake was that, in spite of earning over £300,000 per annum for many years, he still had no savings and did not even own the roof over his family's head. His wife had stayed loyal throughout his sickness but now she wanted to divorce him and start a new life for herself. We arranged to meet the following week.

While I was driving towards his office he called me on my mobile phone. Don't come, I've some urgent company matters to attend to. I told him nothing could be more important than sorting out his marriage and his private life. But he cancelled anyway. He cancelled three more meetings before I gave up on him completely and realized it was pointless to put another appointment in my diary. A few weeks later he left work, sick, and never returned. He died of cancer a few months later, utterly alone.

Within a few years his name was utterly forgotten at that company, his achievements meaningless. How long before the effects of his lifestyle and behaviour to his family will be forgotten and not mentioned by his family? He was a man who could helicopter for the business every day of the week. He just never learned to do it for his own life and family.

How do you know you need help?

How can you know if any imbalances, incorrect instincts or inappropriate automatic responses exist in your own range of behaviours? First, study the way people react to you. If you notice people backing off in a stereotypical way under certain circumstances or failing to react as you would expect when you act in a way calculated to get a different response, ask yourself why? Sometimes, you can tell because, by and large, we do know when we are behaving irrationally. We all tend to tolerate ourselves too easily and delude ourselves that we cannot do anything about it. The telling sign is when people consistently fail to respond to what you consider to be appropriate stimuli when you deliberately behave in a particular manner calculated to get specific reactions. Force yourself to ask what you can do to repair and rebuild any imbalances, incorrect instincts or irrational responses, in your own profile. There are always solutions. What are they?

Refer back to the emotional horizon inquiry in the Chapter on Self-appraisal (p.230). How many questions there remind you of happy or sad times? How does that make you feel? Does it, possibly, make you want to cry? By the way, when did you last cry real tears about any emotional event that happened to you or that you did to somebody else? Or are you phobic about happiness? Are you frightened of success, or of anything that might make you realise that you have nothing left to be afraid of and you are allowed to just enjoy life and have fun, even while being successful? Do you still believe, privately, that emotion and tears form no part of a successful person's business, leadership or management life?

Although there can be no doubt that there is a fashionable preoccupation with emotional intelligence, I would urge you not to dismiss it as a short-term fad. Great leaders need to be equally matured in both their IQ and their EQ. It is as dangerous to your business as to your personal life to have deficiencies in one of the other. Either shortage could damage equally your leadership progress and your emotional life. Both your career and your happiness could be unfulfilled and diminished. You could also be doing lots of harm to others, both your family relations and your subordinates and colleagues.

Read as much as possible of the literature on emotional intelligence and balance (see the References and Bibliography at the end of this book). Investigate your childhood deeply and carefully, first, from your own memories, then from family members (siblings can be particularly useful). Ask those who observed your upbringing. Although they can never give you completely neutral views on your childhood nor your parents' strengths and weaknesses, they can be informative. You can question close childhood friends, the parents of friends', neighbours and others relations of the family. Try to achieve a sense of neutrality about their observations of past events, rather than colour them back to the shades with which you saw them yourself. Work hard to make fresh interpretations of any events and actions from your past that may have caused the current irrational, automated responses in your behaviour patterns that you are trying to eliminate. Keep in mind that it is unlikely that these trauma were caused by any intentional ill will on the part of parents or guardians. They may just be the result of your own accidental or incorrect interpretation of events by yourself. Events and trauma seen through childhood eyes may often seem unbalanced, larger than life and terrifying. Think of all those people who go to see their childhood home and suddenly realize how small it is compared to their memory of the giant home they grew up in.

If you are really unable to get new perspectives and change behaviours which you know are irrational and deleterious to your life, you may need to consider going to a professional therapist. If you do, ensure it is somebody who really understands the nature of business life and its tremendous pressures on leaders.

Getting your emotional life sorted out must be at least as important as your intellectual business skills. After all, you owe it to yourself to try to be happy. It is the right thing to do and it has no potential adverse indicators. I have met some leaders who were particularly unhappy. They thought they would never know happiness and had grown accustomed to thinking that they, somehow, had missed an allocation of the 'happiness gene'. They were enormously buoyed up by my insistence that everybody has a right to be happy and that they owed it to themselves to find out what was preventing them from enjoying their lives. In several cases these people managed to change their lives and, as I would put it, start living a full life of satisfaction at work and contentment at home.

A philosophy of rounded contentment

Most of us have asked ourselves the perennial question 'what is it that makes us happy?' Everybody's answer will be different. In essence, most answers amount to something like 'being happy is mainly being busy doing a balance of all the things I enjoy doing'. For many people, it also means having an important and profound social relationship with a partner, perhaps children, family and friends. Occasionally we meet people who have never been happy, yet who appear to be leaders. I suggest they could be dangerous to themselves and their organizations. Why? Because if happiness is based upon a life balanced between social, private and business time, between serious work and fun pursuits, between highs and lows (because life is about both), then an unhappy person is also somebody who is unbalanced. The essence of great leaders is that they retain high quality judgment at all times. The whole meaning of leadership is judgment about the balance of resources, the state of the markets, the minds of consumers, the attitudes of the stakeholders and the optimal way forward.

Is it impossible to be emotionally mature and live a solitary life? Consider the example of Sir John Browne who 'turned BP Amoco into one of the world's great companies'. (*Sunday Times*, 21 January 2001). He took the business from £20 billion market value in 1995 when he took over to £129 billion just 5 years later. Classically, as outlined earlier, he is the single son of his adoring parents. His mother was the lucky and only family survivor of the Nazi holocaust, having been imprisoned in Auschwitz (his mother was 25% Jewish). Aged 52 now, he never married and lived with his mother until she died last year, from the time that his father died 20 years ago.

When asked about his personal life he admits that 'he fell in love once but it did not work out. He met an American academic who broke his heart and he has never recovered ... In the end, if I had wanted to get married I would have. Whether I will get married remains to be seen. Maybe this (interview) is an advertisement'. Two comments are due. One, he obviously has not ruled out a more conventional, less solitary existence, he just hasn't found the right person yet. Secondly, I am told by senior executives who work with him that he works prodigious hours many days a week. Is it possible that this is setting a poor example of an imbalanced life to those who have a more normal home life and who work with and around him? It all depends upon the degree of true emotional maturity he is able to muster and whether he expects the same performance from his colleagues as he chooses, time-wise, to put in himself.

It seems a curious requirement that good leaders have to be happy. But their happiness, like other people, has to be about utilizing their talents and skills, energy and pure brainpower, capacity for love and objective and wise judgment. We cannot forget that happiness usually requires a minimum of material comforts such as a home, adequate food and clothing. Leaders are also more likely to secure adequate supplies of those.

The loneliness of leadership

The leadership life can be lonely. (Consider the rather sad Sir John Browne above.) Why? Because there are very few people a leader can confide in safely without damaging the organization. This loneliness factor is the single most frequent reason for leaders employing coaches to help them reflect upon their problems. It has become particularly fashionable at the beginning of the twenty-first century.

How does the loneliness arise? If a leader is unique and special, by definition, there will be few people who will understand the organization as he or she does. Worse, there is a limited range of people able to empathize with his role and problems. Few people feel like sympathizing with a person who is being paid more than anybody else in the organization to worry on behalf of the business anyway? Furthermore, most leaders are strong characters (they need to be) and they usually dislike anything which looks or feels like 'whining'. There are also dangers attached to their appearing to be weak or worried about events surrounding the business. There are too many employees who would jump at any opportunity to fawn to the boss by 'being a good listener'. Any leader worth his or her salt would hate that. They have to put up with the fawning anyway. Presenting extra opportunities for sycophancy could be too much to bear. There is also a continuous and real danger that data supplied to the leader is falsified to give him the impression that the results he aspires to are already being achieved. Confiding in people just gives them another opportunity to lie.

The political dimension is another major cause for loneliness. Who can a leader safely confide in? Often a spouse cannot understand the nature of the problems because they are so complex and there is a need for confidentiality. Confiding in a non-executive Chair or President of the organization could be dangerous, for they are also the people who will make judgments about renewing the leader's contract or deciding his or her bonus for the year. Confiding in subordinates is equally invidious and dangerous. Information is often best disseminated on a 'need to know' basis.

How to overcome the worst aspects of leadership loneliness

Some leaders choose to trust coaches. There are some who can be trusted, although they are rare. Others choose to confide in their partner, although this does seem a heavy (and unpaid) burden, especially for those partners who have their own career to manage. Others choose to carefully trust one of the non-executive directors. Hopefully, it's one they can truly call a 'friend'. Some leaders find another leader in an unrelated field and the two confide in each other and provide mutual benefits to each other as listening ears. Other palliatives to alleviate (rather than remove) the loneliness factor is to go on many holidays or short breaks. That helps to keep things in perspective. One realizes that the organization will survive in the leader's absence (they always do). Other bosses play large quantities of golf.

One strongly advocated methodology, is to simply lay less emphasis on confidentiality. Most organizations place too great a stress on the need for secrecy. Some leaders obsess about it. It certainly accentuates the sense of loneliness, because, by definition, the leader carries most secrets in his head as a consequence of his or her ultimate responsibility for everything in the company that is most important. When you examine them, we find that most of the files which are marked *confidential* are not really important or private at all and it would harm nobody if everybody knew about them. While on this subject of confidentiality, isn't it interesting how so many companies will announce their strategy to their shareholders and any of their competitors who have the intelligence to read their annual report, while not thinking it worthwhile to confide their strategy to their employees?

Connections between correct behaviour and ethics

The beginning of an answer to important questions such as 'what's the point of living?' is to acknowledge that we really do have choices to be happy or sad. Neither condition is a given, nor are they governed as much as many people think by simple equations such as 'wealth gives happiness' and a 'lack of wealth means misery'. It is generally agreed that the existence of therapies to help people avoid distress has had great consequential benefit for humankind. These breakthroughs in understanding human psychology may be seminally attributed to the work of Freud, Jung and the other founder theorists of different psychological schools of thought.

They proved that peoples' emotional reactions are a consequence of either inherited characteristics, genetic traits, chemical imbalances in their bodies or behaviours learned unconsciously and subconsciously during the impressionable years when they were growing up. Although we cannot control all these childhood 'learned responses' when we acquire them in our childhood (no matter how they get attributed to us), we can control their effects upon us by relearning and modifying our behaviour when we are adults. We merely have to be determined to avoid unnecessary suffering, when we realize that we are suffering or inflicting misery upon others unnecessarily.

At the beginning of the twenty-first century most intelligent people realize they have a right to be happy and that the means exist to achieve happiness. This is true, in spite of the fact that some may have learned responses which make them feel they don't automatically have that right. All have both the opportunity and the choice to be happy. Being happy also implies that one can be good to oneself and do good to others. However, first you have to be sure you know *when* you are happy. Many business people I work with like to believe they are happy when busy at work. But, often, they don't look happy to me.

Usually, when questioned, they agree they are not happy. They are pleased to be *too* busy to think about happiness. They often don't know how to think about such matters at all. Once they learn how to open the debate in their own minds, they realize that what they have been calling 'happiness' is actually only frenetic activity ('busy-ness') dressed up by themselves to substitute for happiness. Happiness is something they think is reserved for the other parts of their life, as an addendum to their business life. Frequently, that is as sadly neglected an area for happiness as their business life.

Assuming a person can help themselves to achieve relief from unhappiness, another key question is 'can you be happy in yourself while behaving badly towards others?' Self-evidently, if you treat yourself badly, you cannot be or make yourself happy. Another consequence of this argument would lead you to conclude that if you treat others badly you are reducing their happiness. If that is true it must mean that treating others badly is an unethical thing to do. But it cannot be in the interests of your business either. This further implies that we ought to try to be good to others (including employees), as well as to ourselves.

Let's recap the sequential logic line so far. Being good is a choice and a wise choice at that. Everybody has a choice to do good in preference to bad. That must surely mean that anybody choosing *not* to exercise their ability to do good rather than bad, would be close to, what those who believe in it, would call evil or sin. This assumes, of course, that all behaviour has a moral content. In other words, good behaviour is also ethically desirable behaviour. This makes being and doing good not only a choice, but also a desirable behaviour as well as a moral imperative.

What are ethics and why are they relevant?

Ethical principles refer to the underlying rules of life which can, could or should govern the way we behave, live and react to others. Can the same principles govern both our business and our private lives? We have to ask, 'why not?' After all, we spend similar amounts of conscious time at both work and play, it would be irrational to choose to be happy and moral in one part of our lives and not in the other.

All behaviour has moral implications because action has effects upon people and things. Thus good behaviour and good actions must be ethically and morally desirable. The contrary is also true: bad actions and bad behaviour are ethically and morally undesirable. By definition, whatever behaviour we choose to adopt implies that we are also adopting its underlying value. That is true even if we choose to ignore the implied underlying value. Nor would ignorance be an excuse (as it isn't in law either). Thus, even if we remain unaware that there is a bad value which results from an action, it remains nevertheless wrong. Nobody has any time for the drunkard who kills an innocent bystander and says, 'Well, I was drunk and didn't know what I was doing at the time!'

All the arguments above must apply equally to business life as to private life. It must surely make sense to behave well and take good decisions that have good consequences rather than bad, both in our personal behaviour and in any organizational decisions we have to make as a leader. Consider the typical, classical leader's dilemma of needing to reduce the size of a business to better balance the human resources with the other resources of the business (both physical and technological). This may be necessary because if we don't decrease some of the jobs, we may end by losing the whole business and everybody's job. During the 'down sizing' exercise (what a ghastly concept!), you come across an employee who is marginal in terms of employability. But this person is the sole breadwinner for a family where the spouse is dying of cancer and one of the two children is physically and mentally handicapped. Is there an ethical or moral issue?

In my opinion, there can be no ethics-free choice of behaviour. If we make the employee redundant, ignoring the underlying moral imperatives, we would be committing an immoral act. There are real and bad consequences for the individual. Those must affect ourselves and the organization. For example, by ignoring our own sense of decency and fairness, the other employees who are kept on will know that the firm takes decisions which are callous and inhumane. This will reduce their feelings of loyalty and the manner in which they work with customers. I have experienced some cases when the employing organization has behaved so cruelly that the employees retaliated by physically sabotaging the organization's technology (IT and buildings), causing tremendous damage to the business' resources and reputation with customers.

Would the reader want to treat the employee with family problems any differently than a friend or acquaintance in our private life? Why not apply the same rationale to a business employee or colleague as we would to a personal friend? Life and behaviour cannot and should not be subdivided into different realms of ethics with two separate and different standards which apply according to the accident of where the interaction takes place, at work or at home. There must be some universal laws which regulate all human interaction. Once we adopt only contingent values which are, like clothes, put on and taken off according to whim or weather, what criteria can you use to differentiate the values you use at work from those which govern your domestic behaviour. How will you decide where the limits of decency are? You cannot, because there are no criteria with which to differentiate. If you adopt a lower or different standard at work from your home values, which will be the 'real' you? Will you be proud of yourself as a parent or partner in marriage, but ashamed of yourself as a leader, manager or work colleague?

I would go so far as to advocate that there should always be a mental 'ethics' file in every leader's head that is used to filter or 'litmus test' every decision or action s/he takes, to ensure that all potential breaches of decency and cruelty will be avoided and that the circumstances of every individual in the organization are kept in mind at all times.

If behaviour at home reflects best values, why would you want to take second-rate ethics to work with you? Don't you need them even more at work where the objectives are, after all, mainly, just to make more money? If you're a leader, what are you doing to your employees with these 'second rate ethics'? If your ethics at work are your better ethics, what kind of self-respect can you have if you value your personal life less than your business life? Remember that as a leader, if your life is unbalanced, you may find it impossible to take rational decisions on behalf of your employees who must be, at least, one of your most important resources.

You never know when something could go wrong. Would you want your wife or husband in a divorce court of law telling the world about the worst aspects of your personality? A good life in the round, both at work and domestically, is the simplest. All double standards are a form of duplicity. Ultimately, you will be your own victim. Why do it to yourself? Double or contradictory standards are dangerous to the leader's mental health and invidious to the welfare of the organization. They are generally bad practice. Which arouses the question, 'When did you last examine your ethics?'

To summarize, there can be no values-free behaviour. If the objective of living is to have a rounded, happy and good life, nobody will want to employ differentiated and potentially contradictory values in other parts of his or her life. This would present the nonsense of living decently for some aspects of life and indecently for others. Consequently it behoves everybody to think through what their values and ethics really are. They should then live their lives by those standards. This is even more relevant, if one is a leader because those decisions and behaviours, by definition, affect many other people's lives as well as the leader's own. (Try Questionnaire 13.1.)

Cleverness and wisdom

I distinguish carefully between *clever* and *wise* people. It is becoming an accepted notion that great leaders need high quality emotional maturity (including empathy) and that it is more important than pure intellectual calculating power. This highlights a distinction I make between cleverness and wisdom. Clever people are the classical high

Questionnaire 13.1: A values questionnaire

Number	Question	Yes	No	Varies	Total score
1	I believe there are limits to how much time anybody should spend at work	1	3	2	
2	I shout at home but never at work	3	0	1	
3	If I have a choice, I'd always take an economic rather than a compassionate decision	3	0	1	
4	My family always comes first	0	3	2	
5	I regularly work more that 60 hours a week	3	1	2	
6	I mainly see my family at weekends	3	1	2	
7	I try not to mix personal and business socializing	0	3	2	
8	I see (saw) little of my children during weekdays	3	0	2	
9	I am religious but I would not share that information with colleagues at work	0	3	1	
10	I am sometimes distracted by gender considerations at work	3	0	2	
11	I suspend all rules for the company Christmas party	3	0	2	
12	My salary depends on what the market will bear regardless of what the company can afford	3	0	2	
13	You cannot keep expenses records to the nearest penny/cent, it's impossible	3	0	2	
14	You have to discard people development, if the firm is really sick	3	0	1	
15	I see no limit to the level of job I could achieve	3	0	2	
16	You have to tell lies at work and home	3	0	2	
17	Rules do not apply to leaders – they create rules	3	0	2	

Total

Interpretation

Scores over 36 suggest you must carefully and immediately rethink your value system

Scores below 20 suggest that you have thought through your ethics and behaviours

Scores between 20 and 35 suggest that you should reflect upon your ethical values, consider your behaviour carefully and try to adjust them for their effects upon your followers achievers at university who gain high honours and come top of the class. Wise people have emotional maturity and leave college with a profound understanding of human nature. They know what they wish to achieve in life and how they intend to do it. Cleverness is based on the mental accumulation of facts and the power to juggle them. Wisdom is based upon the insight of knowing what to do about the facts for everybody's good. Cleverness is the cold, calculating logic of syllogisms and specious objectivity, maximizing shareholders' wealth alone. Wisdom is the ability to take optimal decisions on the grounds of both business and humanity, looking after both physical and material wealth for everybody concerned in one's business or private projects.

Selecting a partner

Some readers will be outraged at the claim made here. My experience suggests that there is such a thing as an *appropriate partner* for a leader. The best leaders select carefully. Some readers will consider that choosing a partner for life as a background scenario to a leadership career is close to blasphemy. I am not suggesting that business leaders should go out looking to acquire a perfectly suitable *business* partner rather than a partner for life, a 'trophy spouse'. Rather, the pattern I have observed in many leaders I have worked with is that just waiting to fall in love with whoever turns up may be invidious and few top leaders seem to do it. In reality, what really happens is, that *wise* people tend to be careful who they fall in love with. They don't just callously select a spouse or partner on the basis of their career nor on the basis of the type of the private life they wish to lead (although both will apply to some extent). It isn't that they do not let their heart lead them. They just control their heart better and only allow their feelings to lead them where the possible outcomes are complementary to their objectives, desires, way of life and value system. In other words, they do fall in love, but only with the right person!

They know it is the right person because they understand themselves well and they know when they have found somebody who will know how to cope with their career, even if they have an equal or even greater career of their own to pursue. The right partner will respect the inner drive and energy of the person they are attached to; they will care as much or more about the leader's happiness as their own. They will, in short, be faithful to what they need them to be, when they need to be a successful partner to the leader. In many modern couples, where both partners may have equally demanding careers, the ideal partner will be adaptive enough to fulfill the roles of the *company spouse* when that role is required by their partner. With luck, and choice, the partner will probably have similar strong ethical values which are aligned with our own. Above all, they are likely to be highly self-sufficient. And they will reflect and radiate a harmonious moral tone in the aspects of their life which fit their life as a couple.

I am only stating the observations I have made of the successful leaders I have known. If you want to be successful and use different guidelines to those I outline above you will, of course, do so. But remember, it's hard enough to become a great leader. Why would anybody make it harder for themselves by pairing up with a partner who is going to make it twice as hard (and far less likely)?

Summary

This chapter has emphasized the need for leaders and all those preparing and managing a leadership career, to pay careful attention to the trauma of their past which cause inappropriate reactions to current events. I urge that they strive to achieve emotional balance in their lives, both for their personal happiness and the welfare of their business organization. We then lay out the bases for the need to behave as ethically at work as in our private life, with the ever present assumption that ethics in business life as much as in private life are a *sine qua non*. Finally, I advocate that people who aspire to become leaders, eventually, should choose their partners in life carefully and with a view to the special needs that will arise as a consequence of the demands of a leadership career. Don't make it harder for yourself than it needs to be. It's already hard enough to become a great and successful leader.

Concluding thoughts

As an author I am always overwhelmed with the possibility that I have not explained my ideas clearly or that some of the things I have stated as facts are really my opinions and possibly subject to error. However, if we allowed too many aspects of self-consciousness to take over, we would never pick up the pen, or, in my case, open a new directory on the computer.

The overall thesis of this book is that quality leadership is rare and the world is desperately short of sufficient leaders for the multitudinous organizations it has accumulated.

It is my earnest hope that this book will help some leaders improve their quality, that some organizations will choose their leaders better by reference to this book, and that all readers will close it with a more profound knowledge of what it takes to be a leader. I fervently hope that it has clarified for most whether they should stay in or depart from *the leadership race*.

Chapter References

Chapter 1

Blake, R. R. and Mouton, J. S. (1964) *The New Managerial Grid*, Gulf, Houston.

Branson, R. (2000) *Losing My Virginity*, Virgin Publishing, London.

Hamel, G. and Prahalad, C. K. (1994) *Competing for the Future*, Harvard Business School Press, Boston, MA.

Hersey, P. and Blanchard, K. H. (1977) *Management of Organizational Behavior: Utilizing Human Resources*, 3rd edn., Prentice-Hall, Englewood Cliffs, NJ.

Jaques, E. (1976) *A General Theory of Bureaucracy*, Heinemann, London.

Jaques, E. (1982a) *The Form of Time*, Heinemann, London

Jaques, E. (1982b) *Free Enterprise, Fair Employment*, Heinemann, London.

Kuhn, T. (1962) *The Structure of Scientific Revolutions*, University of Chicago Press, Chicago.

Levicki, C. J. (1999) *The Strategy Workout*, 2nd edn., Prentice Hall, London.

McClelland, D. (1961) *The Achieving Society*, Van Nostrand, Princeton, NJ.

Peters, T. J. and Waterman, R. H. Jr (1982) *In Search of Excellence*, Harper & Row, New York.

Popper, K. (1959) *Logic of Scientific Discovery*, Hutchinson & Co., London.

Chapter 2

Axtell, R. E. (1991) *Gestures*, John Wiley, New York.

Cooper, R. K. and Sawaf, A. (1997) *Executive EQ*, Orion Business Books, London.

Goleman, D. (1996) *Emotional Intelligence*, Bloomsbury, London.

Hersey, P. and Blanchard, K. H. (1977) *Management of Organizational Behavior: Utilizing Human Resources*, 3rd edn., Prentice-Hall, Englewood Cliffs, NJ.

Hunt, J. (1981) *Managing People at Work*, McGraw-Hill, London.

Kakabadse, A. (1991) *The Wealth Creators*, Kogan Page, London.

Levicki, C. J. (1998) *The Leadership Gene*, Financial Times/Pitman Publishing, London.

Levicki, C. J. (1999) *The Strategy Workout*, 2nd edn., Prentice Hall, London.

Chapter 3

Goleman, D. (1996) *Emotional Intelligence*, Bloomsbury, London.
Levicki, C. J. (1998) *The Leadership Gene*, Financial Times/Pitman Publishing, London.
Levicki, C. J. (1999) *The Strategy Workout*, 2nd edn., Prentice Hall, London.

Chapter 4

Belbin, R. M. (1991) *Management Teams*, Butterworth-Heinemann, Oxford.
Belbin, M. (1993) *Team Roles at Work*, Butterworth-Heinemann, Oxford.
Berne, E. (1968) *Games People Play*, Penguin, London.
Briggs-Myers, I. (1992) *Gifts Differing*, Consulting Psychologists Press, Inc., Palo Alto, CA.
Burrough, D. and Jelyar, J. (1990) *Barbarians at the Gate*, Jonathan Cape, London.
Chapman, E. N. (1977) *Your Attitude is Showing*, Science Research Associates Inc., Palo Alto, CA.
Cooper, R. K. and Sawaf, A. (1997) *Executive EQ*, Orion Business Books, London.
Endlich, L. (1999) *Goldman Sachs; The Culture of Success*, Alfred A. Knopf, New York.
Ferrucci, P. (1990) *What We May Be*, Aquarian/Thorsons, London.
Goleman, D. (1996) *Emotional Intelligence*, Bloomsbury, London.
Hector, G. (1988) *Breaking the Bank*, Little Brown & Co, Boston.
Hersey, P. and Blanchard, K. H. (1977) *Management of Organizational Behavior: Utilizing Human Resources*, 3rd edn., Prentice-Hall, Englewood Cliffs, NJ.
Jones, E. (1995) *True and Fair: A History of Price Waterhouse*, Hamish Hamilton, London.
Kiersey, D. and Bates, M. (1984) *Please Understand Me*, Prometheus Nemesis Book Company, Del Mar, CA.
Levicki, C. J. (1983) *Managerial Time Horizons and Decision Making and their Effects on Organizational Performance*, Ph.D. Thesis, London Business School, London University.
Lewis, R. and Lowe, P. (1992) *Individual Excellence*, Kogan Page, London.
Schultz, W. C. (1955) *FIRO: A Three-Dimensional Theory of Interpersonal Behavior*, Holt, Rinehart & Winston, New York.

Chapter 5

Belbin, R. M. (1991) *Management Teams*, Butterworth-Heinemann, Oxford.
Belbin, M. (1993) *Team Roles at Work*, Butterworth-Heinemann, Oxford.
de Geus, A. (1999) *The Living Company*, Nicholas Brealey Publishing, London.
Heider, J. (1992) *The Tao of Leadership*, Gower, Aldershot.
Hersey, P. and Blanchard, K. H. (1977) *Management of Organizational Behavior: Utilizing Human Resources*, 3rd edn., Prentice-Hall, Englewood Cliffs, NJ.

Jaques, E. (1976) *A General Theory of Bureaucracy*, Heinemann, London.

Jaques, E. (1982a) *The Form of Time*, Heinemann, London.

Jaques, E. (1982b) *Free Enterprise, Fair Employment*, Heinemann, London.

Kakabadse, A. (1991) *The Wealth Creators*, Kogan Page, London.

Levicki, C. J. (1983) *Managerial Time Horizons and Decision Making and their Effects on Organizational Performance*, Ph.D. Thesis, London Business School, London University.

Levicki, C. J. (1998) *The Leadership Gene*, Financial Times/Pitman Publishing, London.

Levicki, C. J. (1999) *The Strategy Workout*, 2nd edn., Prentice Hall, London.

McClelland, D. (1961) *The Achieving Society*, Van Nostrand, Princeton, NJ.

Chapter 6

Brown, J. (1986) *I Only Want What's Best for You*, Cedar, London.

Chapman, E. N. (1977) *Your Attitude is Showing*, Science Research Associates Inc., Palo Alto, CA.

Ferrucci, P. (1990) *What We May Be*, Aquarian/Thorsons, London.

Goleman, D. (1996) *Emotional Intelligence*, Bloomsbury, London.

Gruber, H. E. and Voneche, J. J. (1977) *The Essential Piaget*, Basic Books Inc., New York.

Harris, T. A. (1973) *I'm OK – You're OK*, Pan, London.

Hearnshaw, L. S. (1979) *Cyril Burt, Psychologist*, Cornell University Press, New York.

Kiersey, D. and Bates, M. (1984) *Please Understand Me*, Prometheus Nemesis Book Company, Del Mar, CA.

McClelland, D. (1961) *The Achieving Society*, Van Nostrand, Princeton, NJ.

Whyte, W. H. Jr (1956) *The Organization Man*, Simon & Schuster, New York.

Chapter 7

Covey, S. R. (1976) *The 7 Habits of Highly Effective People*, Fireside, New York.

Covey, S. R. (1989) *The 7 Habits of Highly Effective People*, Simon & Schuster, New York.

Jaques, E. (1976) *A General Theory of Bureaucracy*, Heinemann, London.

Jaques, E. (1982a) *The Form of Time*, Heinemann, London.

Jaques, E. (1982b) *Free Enterprise, Fair Employment*, Heinemann, London.

Lawrence, P. R. and Lorsch, J. W. (1967) *Managing Integration and Differentiation*, Harvard University Press, Boston.

Levicki, C. J. (1983) *Managerial Time Horizons and Decision Making and their Effects on Organizational Performance*, Ph.D. Thesis, London Business School, London University.

Levicki, C. J. (1999) *The Strategy Workout*, 2nd edn., Prentice Hall, London.

McClelland, D. (1961) *The Achieving Society*, Van Nostrand, Princeton, NJ.

Chapter 8

Harvey-Jones, J. (1988) *Making It Happen*, Fontana Collins, Glasgow.

Heider, J. (1992) *The Tao of Leadership*, Gower, Aldershot.

Holt, D. (1987) *Management, Principles and Practices*, Prentice-Hall, NJ.

Jones, G. R., George, J. M. and Hill, C. W. L. (1998) *Contemporary Management*, McGraw-Hill, Boston.

Kotter, J. (1999) *What Leaders Really Do*, Harvard Business Review Book, Boston.

Levicki, C. J. (1999) *The Strategy Workout*, 2nd edn., Prentice Hall, London.

Syrett, M. and Hogg, C. (eds) (1992) *Frontiers of Leadership*, Blackwell, Oxford.

Chapter 9

Braybrooke, D. and Lindblom, C. D. (1969) *A Strategy of Decision*, Free Press of Glencoe.

Hamel, G. and Prahalad, C. K. (1994) *Competing for the Future*, Harvard Business School Press, Boston, MA.

Hickson, D. J., Butler, R. J., Gray, D., Mallory, G. R. and Wilson, D. C. (1986) *Top Decisions*, Basil Blackwell, Oxford.

Jaques, E. (1976) *A General Theory of Bureaucracy*, Heinemann, London.

Jaques, E. (1982a) *The Form of Time*, Heinemann, London.

Jaques, E. (1982b) *Free Enterprise, Fair Employment*, Heinemann, London.

Kluger, R. (1997) *Ashes to Ashes*, Vintage Books, New York.

Lawrence, P. R. and Lorsch, J. W. (1967) *Managing Integration and Differentiation*, Harvard University Press, Boston.

March, J. G. (1988) *Decisions and Organizations*, Basil Blackwell, Oxford.

Simon, H. (1965) *The Shape of Automation*, Harper & Row, New York.

Wildavsky, A. (1964) *The Politics of the Budgetary Process*, Little Brown, Boston.

Chapter 10

Belbin, R. M. (1991) *Management Teams*, Butterworth-Heinemann, Oxford.

Belbin, M. (1993) *Team Roles at Work*, Butterworth-Heinemann, Oxford.

Berne, E. (1968) *Games People Play*, Penguin, London.

Briggs-Myers, I. (1992) *Gifts Differing*, Consulting Psychologists Press, Inc., Palo Alto, CA.

Chapman, E. N. (1977) *Your Attitude is Showing*, Science Research Associates Inc., Palo Alto, CA.

Covey, S. R. (1989) *The 7 Habits of Highly Effective People*, Simon & Schuster, New York.

de Geus, A. (1999) *The Living Company*, Nicholas Brealey Publishing, London.

Ferrucci, P. (1990) *What We May Be*, Aquarian/Thorsons, London.

Folsing, A. (1997) *Albert Einstein*, Penguin Books, London.

Goleman, D. (1996) *Emotional Intelligence*, Bloomsbury, London.

Harris, T. A. (1973) *I'm OK – You're OK*, Pan, London.

Kiersey, D. and Bates, M. (1984) *Please Understand Me*, Prometheus Nemesis Book Company, Del Mar, CA.

Levicki, C. J. (1998) *The Leadership Gene*, Financial Times/Pitman Publishing, London.

Levicki, C. J. (1999) *The Strategy Workout*, 2nd edn., Prentice Hall, London.
McClelland, D. (1961) *The Achieving Society*, Van Nostrand, Princeton, NJ.
McGregor, D. (1960) *The Human Side of Enterprise*, McGraw-Hill, New York.
Peters, T. J. and Waterman, R. H. Jr (1982) *In Search of Excellence*, Harper & Row, New York.
von Oech, R. (1983) *A Whack on the Side of the Head,* Creative Think, Van Nuys, CA.

Chapter 11

Belbin, R. M. (1991) *Management Teams*, Butterworth-Heinemann, Oxford.
Belbin, M. (1993) *Team Roles at Work*, Butterworth-Heinemann, Oxford.
Briggs-Myers, I. (1992) *Gifts Differing*, Consulting Psychologists Press, Inc., Palo Alto, CA.
Chapman, E. N. (1977) *Your Attitude is Showing*, Science Research Associates Inc., Palo Alto, CA.
Cooper, R. K. and Sawaf, A. (1997) *Executive EQ*, Orion Business Books, London.
Covey, S. R. (1989) *The 7 Habits of Highly Effective People*, Simon & Schuster, New York.
Ferrucci, P. (1990) *What We May Be*, Aquarian/Thorsons, London.
Goleman, D. (1996) *Emotional Intelligence*, Bloomsbury, London.
Harris, T. A. (1973) *I'm OK – You're OK*, Pan, London.
Jaques, E. (1976) *A General Theory of Bureaucracy*, Heinemann, London.
Jaques, E. (1982a) *The Form of Time*, Heinemann, London.
Jaques, E. (1982b) *Free Enterprise, Fair Employment*, Heinemann, London.
Levicki, C. J. (1983) *Managerial Time Horizons and Decision Making and their Effects on Organizational Performance*, Ph.D. Thesis, London Business School, London University.
Levicki, C. J. (1999) *The Strategy Workout*, 2nd edn., Prentice Hall, London.
Lewis, R. and Lowe, P. (1992) *Individual Excellence*, Kogan Page, London.
Russell, B. (1946) *History of Western Philosophy*, George Allen & Unwin, London.
Schultz, W. C. (1955) *FIRO: A Three-Dimensional Theory of Interpersonal Behavior*, Holt, Rinehart & Winston, New York.

Chapter 12

Bagehot, W. (2001) *The English Constitution*, Oxford World Classics, OUP, Oxford.
Braybrooke, D. and Lindblom, C. D. (1969) *A Strategy of Decision*, Free Press of Glencoe.
Gibrat, R. (1931) *Les Inégalités Economiques*, Recueil Sirey, Paris.
Heider, J. (1992) *The Tao of Leadership*, Gower, Aldershot.
Hickson, D. J., Butler, R. J., Gray, D., Mallory, G. R. and Wilson, D. C. (1986) *Top Decisions*, Basil Blackwell, Oxford.
Kakabadse, A. (1984) *The Politics of Management*, Gower, Aldershot.
Levicki, C. J. (1999) *The Strategy Workout*, 2nd edn., Prentice Hall, London.

Longman (1984) *The Longman Dictionary of the English Language*, Longman, Essex.

Peter, L. J. and Hull, R. (1979) *The Peter Principle*, Pan, London.

Peters, T. J. and Waterman, R. H. Jr (1982) *In Search of Excellence*, Harper & Row, New York.

Pettigrew, A. M. (1973) *The Politics of Organizational Decision-Making*, Tavistock, London.

Chapter 13

Adair, J. (1988) *Effective Leadership*, Pan, London.

Briggs-Myers, I. (1992) *Gifts Differing*, Consulting Psychologists Press, Inc., Palo Alto, CA.

Chapman, E. N. (1977) *Your Attitude is Showing*, Science Research Associates Inc., Palo Alto, CA.

Covey, S. R. (1989) *The 7 Habits of Highly Effective People*, Simon & Schuster, New York.

Ferrucci, P. (1990) *What We May Be*, Aquarian/Thorsons, London.

Goleman, D. (1996) *Emotional Intelligence*, Bloomsbury, London.

Harris, T. A. (1973) *I'm OK – You're OK*, Pan, London.

Kiersey, D. and Bates, M. (1984) *Please Understand Me*, Prometheus Nemesis Book Company, Del Mar, CA.

McClelland, D. (1961) *The Achieving Society*, Van Nostrand, Princeton, NJ.

Schultz, W. C. (1955) *FIRO: A Three-Dimensional Theory of Interpersonal Behavior*, Holt, Rinehart & Winston, New York.

Bibliography

Adair, J. (1988) *Effective Leadership*, Pan, London.

Axtell, R. E. (1991) *Gestures*, John Wiley, New York.

Belbin, R. M. (1991) *Management Teams*, Butterworth-Heinemann, Oxford.

Belbin, M. (1993) *Team Roles at Work*, Butterworth-Heinemann, Oxford.

Berne, E. (1968) *Games People Play*, Penguin, London.

Blake, R. R. and Mouton, J. S. (1964) *The New Managerial Grid*, Gulf, Houston.

Braybrooke, D. and Lindblom, C. D. (1969) *A Strategy of Decision*, Free Press of Glencoe.

Briggs-Myers, I. (1992) *Gifts Differing*, Consulting Psychologists Press, Inc., Paolo Alto, CA.

Campbell, A., Devine, M. and Young, D. (1990) *A Sense of Mission*, Hutchinson, London.

Chapman, E. N. (1977) *Your Attitude is Showing*, Science Research Associates Inc., Palo Alto, CA.

Covey, S. R. (1989) *The 7 Habits of Highly Effective People*, Simon & Schuster, New York.

Cox, D. L. (1993) *Management Fleas and Leadership Flies*, Tresises, Burton-on-Trent and Derby.

Crainer, S. (1996) *Key Management Ideas*, Pitman Publishing, London.

Davis, W. (1984) *The Corporate Infighter's Handbook*, Sidgwick & Jackson, London.

Ferrucci, P. (1990) *What We May Be*, Aquarian/Thorsons, London.

Gibrat, R. (1931) *Les Inégalités Economiques*, Recueil Sirey, Paris.

Goleman, D. (1996) *Emotional Intelligence*, Bloomsbury, London.

Hamel, G. and Prahalad, C. K. (1994) *Competing for the Future*, Harvard Business School Press, Boston, MA.

Harris, T. A. (1973) *I'm OK – You're OK*, Pan, London.

Heider, J. (1992) *The Tao of Leadership*, Gower, Aldershot.

Hersey, P. and Blanchard, K. H. (1977) *Management of Organizational Behavior: Utilizing Human Resources*, 3rd edn., Prentice-Hall, Englewood Cliffs, NJ.

Hickson, D. J., Butler, R. J., Gray, D., Mallory, G. R. and Wilson, D. C. (1986) *Top Decisions*, Basil Blackwell, Oxford.

Jaques, E. (1976) *A General Theory of Bureaucracy*, Heinemann, London.

Jaques, E. (1982a) *The Form of Time*, Heinemann, London.

Jaques, E. (1982b) *Free Enterprise, Fair Employment*, Heinemann, London.

Kakabadse, A. (1984) *The Politics of Management*, Gower, Aldershot.

Kakabadse, A. (1991) *The Wealth Creators*, Kogan Page, London.

Kepner, C. H. and Tregoe, B. B. (1965) *The Rational Manager*, McGraw-Hill, New York.

Kiersey, D. and Bates, M. (1984) *Please Understand Me*, Prometheus Nemesis Book Company, Del Mar, CA.

Koch, R. and Campbell, A. (1994) *Wake Up and Shake Your Company*, Pitman Publishing, London.

Lawrence, P. R. and Lorsch, J. W. (1967) *Managing Integration and Differentiation*, Harvard University Press, Boston.

Levicki, C. J. (1983) *Managerial Time Horizons and Decision Making and their Effects on Organizational Performance*, Ph.D. Thesis, London Business School, London University.

Levicki, C. J. (1998) *The Leadership Gene*, Financial Times/Pitman Publishing, London.

Levicki, C. J. (1999) *The Strategy Workout*, 2nd edn., Prentice Hall, London.

Lewis, R. and Lowe, P. (1992) *Individual Excellence*, Kogan Page, London.

March, J. G. (1988) *Decisions and Organizations*, Basil Blackwell, Oxford.

McClelland, D. (1961) *The Achieving Society*, Van Nostrand, Princeton, NJ.

McGregor, D. (1960) *The Human Side of Enterprise*, McGraw-Hill, New York.

Moore, C. L. (1984) *Executives in Action*, Macdonald & Evans Ltd, Plymouth.

Peter, L. J. and Hull, R. (1979) *The Peter Principle*, Pan, London.

Peter, T. (1992) *Liberation Management*, pp. 160–165. Macmillan, London.

Peters, T. J. and Waterman, R. H. Jr (1982) *In Search of Excellence*, Harper & Row, New York.

Pettigrew, A. M. (1973) *The Politics of Organizational Decision-Making*, Tavistock, London.

Schultz, W. C. (1955) *FIRO: A Three-Dimensional Theory of Interpersonal Behavior*, Holt, Rinehart & Winston, New York.

Tichy, N. M. and Cohen, E. (1997) *The Leadership Engine*, Harper Business, New York.

White, R. P., Hodgson, P. and Crainer, S. (1996) *The Future of Leadership*, Pitman Publishing, London.

Wildavsky, A. (1964) *The Politics of the Budgetary Process*, Little Brown, Boston.

Wildavsky, A. (1975) *Budgeting, A Comparative Theory of Budgetary Processes*, Little Brown, Toronto.

Williams, J. D. (1954) *The Compleat Strategyst*, McGraw-Hill, New York.

Biographies of companies and leaders

Bayer, T. (1991) *Maxwell: The Outsider*, Mandarin, London.

Bramson, A. (1990) *Pure Luck*, Patrick Stephens Ltd, Wellingborough.

Burrough, D. and Jelyar, J. (1990) *Barbarians at the Gate*, Jonathan Cape, London.

Colier, P. and Horowitz, D. (1976) *The Rockefellers*, Signet, New York.

Davies, H. (1981) *The Grades*, Weidenfeld & Nicolson, London.

Eberts, J. and Ilott, T. (1990) *My Indecision is Final*, Faber & Faber, London.

Gittin, N. and Masters, K. (1997) *Hit and Run*, Simon & Schuster, New York.

Heller, R. (1993) *The Super Chiefs*, Truman Talley/Plume, New York.

Kessler, R. (1987) *Khashoggi*, Corgi, London.

Lenzner, R. (1985) *The Great Getty*, Signet, New York.

Love, J. F. (1995) *McDonald's: Behind the Arches*, Bantam, New York.

Malik, R. (1975) *And Tomorrow the World?*, Millington, London.

Maney, K. (1995) *Megamedia Shakeout*, John Wiley, New York.

McLachlan, S. (1983) *The National Freight Buy-Out*, Macmillan, London.

Morita, A. (1994) *Made in Japan*, Harper Collins, London.

Shawcross, W. (1992) *Murdoch*, Chatto & Windus, London.

Sloan, A. P. (1965) *My Years with General Motors*, MacFadden-Bartell, New York.

Thompson, P. (1990) *Sharing the Success*, Fontana.

Vanderbilt II, A. (1991) *Fortune's Children*, Sphere, Falmouth.

Walton, S. (1993) *Made in America*, Bantam, New York.

Index